HAYEK'S POLITICAL ECONOMY

In a society where no central agency co-ordinates the human activity of producing, selling and buying, why is there order and not chaos?

This fundamental question has taxed generations of economists. Hayek's notion of spontaneous order goes some way to providing an answer.

Hayek's Political Economy argues that, after explicitly rejecting positivism, Hayek was free to embrace reality and offer an explanation of the processes involved in bringing about order. This explanation required an elaboration of three main points.

- a methodology that allowed him to engage with reality and thereby abandon notions of equilibrium and instrumental rationality;
- 'knowledge' and how it could be communicated to millions of unconnected individuals without any central means of co-ordination;
- the recognition that knowledge is communicated not only by the price mechanism, as he originally thought, but also by a network of social rules of conduct.

This book draws many of Hayek's insights together by locating them within the newly emerging methodological perspective of critical realism. The author argues that understanding how agents communicate knowledge and cope with ignorance leads directly to a focus upon social rules which are essential in addressing the question of order. The final chapter illustrates how it is possible to abandon the notion of equilibrium without falling into analytical anarchy.

Steve Fleetwood spent most of his adult life as a professional cycle racer. After retiring from his sporting career, he studied social studies and economics at Liverpool Polytechnic and Cambridge University. He has a PhD from Cambridge and is now Senior Lecturer at De Montfort University.

ROUTLEDGE STUDIES IN THE HISTORY OF ECONOMICS

1 ECONOMICS AS LITERATURE
Willie Henderson

2 SOCIALISM AND MARGINALISM IN ECONOMICS: 1870–1930
Edited by Ian Steadman

3 HAYEK'S POLITICAL ECONOMY
Steve Fleetwood

4 ON THE ORIGINS OF CLASSICAL ECONOMICS
Distribution and Value from William Petty to Adam Smith
Tony Aspromourgos

5 THE ECONOMICS OF JOAN ROBINSON
Maria Cristina Marcuzzo, Luigi Pasinetti and Alessandro Roncaglia

HAYEK'S POLITICAL ECONOMY

The socio-economics of order

Steve Fleetwood

ROUTLEDGE

London and New York

First published 1995
by Routledge
11 New Fetter Lane, London EC4P 4EE

Simultaneously published in the USA and Canada
by Routledge
29 West 35th Street, New York, NY 10001

Typeset in Garamond by
Ponting–Green Publishing Services, Chesham, Bucks
Printed and bound in Great Britain by
TJ Press Ltd, Padstow, Cornwall

British Library Cataloguing in Publication Data
A catalogue record for this book is available from the British Library

Library of Congress Cataloguing in Publication Data
Fleetwood, Steve, 1955–
Hayek's political economy: the socio-economics of order / Steve Fleetwood.
p. cm.
Includes bibliographical references and index.
1. Hayek, Friedrich A. von (Friedrich August), 1899– .
2. Economics – History – 20th century. 3. Austrian school of economists – History. I. Title.
HB101.H39F58 1995
330'.092 – dc20 95–11821

ISBN 0–415–12909–5
ISSN 1349–7906

To my wife Anne

CONTENTS

ILLUSTRATIONS

FIGURES

TABLE

ACKNOWLEDGEMENTS

I wish to thank Tony Lawson not only for his guidance as my PhD supervisor, but also for his inspiration, and provocative criticism; Mrs O'May, for financing the PhD project through the D. O'May Studentship at Wolfson College, Cambridge; and Mark Peacock, Steve Pratten and Jochen Runde for their incisive comments upon various drafts.

1

INTRODUCTION

> That there is some kind of order, consistency and constancy in social life is obvious. If there were not, none of us would be able to go about his affairs or satisfy his most elementary wants.
>
> (Anon., quoted in Hayek, 1960, 160)

This book is an investigation into the way in which the notion of socio-economic order is dealt with in the work of F. A. Hayek. Rather than merely describe the notion of order that develops in Hayek's work over the course of some fifty years in substantive terms (i.e. at the level of economic theory not meta-theory), I opt for a different approach. I link the various phases that his substantive economics displays to the philosophical positions he adopts, demonstrating that at certain times certain substantive developments are placed out of bounds, whilst at other times certain substantive developments are encouraged by the underlying philosophical presuppositions. In this way, the strengths and weaknesses of his substantive economics in general, and his notion of socio-economic order in particular, are grounded in the strengths and weaknesses of his differing philosophical positions. I believe that this approach has a valuable lesson for economists as it highlights the impact that philosophy necessarily has upon the actual doing of substantive economics.

THE ORIGIN OF THE INQUIRY INTO SOCIO-ECONOMIC ORDER

The term *socio-economic order* refers to a state of affairs where socio-economic activity displays some form of regularity, pattern, system or arrangement. As the epigraph indicates, socio-economic activity must be relatively co-ordinated since the socio- economy is, typically, orderly and not chaotic.

Socio-economic order as a concern, perhaps even as the 'quintessential concern of social science' (Clark, 1989, 598), emerges with the decay of the feudal mode of production primarily in western Europe in the late seventeenth century. Feudal society refers not so much to one overarching society, but to a nested series of societies, each with a central authority regulating the activity of the mass of individuals within its ambit. Since this regulation occurs directly and consciously between an association of individuals, the feudal mode of production might best be described as a mode or order of association. The fundamental institution of this mode is the manorial system, a system based upon the practice of *corvée*, whereby the serf was compelled to perform a specific set of labouring tasks on the lord's land for a specified period of time. This practice was central in regulating labour activity, and type and quantity of produced output. Socio-economic order under feudalism, then, is maintained by conscious regulation and association.[1]

By the eighteenth century, however, the feudal mode of production in Britain had crumbled, and was in the process of doing so in Europe. This development presented a puzzle to Enlightenment thinkers: how is socio-economic order maintained in the absence of direct and conscious regulation and association between individuals? The 'Leviathan' of the sovereign state had dramatically weakened, yet the Hobbesian fear of 'a war of every man against every man . . . [where] life is . . . solitary, poor, nasty, brutish, and short', had not materialised (*A Dictionary of Philosophy*, 1983). Thinkers such as Locke, Hume and Rousseau, taking Hobbes as their starting point, update natural law philosophy and seek an explanation in terms of a social contract. According to Rousseau:

> Some form of association must be found as a result of which the whole strength of the community will be enlisted for the protection of the person and property of each constituent member, in such a way that, when united to his fellows, renders obedience to his own will, and remains as free as he was before.
>
> (Quoted in Kay and Mott, 1982, 32)

The mid-nineteenth century sees the emergence of Adam Smith as one of the leading philosophers of the Enlightenment, synthesising much of Enlightenment thought into a coherent social science. Although influenced by the philosophy of Natural Law, Smith changes the direction of inquiry and begins to look elsewhere for the cause of order. He turns from what would now perhaps be called political science, to political economy and begins a new chapter in the history of social science. According to Heilbronner:

> Smith . . . found the secret of a self regulating economy in the very attribute of a society of perfect liberty that seemed at first to pose the greatest threat to order. This was its social and spatial mobility – characteristics that appeared to many contemporary observers to be the source of potential disruption and disorder.
>
> (Heilbronner, 1986, 151)

The very isolated, atomised, dynamic and mobile nature of individuals, that is, their lack of association leads not to chaos, but to a socio-economic order, via mechanisms which are to be uncovered through political economy. Socio-economic order is to be understood by learning the secret of a self regulating economy, more specifically the mechanism of competition. Smith finds the source of society's orderliness not in the state (*pace* Hobbes) nor in the social contract (*pace* Rousseau) but in the very institution that most enlightenment thinkers presume to be the very source of disorder, i.e. the economy. Smith, then, begins the modern inquiry into socio-economic order by probing into the institutions of political economy. This raises the question of who, if anyone, is currently addressing Smith's project?

SMITH'S HEIRS

Smith's project, the quest for an explanation of socio-economic order, has continued into the twentieth century, where it is possible to identify two broad trends. On the one hand it has been taken up by social theorists, on the other by what may be generally termed economists. The social theorists, due to their relative neglect of economic phenomena, are in a sense continuing the quest initiated by Smith's predecessors Hobbes and Rousseau, that is, they are concerned with explaining order in socio-political terms. Amongst economists, the schools of thought claiming to be continuing Smith's project are: Marxists,[2] General Equilibrium (GE) theorists[3] and Austrians, particularly Hayek.

Although interest in Hayek's work appears to be undergoing something of a revival, he is nevertheless a difficult economist to come to terms with. There are two main reasons for this. The first is that he is not an economist in the orthodox sense of the word, but an all-round social scientist. In order fully to understand Hayek's work, it is necessary to cross subject boundaries – something that many contemporary economists are unwilling to do. He writes:

> although the problem of an appropriate socio-economic order is today studied from the different angles of economics, jurisprudence, political science, sociology and ethics, the problem is one which can be approached successfully only as a whole.
>
> (Hayek, 1973, 4)

> He who is only an economist cannot be a good economist. There is hardly a single problem which can be adequately answered on the basis of a single special discipline.
>
> (Hayek, 1967a, 267)

As will become clear, this thesis takes Hayek at his word, and follows him through economics, philosophy, social theory and cognitive psychology. The second reason why Hayek is difficult to come to terms with is that, because his work spans approximately sixty years, and undergoes a series of changes, it is not possible to refer simply to 'Hayek's work'. To facilitate this study I have found it necessary to classify Hayek's work into three periods. The period up to 1936 (a period hardly discussed here), describes the work of *Hayek I*; the period from 1936 to 1960 describes the work of *Hayek II*; and the period after 1960 describes that of *Hayek III*. These dates are not to be taken literally; they merely constitute useful benchmarks. It is not the case that between 1935 and 1936 or 1959 and 1960 Hayek somehow makes an intellectual leap, discarding all his previous thoughts. It is, rather, that around these dates, a series of insights that Hayek is working on accumulate to the extent that it is possible to detect something of a sea change. I shall emphasise the evolution of Hayek's ideas, bearing in mind that some existing ideas remain intact, some existing ideas are modified, and some existing ideas are discarded. It is this process of overlapping change and continuity in Hayek's work that prompts Lawson to refer to Hayek's 'continuing transformation' (Lawson, 1994c).

Whilst it is now quite commonplace to date Hayek II from his 1936 paper, it is, I believe, novel to claim the emergence of Hayek III and to mark this point from *The Constitution of Liberty* published in 1960. It is in this book that his recognition of the role played by social rules of conduct in the maintenance of spontaneous order first emerges, something that in turn is tied to his shift in philosophical position.[4]

SITUATING HAYEK IN THE CONTEMPORARY CONTEXT

This book is not an exercise in the history of economic thought; it has implications, lessons perhaps, for contemporary economics. It is, I believe, no longer controversial to suggest that mainstream economics is in a state of disarray, and a (small) but significant number of economists are searching for an alternative approach. Mathematical economics is becoming increasingly irrelevant to the economics of the real world, using the smokescreen of the necessity of abstraction to license the use of premises that, whilst analytically tractable and in this sense convenient, are often pure fictions. Econometrics arguably searches in vain for constant relationships between variables that endure when models are confronted with new data.[5] What these different approaches have in common, however, and what is arguably the source of their shortcomings, is their shared grounding in the philosophy of empirical realism, manifested in the approach known as positivism.

This is where the work of Hayek becomes relevant. As long ago as 1936 Hayek begins to abandon mainstream economic theory. The real significance of this abandonment, however, is the fact that his break is encouraged by a break with positivism and therefore with the empiricist philosophy that underpins it. His 1942a paper is primarily an attack upon 'scientism', by which he means the illicit extension of the positivist methods of natural science to social science. Some fifty years after Hayek breaks with mainstream economics, his ideas are attracting the attention of economists who are searching for an alternative approach.

The distinctiveness of Hayek's economics lies in the distinctiveness of his philosophy, and it is, therefore, incumbent upon those who would learn from him to treat the latter seriously. This thesis takes Hayek's philosophy seriously, noting the articulation that occurs between his changing philosophical positions and his substantive economics, particularly his notion of socio-economic order.

THE ARGUMENT OF THE BOOK IN A NUTSHELL

From 1936 onwards Hayek is engaged in an investigation of socio-economic order. Yet before 1960 he has not developed the theoretical (philosophical or economic) apparatus to complete this investigation. The period from 1936 to 1960 can, with hindsight, be perceived as a preparatory stage in the development of his mature notion of order, incorporating two main lines of development. Pursuing one (negative) line, Hayek breaks from mainstream economics, notably in terms of knowledge assumptions, equilibrium and the theory of human agency encapsulated in *Homo economicus*. Pursuing the other (positive) line, Hayek begins to develop an awareness of the importance of knowledge. Hayek is deeply concerned with the way knowledge is produced, discovered, acquired, transformed, conveyed, communicated and stored by and between agents and across time. For brevity I refer simply to the way knowledge is *discovered, communicated and stored*. I shall also refer to the institutions that facilitate this discovery, communication and storage.

What he lacks at this point in time, however, is any adequate grasp of social structures, particularly social rules of conduct. This lack, combined with the developing awareness of the importance of knowledge, creates a problem. He begins to understand the complex nature of knowledge, and to recognise that the '*telecommunications system*' (his term for the price mechanism) *alone* cannot facilitate the discovery, communication and storage of the quality and quantity of knowledge necessary for socio-economic co-ordination in a complex society. But as yet he has no means of integrating his developing awareness of the importance of knowledge with any social structures that might augment the telecom system. He is forced, as it were, to make exaggerated claims about the role and efficacy of the telecom system in facilitating the discovery, communication and storage of knowledge.

After 1960, however, Hayek successfully integrates the notion of social structures into his analysis, thereby allowing the development of a notion whereby human agents navigate their way in the socio-economic world by following social rules of conduct. This development appears to be a turning point in his work. These rules serve as the structures that augment the telecom system, allowing knowledge to be communicated when agents possess it, and ignorance to be coped with when they do not. He begins to sketch a complex articulation between the underlying structure of rules and the telecom system that underpins the operation of the market process.

Encouraging this sea change in terms of substantive economic theory is a change in his philosophical and methodological (for brevity, I refer to this combination as philosophical) position. Prior to 1936 Hayek might be defined as a positivist – although I shall not elaborate upon this.[6] Between 1936 and 1960 he adopts a synthesis of *subjective idealist epistemology* and (augmented) *empirical realist ontology*. After 1960 he veers towards a philosophical position that I call *quasi-critical realist*. In each of the periods, then, Hayek's substantive work is tethered to a philosophical position. Elaborating upon the nature of this tether is one of the main aims of the thesis.

Prior to 1936, Hayek's adherence to 'narrow technical economics' might be due to his adoption of positivism,[7] and thereby to an implicit adoption of an (empirical realist) ontology that effectively permits only of events given in sense experience. The only domain of reality that Hayek's empiricist ontology permits him to investigate is that of the empirical, that is, he must couch his investigation in terms of the events of experience. This encourages the use of the concept of equilibrium as the organising principle of socio-economic activity.[8] Hayek I, then, like other positivist economists, attempts to investigate the compatibility of actions that appear to constitute socio-economic order in the guise of equilibrium. Recognising Hayek's shift from positivism in the late 1930s is essential to comprehending his break with mainstream economics.

After 1936 Hayek develops an epistemology and ontology that permits not only events given in sense experience, but also conceptions or ideas held by agents. He now recognises a further domain of reality, that is, a domain (metaphorically) deeper than, or beneath, the flux of events, namely the conceptions created by agents. He can now no longer treat 'the data' as something independent from human identification, that is, as an objective and technical phenomenon (as an engineer might) but as inextricably linked to subjective agents' conceptions. He recognises that mainstream economics treats knowledge in an extremely superficial way and begins to challenge the use of its knowledge assumptions. Once underway, a critique of the notion of equilibrium and the theory of human agency soon follow. However, his adoption of subjective idealism and (augmented) empirical realist ontology leads from one problem into another.

It was noted above that Hayek needs, but prior to 1960 does not have, a developed notion of social structure in general and social rules of conduct in particular. This is by no means accidental. The subjective idealist epistemology that he adopts manifests itself in his social science as hermeneutic foundationalism, that is, the view that reality is exhausted by agents' conceptions. This position prevents him from developing an adequate ontology, and thereby a notion of social structures as *real* entities that exist independently of agents' identification of them. Hayek II, then, faces a problem in that whilst he (tentatively) rejects equilibrium as a valid notion of order, he has nothing with which to replace it. The result is that he writes virtually nothing about socio-economic order in this period.

He is, then, impaled on a fork of his own making. The theoretical apparatus he needs for his substantive theory is placed out of bounds by the philosophical position he adopts. With hindsight, it is quite clear that if Hayek is to develop the notion of social structures in the form of social rules of conduct, then he has to abandon this philosophical position. And this is precisely what he does around 1960.

Hayek III adopts a quasi-transcendental realist philosophy. His subjective idealist epistemology and hermeneutic foundationalism evaporate and he (further) augments his ontology of events and conceptions to include (metaphorically) deep structures in the form of social rules of conduct. At this point he can finally proffer an alternative to equilibrium by going 'beneath' the events, but this time to the real (as opposed to merely conceptual) structures that govern these events. Instead of being preoccupied with the events of experience (as is Hayek I the positivist), or agents' conceptions (as is Hayek II the subjective idealist) he becomes preoccupied with the underlying or 'deep' structures that give rise to the events of experience (i.e. Hayek III the quasi-transcendental realist). He develops something approaching the Transformational Model of Social Activity (TMSA), ending up with a sophisticated social theory that allows him to combine the themes of knowledge (kinds), ignorance, rules and the telecom system in his elaboration of the market process or catallaxy in what I call a *transformational conception of spontaneous socio-economic order.*

2

PHILOSOPHY

EPISTEMOLOGY AND ONTOLOGY

Why bother with philosophy: why not go straight into an investigation of Hayek's thought on matters of socio-economic order? There are two reasons. The first is that Hayek's break with mainstream economics between 1936 and 1942 is itself explicitly philosophical, taking the form of a rejection of 'scientism' – i.e. the application of the natural scientific method to social science. He writes:

> And although in the hundred and twenty years or so, during which this ambition to imitate Science in its methods rather than its spirit has now dominated social studies, it has contributed scarcely anything to our understanding of social phenomena . . .
>
> (Hayek, 1942a, 268)

If, therefore, Hayek himself claims to break from mainstream economics due to matters of a philosophical nature, it is incumbent upon commentators to understand Hayek's thoughts on such matters.

Second, all thinkers adhere to a philosophical position (whether they are conscious of it or not), and any philosophical position encourages, or predisposes, its adherents to formulate thoughts in certain ways. Thinkers have to think, and do so with the aid of a set of concepts and categories that are based in one philosophical position or another – or perhaps a mixture.

The branch of philosophy concerned with these matters is metaphysics, which according to Harré is 'the study of the most general categories with which we think' (1988, 100).[1] Concepts are the tools which enable one to think in the first place. They exist prior to scientific practice and are necessary in order to make sense of the diverse entities in the world. As Harré puts it:

> We have to choose some concepts with which to think about the world, and this amounts to . . . accepting a system of picturing and conceiving the structures of the world. Any set of concepts we choose, no matter how much they may lack systematic connection, involves

> metaphysical... assumptions. If we employ thing-concepts, we are already embroiled in a metaphysics that assumes the continuity of individuals in time...
>
> (ibid., 16)

No thinker, therefore, simply creates theory *ab initio*: fundamental (and often implicit) philosophical presuppositions shape the formulation of both the problems and the solutions subsequently advanced. Moreover, if and when these philosophical presuppositions undergo a change, they often encourage a change in substantive theory, something which, as will become clear, occurs with Hayek. In this case, understanding the nature of the philosophical change allows one to grasp more fully the nature of the ensuing change in economic theory.

At the heart of metaphysics lie two basic questions: What exists? and: What can be known? These questions relate to the respective disciplines of ontology and epistemology. Ontology is concerned quite simply with the inquiry into the nature of being, into what exists. All theory presupposes an ontology, the key question being: What entities are taken to exist? Epistemology on the other hand is concerned with knowledge, its nature and limits. It is the inquiry into how one obtains knowledge about what exists. Ontology and epistemology, then, will be the key categories used in understanding Hayek's philosophy.

With the rise to hegemony of empiricism, beginning in the seventeenth century, the major philosophical preoccupation shifts from matters of ontology (in the Aristotelian tradition) to matters of epistemology; from questions of what exists, to questions of how one can know (about) what exists. The net result of this 'epistemological turn' has been an eclipse of ontology. The preoccupation with matters of an epistemological nature remains in vogue today, shaping much philosophical and scientific discourse, particularly in the 'sciences' such as economics that adhere to positivism – of which more below.

This eclipse of ontology, however, does not mean that matters of ontology are banished from theory. This would be quite impossible for two reasons. The first reason relates to substantive theory. All substantive theory necessarily presupposes some conception of the nature of the reality under investigation, that is an ontology, irrespective of whether the adherent of the theory is aware of this ontology or not. For example, a theory that denies the existence of 'society', typically, presupposes an ontology of unconnected atomic particles or individuals. The second reason relates to epistemology. Any set of claims that constitute an epistemology, that is a theory of how one knows the reality under investigation, must presuppose that the reality in question is of such a kind that can be known in the way suggested by that epistemology. For example, advancing the epistemological claim that reality can be known via the recording of regular patterns in the events of experience, presupposes an ontology of regular, unconnected, atomic episodes or events/actions.[2]

Whilst, however, epistemology and ontology are inextricably linked, the empiricist-inspired preoccupation with epistemology tends to make ontology a derivative of the adopted epistemological position. Positivism, rooted as it is in empiricism, is no exception. It subscribes, implicitly, to a particular ontology, namely that being consists of events given in sense experience. What exists is what is perceived.

I shall argue that Hayek II's philosophical base consists of a synthesis of a Kantian inspired subjective idealist epistemology and, secreted within it, an (augmented) empirical realist ontology of events given in sense experience. This philosophical synthesis informs his method and subsequently his economic thinking. However, before any of this can be done, these two philosophical positions need to be elaborated and defined more accurately.

KANT'S SUBJECTIVE-IDEALIST EPISTEMOLOGY

Kant's subjective idealism might be conceived of as more 'realist' in comparison to Berkeley's version of idealism in that he permits the existence of the mind-independent thing-in-itself, even though the latter is destined to remain unknowable.[3] The thing-in-itself allows Kant not so much to solve the materialist–idealist antinomy as to neatly sidestep it. He shifts the focus away from the vexed matter of ascertaining what exists (or for that matter of whether anything exists at all) in the external world, towards the slightly different one of explaining the possibility of experiencing that world. That is, he shifts attention towards the particular epistemological question of how knowledge is derived (i.e. via the categorical structure of the mind) when the object of that knowledge remains unknowable.[4]

Bakhurst succinctly illustrates what the possibility of experiencing the world means: it involves explaining how an agent 'individuates and identifies events in the sensuous manifold, or how the subject [agent] conceives of this patch of, say, the visual field as an experience of such and such a kind' (Bakhurst, 1991, 195). As is well known, Kant explains this possibility by employing the synthesising process performed by the pure categories of the understanding which act to filter sense experience, to render a thing-in-itself into a thing-for-us.

Herein lies the 'subjective' aspect of Kant's subjective idealism, giving the idealism what Stern refers to as an 'ontological twist' (Stern, 1990, 21). That is, the mind of the transcendental subject structures the object, the external world, thereby creating an object or thing-for-us. As Stern puts it, for Kant 'the subject has a vital ontological role to play in bringing the object into being' (ibid., 111). The unity of the object rests upon the unity of the transcendental subject or, more accurately, the unity and organisation of the subjective mind. I shall, throughout the book, refer to this process of synthesis simply as *the subject structuring the object*.[5]

The process of the subject structuring the object turns on the claim that the cognitive apparatus of the transcendental subject is structured prior to experiencing the (unstructured) object and, moreover, is structured in such a way as to make the object experienceable as something in particular rather than as a mere jumble of sense experiences. As Kant put it:

> [A]ll combination . . . is an act of the understanding. To this act the general title 'synthesis' may be assigned, as indicating that *we cannot present to ourselves anything as combined in the object which we have not ourselves previously combined*, and that of all presentations, combination is the only one which we cannot be given through objects. Being an act of the self activity of the subject, it cannot be executed save by the subject itself.
>
> (Quoted in Stern, 1990, 23, emphasis added)

Although there is far more to Kant's epistemology, for the purposes of illustrating the (possibly implicit) influence he has on Hayek, the former's epistemology might be characterised as follows:

1 The raw material which is to be worked up into knowledge presents itself in the form of sense experience. Thus, whilst Kant does not confine knowledge to that given in experience, knowledge can only be about the phenomena of experience. However, (if it leads to anything) raw sense data can lead only to a jumbled, chaotic conception.
2 Sense experience is acted upon by the pure categories of the understanding and only then does one possess knowledge of something. The manifold of otherwise chaotic conceptions is brought under a concept.
3 The combination of sense experience and the pure categories operate to structure the external world and create an object 'for us'. Herein lies the subjectivist aspect of subjective idealism. *The transcendental subject structures the object.*
4 The external world 'for us' becomes a projection of the subjective mind. Herein lies the idealist aspect of Kant's subjective idealism as the world becomes what agents conceive it to be.
5 The thing-in-itself is unknowable, by which Kant means unknowable in the Aristotelian sense of uncovering a thing's essence. With this device, Kant shifted the question from What exists? to: How is experience of what exists possible?
6 Kant's subjective idealism has the effect of collapsing the domain of the ontic into that of the epistemic. What there is to know becomes dependent upon how it can be known, a collapse referred to by Bhaskar as the 'epistemic fallacy' (Bhaskar, 1989a, 133). Despite this fallacy, however, Kant has not banished ontology; merely, if implicitly, accepted a particular version of it – namely one of sense impressions.

TWO ONTOLOGIES

If, like empiricists, one does not start with a claim in ontology but a claim in epistemology, then an implicit ontology will nevertheless be adopted, deriving from that epistemology. This section elaborates the ontological position that is engendered by the 'epistemological turn' in philosophical thought, namely empirical realism. Such an elaboration is facilitated by the construction of a framework of ontological perspectives, thereby allowing for empirical realism to be located. The construction I shall make is based upon the work of Meikle (1985) and Bhaskar (1978, 1989a).

According to Meikle (1985, 8–10), there are only two basic ontological positions: atomism and essentialism.[6] These two positions may be traced to the ancient Greeks, and specifically to the debate between the atomists Democritus and Epicurus and to Aristotle. Whereas the atomists conceived of matter as atomistic small bits that combine and repel in the void, Aristotle argued that matter could not be conceived of in terms of its constituent parts, and that the category of form or essence was necessary.

Giving the discussion less of a metaphysical and more of a philosophy of science approach, Bhaskar locates essentialism under transcendental realism and atomism under empirical realism. He then goes on to break down the latter into two components: classical empiricism, with its origin in Hume; and transcendental idealism, with its origin in Kant and manifesting itself (via neo-Kantianism) in positivism of one form or another. Before outlining these components, which amount to the two main traditions in the philosophy of science, Figure 2.1 will simplify the ensuing exposition.

EMPIRICAL REALISM

Bhaskar defines the ontology underlying classical empiricism as empirical realism, which he explains as follows:

> To say that every account of science . . . presupposes an ontology is to say that science abhors an ontological vacuum. The empiricist fills the vacuum he creates with his concept of experience. In this way an implicit ontology . . . is generated. First, knowledge is reduced to that of atomistic events apprehended in sense experience. Second, these events are then identified as the particulars of the world. In this way, our knowledge of reality is literally identified, or at best taken to be in isomorphic correspondence with the reality known by science . . . [T]he epistemic fallacy thus covers or disguises an ontology based on the category of experience, and a realism based on the presumed characteristics of the objects of experiences, vis atomistic events, and their relations, vis constant conjunctions.
>
> (Bhaskar, 1978, 40–1)

This is an extremely important comment, requiring some elaboration to bring

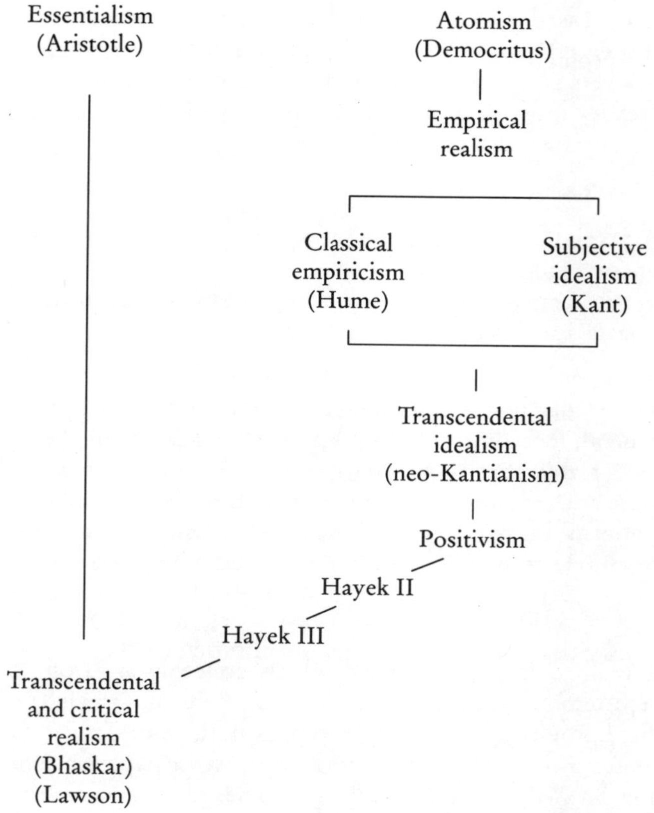

Figure 2.1 The family tree of relevant philosophical perspectives

out its salience. The following six points appear to capture the essential characteristics of empirical realism:

1 Every scientific statement presupposes an ontology of some kind, whether the scientist recognises it or not.
2 The empiricist, on occasion explicitly (Hume), but usually implicitly (Kant), presupposes an ontology grounded in sense experience. Knowledge about the extended world is reduced to knowledge about what can be perceived, so that to exist is to be perceived. What cannot be perceived cannot be known about and is therefore inadmissible to science.
3 What can be perceived are unique, unconnected, fragmented, punctiform, atomistic episodes or events. Events given in sense experience cannot be other than atomistic, since any connection or relation between them is impervious to sense observation.
4 Knowledge of reality given as events in sense experience is taken to be

isomorphic with, or fused with, the reality known to science. This epistemology has implications for ontology. If, epistemologically speaking, sense experience delivers atomistic events, and these events are fused with reality, then that reality must be atomistically constituted. The ontology that derives from the epistemology is one of atomism.

Two more points follow on from these:

5 Because events are taken to constitute reality, experience of them is taken to be certain and incorrigible.
6 If knowledge of reality is given as events in sense experience, then these events form the basis for scientific knowledge. Lawson explains this succinctly:

> [I]f particular knowledge is of events sensed in experience, then any possibility of general, including scientific knowledge must be of the constant patterns, if any, that such events reveal. On this Humean view, clearly, these are the only forms of generalisations conceivable. Such constant patterns, i.e. regularities of the form 'whenever event x then event y', of course constitute the Humean or positivist account of causal laws.
>
> (Lawson, 1995a)

In short, empirical realism is a philosophy which conceals an atomist ontology within an epistemology grounded in the limitations of knowledge. General or scientific knowledge is available only on the possibility of discovering regular patterns in the flux of events given in sense experience of the form 'Whenever event *X* then event *Y*', referred to here as *Humean laws* – since Hume encouraged this view. Economics, from the empirical realist perspective, proceeds by using Humean law(s) to deduce consequences from initial axioms, buttressed by assumptions.

TRANSCENDENTAL IDEALISM AND POSITIVISM

The synthesis of subjective idealist epistemology and empirical realist ontology, when transposed into the field of philosophy of science gives rise to transcendental idealism – a neo-Kantian position. Transcendental idealism differentiates its ontology from that of classical empiricism by a refusal to take objects or events given in sense experience as the *sole* objects of scientific inquiry. However, it shares with it the presupposition that event regularities are ubiquitous and therefore that laws are of the Humean form. The manifestation of this philosophy of science in the sciences themselves and in mainstream economics is positivism.

Transcendental idealism, in its guise as positivism, employs a creative stage in the modelling exercise, whereby a tractable mechanism is postulated to produce the event regularities under scrutiny. Here, entities not amenable to direct perception, such as social structures, mechanisms, magnetic fields, atoms or Walrasian auctioneers, are taken to be useful to science. Of significance, however, is the absence of a requirement that such mechanisms be real. A theory might simply use tractable but fictitious theoretical constructs to facilitate model building and the *ex post* rationalisation of event regularities.

On the basis of the framework outlined here, then, both classical empiricism and transcendental idealism share a common grounding in an empirical realist ontology. This common grounding permits both positions to be labelled empirical realism. Transcendental idealism merely goes further and admits the usefulness of imaginary theoretical constructs in the practice of science.

CLARIFICATION OF CATEGORIES AND TERMINOLOGY[7]

The final section of this chapter aims to clarify some of the categories and specific uses of terminology that will be employed throughout this book.

The term 'efficient' cause refers to the common-sense notion whereby, for example, the cause of a glass shattering is the hand that knocked it from the table. This stands in contrast to 'material' cause, which might be thought of as an enabling condition, or a condition for action. Thus the table from which the glass fell is a material cause of the glass breaking.

The *social* scientific analogue of 'events' (the latter being used primarily with respect to *natural* science) is 'actions'. Since, however, Humean law, styled as 'Whenever event *X*, then event *Y*', is often used by positivists in both social and natural sciences, the distinction between events and actions becomes blurred. When discussing social science, then, I shall make reference to events/actions.

The terms 'ideas', 'attitudes', 'meanings', 'descriptions', 'beliefs', 'opinions', and so on, held by agents that permeate all Hayek's late 1930s and early 1940s work will be referred to simply as agents' *conceptions*.

The term 'real' denotes entities that have a real existence. Thus, stones and wombats are real, as are the *conceptions* of God and fairies that agents might hold, although God and fairies themselves are not real.

The world is taken to consists of the following real entities:

- brutely *physical*, that is, physical non-conceptual entities that exist totally independently of their identification by agents;
- artefacts such as tools that are in part brutely physical and in part conceptual. Their existence is partially dependent upon their identification by agents;
- brutely *social*, that is, conceptual non-physical entities. Their existence may or may not be dependent upon their identification by all agents. For

example, the rules of the highway code are entirely dependent upon, but social structures such as class or rules are independent of, their identification by agents.

The term 'identification' implies (a) that agents have knowledge of the entity, and/or (b) that agents create the entity in the act of cognition (i.e. a subjective idealist position). In combining the types of entities that comprise the world with the term 'identification', to form phrases like 'entities that exist independently of their identification by agents', two points require clarification.

First, the phrase implies that these entities exist without them necessarily (a) being known, and/or (b) being subjectively constructed by any particular agent. Whilst similar, (a) and (b) are not the same. Possessing knowledge of an entity is not the same as subjectively constructing that entity, since there is no real entity to have knowledge *of*. There is, in other words, no object *of* knowledge: only an object *as* knowledge. This, however, makes use of the term knowledge problematic.

If an entity is a subjective creation, then it must (in some sense) be known to the agent A who created it. The possibility then arises, however, that the entity might be known to agent A yet be completely imaginary, for example, God. But then what does it mean to say that agent B has (or even has no) knowledge of God? One cannot have knowledge of something with no existence. There is no object *of* knowledge for A or B, only an object *as* knowledge for A.

If, therefore, one does not use the term *identification*, and rests content with the term *knowledge*, then the statement 'entities exist independently of their knowledge' does not rule out the possibility that whilst such entities might be unknown, their existence might be completely imaginary, i.e. subjective creations. If one uses the term *identification*, this problem does not arise, since the statement 'entities exist independently of their identification' rules out the possibility that entities might be subjective creations, and therefore completely imaginary. Put another way, on my definition, if an entity is said to 'exist independently of its identification by an agent', then it is both (a) real and not merely a subjective creation, and (b) unknown to that agent.

For the second point of clarification, consider the mode of existence of the three types of objects or entities that comprise the world. Brutely physical entities do not at all, artefacts do partially, and brutely social entities may or may not depend for their existence upon their identification by agents.

Since artefacts and some social entities require at the very least partial identification, is it not contradictory to make the statement that 'artefacts and social entities exist independently of their identification', or 'have a mind independent existence'? The statement is not contradictory, once one understands the following. An artefact or social entity might exist independently of its identification by *at least some* agents. Rules of the highway code, for example, continue to exist even though some agents are unaware of them – they are identified, drawn upon and therefore reproduced by others. They could not continue to exist, however, if all agents were unaware of them. But in complete contrast, social rules or social class can exist even if all agents are unaware of them.[8] Agents enter into relations of production with one another in order to work and earn an income. Whether or not they identify the class nature of these relations is irrelevant for the existence of these relations.

The interchangeable terms 'real social material, object, entity or concept' refer to entities that are conceptually non-physical in nature but none the less real – for example, a social rule. The question that cannot be ignored, particularly in a discussion of social material, however, is: What exactly is meant by the term 'real'? My use of the term 'real' social material connotes the following. An entity is said to be real if it makes a difference to action. For example, if one possesses the conception or idea that God wants people to respect the Sabbath, then one might opt not to work on Sundays. Even if this idea is completely imaginary, it is still causal and therefore real. Now whilst this is correct as far as it goes, it does not go far enough, because it fails to capture a distinction that is important in understanding subjective idealism. The crucial point to focus upon is not the nature of the conception or idea itself, but the way it is treated by the social scientist. This reveals the social ontology presupposed by the scientist.

Consider (very briefly), for example, the issue of social class from both Marxist (materialist/transcendental realist) and Weberian (subjective idealist) perspectives. For the Marxist, there is a set of social structures (i.e. relations and forces of production) that determines the class position of agents. Not only do these structures exist independently of their identification by agents, they shape the class consciousness of agents – 'being determines consciousness', as Marx puts it. Ideas about class, then, do not originate in the cognitive activity of the mind; they have some form of material grounding.

For the Weberian, by contrast, since social structures that exist independently of their identification cannot be conceived of, class cannot be said to be grounded in a social structure or relation. Class cannot be treated as anything other than the product of ideas about class: there is nothing beyond agents' conceptions in which to ground it. Subjective idealists do not, of course, see a problem in this because they accept the primacy of ideas. They actually accept that ideas or conceptions originate in the cognitive activity of the transcendental subject.

Ideas about class, therefore, since they make a difference to action, are real from both materialist and subjective idealist perspectives, but it is clear that they have very different implications in each case. In order to differentiate, therefore, between the use of the term 'real' by these opposed perspectives, I shall refer to social material that is presumed to be materially grounded as *real social material*, and social material that is presumed to originate in the structured mind as *ideal social material*. Use of the term 'ideal social material' then (and this is important) does not mean unreal; it simply means that the concept is presumed to have no material grounding, that its origin lies in the cognitive activity of the agent.

The term *hermeneutic foundationalism* is a version of extreme subjectivism. It involves the claim that the social world is entirely conceptual in nature, that is, the social world is not merely concept-*dependent*, but concept-*determined*. Put another way, the social world is *exhausted* by the conceptions that agents hold. It is, I shall argue, the expression at the level of social theory of an underlying subjective idealist philosophy.

Since I shall argue that Hayek II adopts hermeneutic foundationalism as his social theory and subjective idealism as his underlying philosophy, a few comments on subjective idealism at this stage might prevent a possible misunderstanding.

Subjective idealism, as I defined it above, means that the structured mind of the transcendental subject structures the (possibly unstructured) object. The term 'structures' does not mean 'physically creates', 'physically brings into being', or some such. If the mere act of thinking brought a social or physical object into existence, this would not be subjective idealism but magic. All that is involved in my description of subjective idealism is that whilst the existence of an external entity is (of course) recognised, *any structure humans perceive in it is the result of the cognitive capacity of the mind, not the objective properties of the entity.*

I do not use the term 'subjective idealist' pejoratively. To continue with an example used above, the subjective idealist conception of class in its Weberian form has a strong tradition in social science, and it is not an absurd position to hold – even though I consider it mistaken. It might appear absurd, however, if my definition of subjective idealism is misconstrued to imply something more akin to Berkeley's 'dogmatic realism', i.e. to magic.

I shall make use of the transcendental form of argument or inquiry. In general, transcendental inquiry is an inquiry into the conditions of the possibility of an entity. In effect one asks: What *must* be the case for *X* to be possible? The '*must*' here requires some clarification. Transcendental realists Lawson, Peacock and Pratten offer a most succinct clarification:

> [Must] does not signify some ahistoric, infallible conception of the acquisition of knowledge . . . A theory which results from transcendental analysis is, at best, the only known theory at the time to be consistent with the acceptable premises. Instead the *must* relates to a two-stage structure of the transcendental argument: the first, positive stage is to show that the existence of some Y makes X intelligible; the second, negative part, is that in which it is shown how counter intuitive, contradictory, or incoherent results follow from the failure to sustain Y.
>
> (Lawson, *et al*., 1995)

In discussing Hayek's philosophy and, specifically, ontology, I shall deploy this form of argument by asking, in effect: What *must* Hayek be presupposing about the nature of being in order that he can hold such and such a substantive claim? What Hayek *must* be presupposing, then, does not signify an infallible claim on my part; it has to be reasoned for – and reasoned against by other commentators who oppose my argument.

CONCLUSION

Economists can (try to) ignore philosophy (including methodology, ontology and epistemology), but philosophy matters and hence will not ignore economists or their economic theory. It is important to recognise in particular that an ontology is implicit in, and colours all, substantive theory. Unlike most mainstream economists, Hayek formally and explicitly breaks with positivism and this has profound effects on his notion of socio-economic order. An understanding of his economics, therefore, makes an understanding of his philosophical and methodological position non-optional. Hence Hayek's philosophical and methodological positions will form the subject matter of the next two chapters and pave the way for an investigation of his socio-economics in Chapter 5.

3

THE PHILOSOPHY UNDERLYING HAYEK II's SOCIO-ECONOMIC THEORY

The previous chapter sketched out a subjective-idealist epistemology and an empirical-realist ontology. This chapter aims to establish that Hayek II's philosophical position consists of a synthesis of these two elements, as a prelude to drawing out in Chapter 5 the implications of this philosophical position for his socio-economic thinking.

The main complicating factor in ascertaining Hayek's philosophical position is his differential treatment of natural and social science. As will be demonstrated, Hayek virtually cedes natural science to positivism in two senses. He does this, first, in the sense that he accepts the ubiquity of constant conjunctions of events as the basis of (Humean) law, and second, in his use of fictitious entities in model-building.

Whilst he attempts to develop an alternative to positivism for social science, this alternative proves to be inadequate due to his uncritical acceptance of certain aspects of positivism in natural science which he (implicitly) transfers to social science. By drawing out his thinking on both natural and social science we are better placed to evaluate his thinking on the latter.

I shall set out the chapter in two parts: the first discusses Hayek's philosophical position in natural sciences, whilst the second does the same for social sciences.

HAYEK'S PHILOSOPHICAL POSITION IN NATURAL SCIENCE

Table 3.1 may assist the reader to see the structure of the following exposition with more clarity.

This section will demonstrate that Hayek:

- rejects the unknowability of the thing-in-itself, that is, he claims that science can come to know the object under investigation;
- accepts the ubiquity of constant conjunctions of events as the basis of (Humean) law;
- accepts the transcendental idealist/positivist use of theoretical constructs;
- accepts the empirical-realist ontology of events given in sense experience.

Table 3.1 Hayek's conception of epistemology, ontology and law in both natural and social science

	Epistemology	*Ontology*	*Law*
Natural science	Rejects unknowable thing	Events	Event regularities (Humean)
Social science	Claims unknowability is irrelevant. Subjectivism and idealism are maintained	Events and conceptions	None

These points will not be tackled one at a time, but will all emerge from investigation into the issue of the unknowable thing-in-itself.

Hayek differs from Kant in that he appears to claim that the thing-in-itself is knowable, although he emphatically does not claim that this thing can be known in the Aristotelian sense of the uncovering of an essence. That he appears to think that the notion of an essence is quite meaningless is indicated by his rather impatient remark that 'we shall not be interested in what a thing "is" or "really is" (*whatever that may mean*)' (Hayek, 1952, 4, emphasis added). Whilst he does not use the term 'thing-in-itself' and then explicitly set about demonstrating how such a thing can be known, this is in effect what he does in his elaboration of the procedure of natural science. Translating from Kantian language and problematic into Hayekian language and problematic, it appears that Hayek poses a kind of transcendental question for natural science, namely: How can one come to know something about the object that resides in the physical world over and above what can be known via that sense experience? For brevity, I shall phrase it as follows: *How can the object be known?*

In addressing this question, Hayek takes two seemingly contradictory pathways. Consider the first pathway. The question of how the object can be known appears to be implicit in Hayek's (1942a) paper, especially section 2, and again in *The Sensory Order* (1952, ch. 2, s. 2), where he indicates that the task of science is, via systematic testing, to replace the initial classification given in sense experience with one that proves more adequate to describe the particular regularities occurring between events as an instance of a more general rule. 'Recognising the particular as an instance of a general rule' (1942a, 271) is no more than classifying or identifying an object as such and such. When this is done, the scientist is claiming that the object is known. The process of science, then, is a process designed to come to know the object – irrespective of whether the term 'thing-in-itself' is used. According to Hayek, natural science allows one to 'get down to objective facts' (1942a, 271). The claim that there is a level of 'objective facts' that one can 'get down to' strongly suggests that he accepts the existence of a knowable reality beyond sense experience.

Consider the second pathway. In another place in the same paper Hayek appears to contradict what he claimed in the first pathway:

> The world of science might be described as no more than a set of rules which enables us to trace out the connections between different complexes of sense perceptions . . . [T]o establish such uniform rules that the perceptible phenomena obey . . .
>
> (Hayek, 1942a, 273)

Here the claim that the task of natural science is to establish connections between 'complexes of sense perceptions', that is, between 'perceptible phenomena', strongly encourages the view that science cannot establish connections between real objects, because the latter, unlike the sense experience they generate, cannot be known. This suggests that there is nothing beyond sense experience, only complexes of sense perceptions, a classical empiricist position. As the subjective idealist Ernst Mach once put it: 'Bodies do not produce sensations, but complexes of sensations make up bodies' (quoted in Vries, 1994, 317).

Hayek appears to have a weaker version of this in mind in *The Sensory Order* when he makes continual reference to the objective world as an objective 'order of events' (1952, 173). He claims that similarity of physical properties of events refers to the similarity of the effects which they give rise to (ibid., 5, 15, 23, 47, and passim). Two objects are the same kind of thing, therefore, if they engender the same effects under the same conditions. This carries implications for Hayek's understanding of how it is that one knows the object when it manifests as a complex of sense perceptions.

Hayek suggests that the word 'real' ought to be 'altogether avoided in scientific discussion', writing that 'The contrast . . . is not between 'appearance' and 'reality' but between the differences of events in their effects on us' (ibid., 4–5). What Hayek is driving at in this rather ambiguous discussion is the following: appearance refers to the effect a sequence of events has upon *us*, whilst reality refers to the effect events have upon *each other*. Knowledge of appearances is gained in the lay process of contemplation (or initial classification), knowledge of the object that generated these appearances is gained in the process of science (re-classification) where the effects, the sequence of events generated when one object affects another object, is recorded and something inferred from it.

The two pathways noted above can, however, be reconciled. Hayek appears to accept the possibility of knowing the object even though it is manifest only as a complex of sense perceptions. One can come to know it via these perceptions by recording the brute facts of experience in the form of regular sequences of events engendered by physical objects acting upon one another, or acting under varying conditions – i.e. via experiment. Sense experience, when organised through a scientific process, appears to allow the possibility of coming to know the object. One comes to know the object, then, via the sequences of events given in sense experience generated under certain conditions.

Note here that the entire weight of Hayek's argument is carried by the putative existence of event regularities, since (on the Humean understanding noted in the previous chapter) if events were not regularly conjoined, then general knowledge would not be possible. This, however, raises the following question: How exactly does the process of science in general, and the recording of event regularities in particular, establish the possibility of coming to know the object? Attempting an answer necessitates a closer look at Hayek's conception of natural science.

How science establishes the possibility of knowing the object

For Hayek, the scientific process is one of 're-classifying objects which our senses have already classified in one way' (1942a, 272). In what follows, I shall make use of Hayek's example of the re-classification of two white powders, although of course the point is a general one. He is, I suggest, attempting to demonstrate how the re-classification of sense experience can result in the possibility of coming to know the object under investigation as a 'particular instance of a general rule' (ibid., 271). He is claiming that science can come to know what things are.

The nervous system might respond to an external stimulus and the mind might, for example, classify two different powders as one and the same. At this stage the agent forms a provisional classification, that is, classifies two external objects as the same constant complex of sense qualities. This stage of cognition is an example of classical empiricism in that the domain of the sensory and the real are fused: what one sees is what is. Natural science, however, cannot rest content with this stage: experiment might reveal that the white powders are in fact different, say, salt and cocaine. The provisional classification is not of sufficient depth to sustain scientific inquiry and therefore has to be developed, revised or re-classified.

Now the fact that Hayek registers a distinction between an external object and one's perception of it implies that the events of experience are taken to be *corrigible* – hence the need for a continual revision or re-classification of the sense data. In this case, the external world (revealed via scientific inquiry) and the sense world (revealed via contemplation) cannot be fused, and Hayek cannot be described as a straightforward classical empiricist in the Humean tradition. He can, however, be classified as an empirical realist, subscribing to an empirical-realist ontology.

The reason that this is not obvious is that discussion of re-classification tends to highlight the gulf between classification by lay agents via *contemplation* and re-classification by scientists via *scientific procedure*. This gulf between lay agent and scientist, however, is not actually under examination. What is under examination, rather, is the gulf between the scientific situation (i.e. procedure of experiment) and the non-experimental situation (i.e. reality). And this is where one finds the fusion that characterises empirical realism.

It is not that the external world, and the sense world *derived from contemplation* are fused – so that what is directly experienced in contemplation is what exists. Rather it is that the external world and the sense world *derived from experiment* are fused – so that what is generated and then experienced (i.e. *in*directly perceived) is what exists. This makes the role of constant conjunctions of events highly significant. The fusion is between the events and their constant conjunction generated via experiment, and the events and their constant conjunctions that are presumed to persist outside that experimental situation. It is not events *per se*, but events manifesting as constant conjunctions that are fused with reality, so that the *sequence* generated is what exists. What are taken to be incorrigible, then, are not events *per se*, but their constant conjunctions.

The process of re-classification involves (amongst other things) the creation of conceptual entities, conceptual constructs which cannot be perceived by the senses at all, for example the atomic structure of chemical compounds. Significantly, there is nothing to prevent the use of complete fictions here. Hayek never acknowledges the existential status of things like 'electrons', 'waves', 'atomic structures' or 'electro magnetic fields' (ibid., 273), leading Lawson (1994c, 145) to suggest that they are, for Hayek, merely conceptual constructs. Re-classification, then, involves a creative step and facilitates the formation of a model which assists in the elaboration of event regularities:

> In place of . . . constant complexes of sense qualities . . . new entities, 'constructs' are created which can only be defined in terms of sense perceptions obtained of the 'same thing' in different circumstances and at different times.
>
> (Hayek, 1942a, 273)

This creative step registers the existence of a third (c) domain or world to add to the two (a) and (b) Hayek already mentions, making the domains as follows:

(a) The physical or external world (*e*);
(b) The world of the senses (*s*);
(c) The theoretical world (*t*).

And yet Hayek is keen to point out that what is created in theory is somehow related to what is perceived:

> The new world which man thus creates in his mind, and which consists altogether of entities . . . (electrons, waves, atomic structures, electro-magnetic fields) . . . which cannot be perceived by the senses, is yet in a definite way related to the world of our senses.
>
> (Ibid., 273)

Figure 3.1 may help to clarify the argument that follows, but note three points.

1 The theoretical world contains experimental objects such as salt and water, and conceptual constructs such as chemical compounds, atoms or magnetic fields.
2 The difference between events X_t and Y_t, X_s and Y_s and X_e and Y_e is that they all occur in different worlds or domains. X_t and Y_t occur under experimental conditions. X_e and Y_e allegedly occur in the real world. X_s and Y_s are the sense experiences of both X_t and Y_t and X_e and Y_e.
3 When a particular relation (i.e. a constant conjunction) is established, via experiment, between events X_t and Y_t, this relation is immediately perceived in the sensory domain as a constant conjunction between events X_s and Y_s. And due to the fusion of sensory and external domains (noted above), by implication, events X_e and Y_e are presumed to be constantly conjoined.

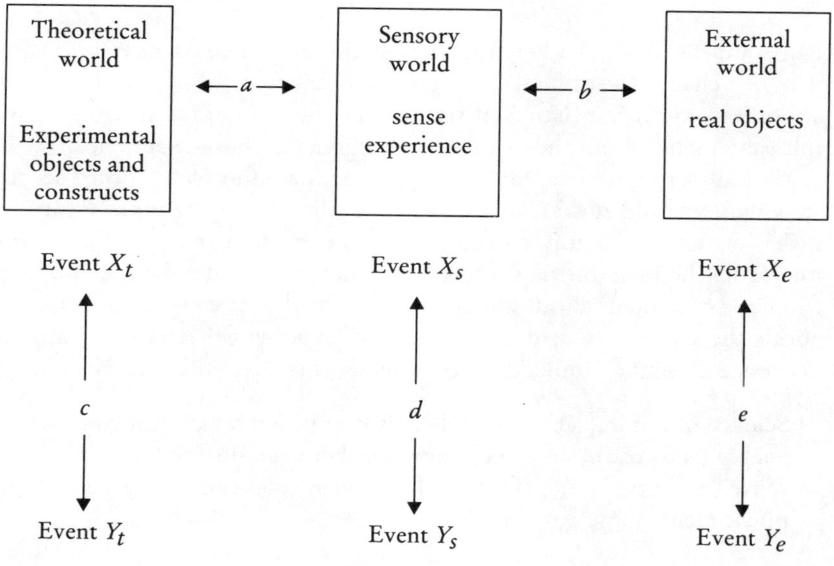

Figure 3.1 The relations between the theoretical, sensory and external worlds are established via the alleged constant conjunction of events appertaining to each world

The point of the scientific exercise is to come to know, to reveal, the object under investigation as something in particular, as salt perhaps. This object cannot, however, be known directly, but only via the events it generates in experimental conditions, apprehended in sense experience.

If science is to be useful, first the theoretical and sense worlds must relate (relation *a*), otherwise statements about events generated in the theoretical world would have no bearing upon events given in sense perception. Second, the sensory and external worlds must relate (relation *b*) otherwise the events generated in the theoretical world and given in sense experience would be completely detached from reality. The important point to note however, is that these relations (*a* and *b*) are established via the (constant) relations between events that occur in each of the worlds – i.e. theoretical (relation *c*), sensory (relation *d*) and external (relation *e*).

Consider the relation between the theoretical and sensory worlds. Hayek suggests that this relation is established in terms of 'rules' and 'keys':

> Although the theories of physical science at the stage which has now been reached can no longer be stated in terms of sense qualities, their significance is due to the fact that we possess rules, a 'key', which enables us to translate them into statements about perceptible phenomena.
>
> (Ibid.)

Rules appear to act as a key, relating the theoretical and sensory worlds, but it is not clear how this relation is supposed to occur. The term 'translate' appears to mean translation of statements obtained in the theoretical world into statements about the external world given in sense experience.

Without a rule, a metaphorical key, to facilitate this translation, theoretical statements would not be 'significant', i.e. they would be purely formal. In order for this translation to occur, statements must be of a specific form: they must take the form of rules. Only when statements take the specific form of rules can statements about the theoretical world be translated into statements about the external world given in sense experience. And rules appear to express the regular connections between events. According to Hayek:

> Science might in fact be described as no more than a set of rules which enable us to trace out the connections between different complexes of sense perceptions . . . to establish uniform rules which the perceptible phenomena obey.
>
> (Ibid.)

'Uniform' or 'general rules', by which Hayek appears to mean 'scientific laws', establish connections between events. According to Hayek, experiment reveals 'what proves to behave in a similar manner in similar circumstances' (ibid., 271–3). This can only mean that event *X*'s are regularly conjoined with event *Y*'s. It appears the rules that are established between events (i.e. relations *c*, *d* and *e*) somehow permit the theoretical, the sense and the external worlds to relate (i.e. relations *a* and *b*) and because of this, they permit the object to be known that is, classified as salt. The question is: How?

According to Hayek, scientists construct and/or obtain, via theory and experiment, a model consisting of the following theoretical components:

- conceptual objects such as atoms and magnetic fields which may or may not have an external referent;
- events X_t and Y_t which are presumed to have external referents, namely events X_e and Y_e;
- laws which are presumed to establish relations, ultimately between events X_e and Y_e. The rule or law is established via the generation of a constant conjunction between the events X_t and Y_t.

Having constructed this model, and tested it in experimental conditions, the scientist presumes that statements derived from the relation between the experimental events X_t and Y_t, are transferable into statements about real events X_e and Y_e. In other words, because under experimental conditions, events X_t and Y_t are constantly conjoined, it is presumed that outside the experimental conditions events X_e and Y_e are similarly constantly conjoined. To stick with the example: whenever a measure of salt (the object under investigation) is placed (event X_t) in a measure of water, it dissolves (event Y_t), thereby proving that the object is in fact salt and not, say, chalk. The object initially classified as chalk is re-classified as salt.

At this point, the argument is complete; the theoretical world is related to the sensory world, the latter is related to the external world, and we come to know something more about the object than its mere appearance – even though we only have access to sense experience. By his elaboration of the natural scientific process of re-classification, Hayek establishes that there is a real object and one can come to know it, to classify it as such and such, via its effects. Of enormous significance, however, is the fact that *only certain kinds of effects are necessary and sufficient for general scientific knowledge to be gained.*

That (positivist) science is able to classify or identify an object from a series of events is due to the latter manifesting in experimental conditions as constant conjunctions. If events merely appeared as a random flux, they could not be classified as anything in particular. If on one occasion salt dissolves in water and on another occasion does not, we cannot know what it is that we are dealing with – without further experiment to obtain an event regularity. *In order therefore for Hayek to maintain that a mind-independent object can be known, whilst simultaneously maintaining that it can be known only via sense experiences, he has to accept the ubiquity of constant conjunctions of events, that is, a Humean notion of scientific law.*

Physical ontology

Once Hayek's understanding of science as re-classification is fully grasped, his ontology is easily ascertained. Only two types of entities are used in science: conceptual constructs such as atoms, and events given in sense experience. The former, since they are merely useful constructs that aid theory formation and have no real existence, cannot therefore be included amongst the entities permitted in ontology. This leaves Hayek with an ontology consisting of the events of sense experience, that is an empirical-realist ontology.

As noted in the previous chapter, the synthesis of subjective-idealist epistemology and empirical-realist ontology, when transposed into the field of philosophy of science gives rise to transcendental idealism – a neo-Kantian position. Transcendental idealism, in its guise as positivism, employs a creative stage in the modelling exercise whereby a tractable mechanism is postulated to produce the event regularities under scrutiny. There is, however, no requirement that such mechanisms be real. A theory might simply use fictitious theoretical constructs to facilitate model building and the *ex post* rationalisation of event regularities. Hayek's position in natural science, turning upon the use of fictitious theoretical constructs and the presumed ubiquity of constant conjunctions of events, is quite clearly that of transcendental idealism.

Since the relation between subjective idealism and transcendental idealism is not clear-cut due to the former being essentially a position in metaphysics and the latter a position in philosophy of science, one cannot read Hayek's subjective idealism directly from his transcendental idealism. I suggest however, that what establishes the link is the fact that the distinctive feature of both subjective and transcendental idealism is that 'the order that obtains in the world, is actually imposed by men in their cognitive activity' (Bhaskar, 1978, 27). This has two moments.

First, order is imposed upon nature via the creation of constant conjunctions of events in experimental situations. Second, the use of fictitious theoretical mechanisms implies that they are constructions of the human mind, that is, structures imposed upon the phenomena of sense experience. As Bhaskar puts it, on this view, 'the natural world becomes a construction of the human mind or, in its modern versions, of the scientific community . . . [N]ature is the product of man' (1978, 25).

Whereas for subjective idealism the structure is imposed on the object by the pure categories of the understanding, for transcendental idealism the structure is imposed on the object by the process of re-classification via conceptual constructs and the generation of constant conjunctions of events.

HAYEK'S PHILOSOPHICAL POSITION IN SOCIAL SCIENCE

Hayek's position in social science might usefully be interpreted as an overreaction to positivism, or more accurately, to scientism. Once Hayek recognises that for social scientists, the external world is not objectively given (*pace* classical empiricism and positivism), he does not stop at the correct view that it is mediated by, or *dependent* upon, agents' subjectively formed conceptions. He overreacts, making the hermeneutic-foundationalist, and as I shall show, subjective-idealist, presumption that the social world is *determined* by, or *exhausted* by, agents' conceptions.

Hayek, in effect, empties his social ontology of *real* social material, leaving a residue of nothing more than conceptions, ideas, beliefs, attitudes and so on, that is, *ideal* social material. The loss of ontology, or more accurately, the collapse of ontology into epistemology, styled by Bhaskar as the 'epistemic fallacy', manifests at the level of social theory in the removal of the mind-independent, external world from the interest field of social science. As Bhaskar put it:

> when the idea of scientific certainty eventually collapsed [as it did for Hayek in the 1940s], the absence of an ontological dimension discouraged anything other than a purely voluntaristic action – in which it was supposed that because our beliefs about the world were not causally determined by the world, then they must be completely free creations of our own minds . . .
>
> (Bhaskar, 1978, 44)

I shall show in the following sub-sections how Hayek empties his social ontology of real social entities. The first sub-section will briefly consider artefacts, whilst the second concentrates upon the more important category of social material to show that Hayek conceives of this as originating with the cognitive activity of the subject. The third sub-section will note that Hayek advocates a method which avoids consideration of social objects that exist independently of their identification. His advocacy of this method indicates his presuppositions *vis-à-vis* the nature of the social world. The final sub-section will consider Hayek's discussion of the mind in Hayek's schema, illustrating the centrality it plays in social inquiry.

Artefacts and subjective idealism[1]

Artefacts such as tools are brutely physical in the sense that they exist, in part, as mind-independent physical entities, *and* conceptual in the sense that they are, in part, dependent upon their identification by human agents. This dual nature makes them difficult to investigate, something that is compounded by Hayek's ambiguity on these matters.

As a result of these difficulties, this sub-section will fail to come to a conclusion on the possible link between Hayek's treatment of artefacts and subjective idealism. There is, however, good reason for including a section with such a negative conclusion. Hayek's thoughts *vis-à-vis* artefacts (for example, hammers), which often cannot be pinned down to any philosophical position, must not be confused or conflated with his statements on social material (for example, policemen), which suggest a subjective-idealist philosophy. Discussing artefacts separately will pre-empt any possible confusion or conflation.

Consider the following sample of comments (there are many more) taken from Hayek (1942a) – and note how the physicality of the external world is understated and cognitive activity overstated:[2]

> So far as human actions are concerned, the things *are* what the people acting think they are.
>
> (Hayek, 1942a, 278)

> [Definitions of instruments such as hammers and barometers] will not contain any reference to its substance, or shape, or physical attribute. They are abstractions from *all* the physical attributes of the things . . . and that their definition must run *entirely* in terms of mental attitudes towards the things.
>
> (Ibid., second emphasis added)

> Any knowledge which we may happen to possess about the true nature of the material thing, but which the people whose action we want to explain do not possess, is as little relevant to the explanation of their actions as our private disbelief in the efficacy of a magic charm will help us understand the behaviour of the savage who believes in it.
>
> (Ibid., 280)

> What is relevant in the study of society is not whether or not these laws of nature are true in any objective sense, but *solely* whether they are believed and acted upon by people. And all the 'physical laws of production' that we meet in economics are not physical laws in the sense of the physical sciences, but peoples beliefs about what they can do.
>
> (Ibid., 281, emphasis added)

> [O]nly what agents know or believe can enter as a motive for their conscious action.
>
> (Ibid., 284)

Hayek goes to great lengths to establish what he obviously feels are some of the most important points as far as social science is concerned, namely: (a) that conceptions, ideas, beliefs, and so on held by agents are not the same as physical objects; (b) that agents are motivated solely by conceptions and not by physical objects *per se*; so (c) the physical nature or brute physicality of objects is therefore not part of the subject matter; in which case (d) all that is left, and all that matters is what lay agents believe to be the case, that is, their conceptions; so that even if (e) the social scientist 'knows' that the lay agent's belief is incorrect by knowing what the physical object really is, this latter knowledge is irrelevant for understanding how the agent will act.

Whilst these examples suggest the *completely* socially constructed nature of artefacts, there is more to it. He appears to be making the claim that any property appertaining to the physicality of mind-independent entities does not enter the interest field of social science. All that matters 'for the purposes of social study' (Hayek, 1942a, 280) are the conceptions held by agents about them. In other words, he is not denying that the physicality of artefacts exerts a 'pull' as it were on the formation of agents' conceptions and subsequently upon their actions, he is merely ruling this out of the interest field of social science. This claim, however, is not as innocuous as first appears and can, I suggest, be interpreted in two ways.[3]

First, it can be interpreted as a mistake, or perhaps too narrow a focus on the domain of conceptions to the neglect of the mind-independent, external domain. Hayek overreacts to scientism and the crude materialist notion that agents' actions derive from the objective properties of the external world, by downplaying, ignoring, or even removing the external world and its properties from the interest field of social science. Agents are presumed to act *solely* on the basis of their subjective beliefs about the external world. Hayek does not, of course, deny the presence of a mind-independent, and possibly causal external world, he merely, if incorrectly (as I shall show), claims that properties of entities residing in this domain lie outside the interest field of the social scientist. On this interpretation, then, Hayek merely makes a mistake at the level of social theory, and nothing can be inferred about his philosophical presuppositions.

Second, the claim can be interpreted as a consistent manifestation of an implicit philosophical position. As was pointed out in the previous chapter, all scientific thinking necessarily presupposes a particular ontology. The claim that the external world is placed outside the interest field due simply to a mistake still leaves the question of what ontological presupposition is being made. We could in effect ask: Given this mistake, what ontology must be presupposed? Two (sub-)interpretations are possible:

1 Hayek might be committed to a social ontology that consists of ideal entities – i.e. be a *realist about conceptions* constructed by the cognitively active subject. In this case his decision to ignore mind-independent entities in his socio-economic theory is quite consistent with his ontology. There simply is no causally efficacious external world: the external world is present but inert. Hermeneutic foundationalism is, then, a *consistent* manifestation of subjective idealism.
2 Hayek might be committed to a social ontology consisting of real, causally efficacious, mind-independent entities, – i.e. he might be a *realist about mind-independent entities*. He might then choose to ignore the role they play in informing agents' conceptions and therefore actions, in his socio-economic theory. By ignoring his own ontological commitment, however, an inconsistency is generated between ontology and theory.

Let us consider these interpretations and (sub-)interpretations in a little more depth, to find if there are any grounds for any of them. Hayek's presupposition that human actions are based on the state of the external world, and that social scientists might simply choose to ignore this domain simply because it lies outside their interest field could conceal another presupposition – namely that *actions are based upon beliefs and conceptions full stop*. That this might be the implicit presupposition gains credence from two sources. First, from the number of times Hayek repeats the idea that only conceptions matter for human action, and secondly via the transcendental question: What must Hayek be presupposing about the relation between the external world and social action, given the complete absence of this world from his account of social scientific inquiry? If actions are based *even partially* on the properties of the external world, then these properties must, at some stage, be included within the interest field of social science – if social inquiry is to be complete.

A brief comparison with a transcendental realist/materialist perspective is illuminating. For a materialist this one-sided approach is completely unthinkable since the physicality of an artefact is inextricably involved in, although it does not exhaust, any social scientific investigation or definition of it. If an agent (incorrectly) conceives of a hammer as a magic charm and acts upon this misconception, then the social scientist will want to know things such as how such a misconception came to be held; the social practices, power structures or ideological factors that are involved in the formation and maintenance of this misconception; and the consequences in terms of agents' action that follow from it.[4] Inquiries like this are necessary even if the investigation attempts no more than 'to explain the . . . actions of many men' (Hayek, 1942a, 276), since social action is (unless one subscribes to complete voluntarism) likely to be the result of *much more* than agents' (mis)conceptions. That is, external reality, even if it is conceptually mediated, will also cause action and must, therefore, be investigated.

The properties of such an external entity can be ignored only at the cost of inconsistency between an ontology which admits of external, causally efficacious, non-inert properties, and a theoretical approach that simply ignores its own ontological commitments. If Hayek is not to be inconsistent, then he must be a realist about conceptions only, that is, must presuppose an ontology rooted in subjective idealism.

The plausibility of the interpretation that Hayek adopts a subjective-idealist philosophy and not simply a mistaken socio-economic theory, and therefore the (sub-)interpretation that he avoids inconsistency between his ontology and theory, appears to lie in his preoccupation with *cognitive* as opposed to *sensuous* activity. However, the way in which agents form conceptions of the external world, and the grounds for any subsequent action, are not, *contra* Hayek (1942a, 288 and 1952, 5–8), solely a matter of psychology, but also a matter of (a) the properties of that external world, and (b) the way that agents interact with its physical texture – i.e. human praxis.

Taylor offers a neat example of what praxis involves, and why it involves more than just psychology:

> We can draw a neat line between my *picture* of an object and that object, but not between my *dealing* with the object and that object. It may make sense to ask one to focus on what one believes about something, say a football, even in the absence of that thing; but when it comes to playing football, the corresponding question would be absurd. The actions involved in the game cannot be done without the object; they include the object.
>
> (Quoted in Sayer, 1992, 48)

When we act, we interact with the (physical or social) external world so the texture of this world is inextricably linked to the conception we form of it, and the actions we subsequently take. Hayek's refusal to elaborate upon real sensuous activity and his preoccupation with cognitive activity suggest that conceptions are in some sense estranged from the texture of the external world, inviting the interpretation that Hayek is a subjective idealist.

Having laid out the possible grounds for this interpretation, I now draw back from it. I think it is virtually impossible to ascertain whether Hayek is a subjective idealist or is simply mistaken at the level of social theory, due in part to the nature of artefacts, and in part to his own ambiguity on such matters. There are, however, two points to note from this rather negative discussion of artefacts.

The first is to recognise that the charge of subjective idealism *vis-à-vis* Hayek's understanding of artefacts is not without grounds. Whilst I shall not charge Hayek with it, there are moments when he certainly encourages this interpretation. I suggest, therefore, that Hayek is simply mistaken in down-playing the role of external, mind-independent entities in the study of human action. The second point is that an elaboration of the nature of artefacts allows one to avoid any error that could arise by confusing Hayek's thoughts on artefacts with his thoughts on social material. That is, we cannot use examples where Hayek might be treating artefacts as real entities to argue that he treats social material in a similar manner – the two are quite different kinds of thing.

Social material and subjective idealism

When we move from discussing artefacts to discussing social material such as social structures or elements of social structure, for example, policemen, as Hayek does, the claim that underlying his thinking is a subjective-idealist epistemology can be made with some degree of satisfaction. For Hayek, social material, social structure, is an example of what I refer to in Chapter 2 as *ideal social material*. It is real in that it makes a difference but has no material grounding: its origin is the cognitive activity of the transcendental subject not in any mind-independent social structure. This can be illustrated by elaborating upon Hayek's attempt to discuss what he misleadingly calls social 'structure'.

Consider first of all this sample of comments drawn once again from Hayek (1942a):

> Society as we know it is, as it were, built up from the concepts and ideas held by the people. . . . it is the individual concepts, the views people have formed of each other and the things, which form the true elements of the social structure.
>
> (283–4)

> If the social structures can remain the same although different individuals succeed each other at particular points, this is not because the individuals which succeed each other are completely identical, but because they succeed each other in particular relations, in particular attitudes they take towards other people and as objects of particular views held by other people about them.
>
> (284)

> The individuals are merely the foci in the network of relationships and it is the various attitudes of the individuals towards each other (or their . . . attitudes towards physical objects) which form the current recognisable and familiar elements of the structure.
>
> (Ibid.)

> If one policeman succeeds another policeman at a particular post, this means . . . that the new man succeeds him in certain attitudes towards his fellow man and as an object of certain attitudes towards his fellow man which are relevant to his function as a policeman. This is sufficient to preserve a constant structural element . . . we recognise these elements of human relationships only because they are known to us from the working of our own minds . . .
>
> (Ibid.)

> That in this effort to construct these different patterns of social relations we must relate the individual's action not to the objective qualities of the persons and things towards which he acts, but that our data must be man and the physical world as they appear to the men whose actions we try to explain, follows from the fact that only what people know or believe can enter as a motive into their conscious action.
>
> (Ibid.)

> The various types of individual beliefs or attitudes are . . . the elements from which we build up the structure of possible relationships between individuals.
>
> (288)

I interpret these comments as follows. Society is composed of social structures, which in turn are composed of social elements. Different structures are composed from different elements. The elements consist of conceptions, that is, ideas, attitudes, beliefs, and so on, formed by agents about other agents and objects. Social structure consists ultimately of conceptions. Social structures endure, that is, remain the same although individual agents change, because the elements that compose them, i.e. the conceptions, remain in the same relation to one another. There is, it appears, a network of relations that exist not between agents themselves, but between the conceptions held by agents. Hayek adopts a relational conception of social structures, although the relata are mere conceptions.[5]

Consider Hayek's example of the policeman as an element of social structure. He is (quite correctly) unconcerned about the brute physicality of the policeman, he is concerned only with the sociality, with policeman as a social category. In what, however, does this sociality consist?

Agents hold attitudes towards policemen, and towards other agents who hold attitudes towards policemen. Policemen hold attitudes towards agents and towards other policemen, and so on. (The permutations of this network are, of course, far more complex.) A particular agent might, for example, consider policemen to be those people who fight crime, and a particular policeman might also consider his own role to be that of crime fighter. As agents and policemen come to hold this attitude, then this attitude comes to constitute the social-structure policeman. What a policeman is as a social category, an element of social structure, is composed from the attitudes held by agents and policemen. The social category of policeman as a crime fighter is thereby socially constructed. In fact, in one place Hayek actually refers to 'the individual attitudes which form the elements of [the] structure of . . . social complexes' (1943, 43).

Both individual agents and individual policemen will come and go in space and time, but the structural element of policeman will endure because the relations that exist and endure are not between agents and policemen but between their attitudes. Continuity of social structure occurs not because successive people are identical but because the attitudes people have of the situation remain intact.

In other words, 'policeman' as an element of social structure is constituted in the act of thought. Policemen as constitutive elements in the social structure are no more than what agents believe them to be. If policemen form part of the material out of which social structure is fabricated, and policemen as a social category are merely the conceptions held by agents, then social structure is merely conceptual in nature. Now whilst it is true that much social material is conceptually non-physical in nature, in this case, the social category policeman has no material grounding whatsoever and must therefore be interpreted as *ideal* social material: i.e. a manifestation of subjective idealism.

Critics have responded to my interpretation by claiming that just because Hayek suggests that the social scientific approach to the study of policemen is concerned only with agents' conceptions, this does not imply that policemen are reducible to mere conceptions. Once again, however, it is Hayek's silence that is revealing, in the sense that he can suggest a social scientific approach to elements of social material such as policemen, and never even feel the need to discuss anything other than agents' conceptions. A brief comparison with a transcendental-realist/materialist perspective once again illustrates what is hidden within the silence.

A transcendental-realist/materialist (for example, a Marxist) approach that remains entirely within the domain of conceptions is completely unthinkable. Policemen form part of a real social structure, because the position of and set of practices that constitute the social category 'policeman' are grounded in certain social relations that involve mind-independent entities such as the state. If policemen actually exist as the strong arm of the state, and agents (mistakenly) believe they exist to fight crime, then agents' beliefs do not exhaust the social category 'policeman'. There is more to the social category 'policeman' than just the conceptions held by agents, and this extra component must enter the interest field of the social scientist. The conceptions that agents form of policemen, far from constituting the social category 'policeman', are in fact constituted by a range of mind-independent entities such as social relations.

Mind-independent, social entities, then, even if they are completely unknown to the agents under scrutiny, cannot be ignored in a social scientific investigation of agents and their interaction with social structures. Social entities are not ideal but real, and the social ontology must reflect this, otherwise, as appears to be the case with Hayek, we shall attempt to grasp the social world using the wrong ontological categories.

If, however, as Hayek does, a social scientist advocates carrying out a social study which requires no reference to the external, mind-independent, social domain, then we are entitled to consider the possibility that such a domain is ignored because it has no effect on the agent. That social scientists might choose to ignore this domain on the grounds that it lies outside their interest field conceals the possibility that *actions are based upon beliefs and conceptions full stop*. The possibility that this is the implicit presupposition is revealed via a transcendental question: What must Hayek be presupposing about the relation between the external social world and the formation of social structures, given the complete absence of this world from his account of social scientific inquiry? If conceptions are based even *partially* on the properties of the external social world, then these properties must be included within the interest field of social science.

The external, social, domain can be ignored only at the cost of inconsistency between an ontology which admits of a causally efficacious, non-inert, external, social world and a theoretical approach that simply ignores this ontological commitment. Consistency is restored to Hayek's position by recognising that the external world has no causal effect in concept formation, because the subject in the form of the agent structures the object in the form of the social world – i.e. by recognising that Hayek is a subjective idealist *vis-à-vis* social material.

Before turning to methodological considerations, unravelling the thread of the argument in Hayek (1942a) is revealing. Allowing, for the sake of argument, his over-zealous treatment of the conceptual texture of the world investigated by social science, Hayek has established that brutely physical non-conceptual objects and the physicality of artefacts are irrelevant for social science: all that is relevant are the conceptions held by agents.

At this point however, the argument jumps illicitly and (virtually) imperceptibly from a discussion of physical material to social material, but with one crucial point retained. Hayek has removed the necessity for social scientists to consider the external world in its physical non-conceptual form. When he then shifts to discuss the social world, he maintains a similar position, although now the external world that he is dealing with is social not physical. All he has left are the conceptions held by agents. He has no external phenomena such as social structures, because these are the analogue of the physical objects that he has just moved. In other words, in removing the physical non-conceptual, he simultaneously removes the conceptual non-physical including real social material, leaving a residue of ideal social material. Agents' conceptions exhaust society. This is why he can make comments such as: 'The real contrast is between ideas which by being held by the people become the *causes* of a social phenomenon' (1942a, 285, emphasis added).

He moves, therefore, from the correct insight that the social world is concept-*dependent*, to the incorrect or exaggerated claim that the social world is concept-*determined*. It appears that in breaking with positivism and its failure to treat the sociality of objects, Hayek proceeds directly to the opposite extreme and treats all external social objects as purely conceptual.

Methodology and subjective idealism

Further evidence of Hayek's subjective idealism emerges by pursuing the following transcendental question: What must Hayek be presupposing about the nature of the world, for (his version of) the social scientific method to be perceived as successful?

Consider first his proposed methodological approach. As will become clear in the following chapter, for Hayek the subject matter for a social scientist is exclusively the conceptions held by lay agents. Lay agents experience the world, understand it in a particular way, describe it in a particular way and act according to this understanding and definition. Social scientists, then, have to base their own understanding and descriptions on those of lay agents –

which are taken to be unproblematic and incorrigible. Social science has to understand using agents' understandings, and to describe using agents' descriptions. Anything that the observing social scientist happens to know over and above what is given via accessing agents' ideas is, for Hayek, irrelevant in explaining their behaviour.

Of significance here is the fact that Hayek obviously does not find this a handicap. As I demonstrated via the examples of artefacts and social material, he feels that the social world can be understood with this rather emaciated ontology. That Hayek can advocate the investigation of human action without taking into consideration the domain of real social material can only imply that this domain has no influence on the actions of the agent, since if it does, and this is recognised, it must be investigated – at some point.

If the external domain of real social material has no influence on agents' action, then all the phenomena necessary for agents to initiate action must be internal, existing as a demi-urge within the dimension of the conceptual, that is, within agents' ideas. For example, for a materialist, a real social structure such as a rule of action exists externally to (some) agents, and may be drawn upon as a condition or a material cause of action. If, in complete contrast, for a subjective idealist, mind-independent social structures cannot be conceived of, then there can be no material cause of action. Causality lies internal to the agent. In this scenario, it is not the case that agents draw upon external structures and are thereby enabled to initiate action; they construct the conditions for their action in their own minds. The conditions for action, then, are not real but ideal – hence the voluntarism of hermeneutic foundationalism.

An answer can now be given to the initial transcendental question: What must Hayek be presupposing about the nature of the social world, for (his version of) the social scientific method to be perceived as successful? He must be presupposing that the social world is the subjective creation of agents. Once again, it is not merely that Hayek chooses to advocate a method that focuses upon ideas or conceptions and not real social material: it could not be otherwise. Social material is merely ideal, and is constituted by the mind.

The role of the mind and subjective idealism

One of the key claims made by subjective idealists is that the transcendental subject structures the object, a process that involves the existence of a structured and active mind existing prior to its experience of the external world. Hayek (1942a) attempts the construction of a methodological approach which embraces the primacy of the active mind. This is, arguably, a manifestation of Kantian philosophy, as Hayek proceeds to push this active mind centre stage.[6]

He offers an argument to support his assertion of the primacy of mind, by way of a discussion of tools and instruments: hammer and barometers (1942a,

278). He argues that any attempt to refer to them as objective facts, irrespective of what people think of them, is impossible. Definition will always involve, and involve no more than a thinking person, an actual or imaginary effect and the thing itself. Definitions will not refer to any physical properties the object might possess. He gives another example, of an archaeologist trying to determine whether the object under scrutiny is a stone tool or merely a chance product of nature. The scientist attempts to decide by trying to understand the mind of historic man, trying to understand how he would have made the implement.

In both these cases the scientist is, he claims, able to intuit aspects of human activity intimately, via recourse to knowledge of the working of her own mind. The important point to take from this is that Hayek claims that scientists can form concepts about the object (hammer, barometer or historic tool) *solely* by virtue of the fact that all humans possess similar minds (1942a, 279; 1952, 23). He does not halt therefore at the (correct) claim that social material is concept-dependent, but exaggerates this to the (incorrect) claim that the concept-dependence of social material is all that matters.

The objection to my argument can be raised that Hayek does not deny the influence of the physical properties of tools, he merely starts by taking agents' conceptions as data. He presumes the material properties of tools have *already* shaped agents, conceptions, and the task of the social scientist is merely (a) to recover agents' beliefs or meanings, and (b) to trace out the implications of these beliefs. This objection, however, merely triggers a regress. If agents' conceptions were formed at some time in the past (even if only in part) by the material properties of tools, then *at that time* these properties formed part of the interest field of social science. It does not matter when the conceptions were formed: if they were formed with respect to the physical properties of an artefact, then these properties must enter the social scientist's interest field *at some point*. They cannot forever be ignored, not even 'for the purpose of social study' (Hayek, 1942a, 280).

The mistake (or possible subjective idealism) buried in the continual downplaying of the material properties of artefacts is thrown into relief by considering the critical-realist/materialist explanation of such phenomena. The physical structure of a hammer is not irrelevant even to the social process of classifying it as something in particular.[7] An object is called a hammer not merely because agents choose to classify it as such, but rather, they classify it as such because it possesses certain intrinsic properties that make it a potential hammer and also because it has been found, via practical activity, to be suitable for the purpose of hammering. Similarly, the archaeologist attempting to understand the nature of an object proceeds not solely (if at all) by attempting to recover the mind of prehistoric man, by imputing to such man the ideas of contemporary man, but by attempting to recover the practical activity of prehistoric man. This requires understanding of the centrality of social labour in its widest description, that is, practical activity.

In exaggerating the role of the human subject's cognitive activity, whilst ignoring the role of the object and practical human action in social life, Hayek reveals his subjective-idealist leanings. Whilst not discussing Hayek, the following comment by the archaeological anthropologist E. Leacock pinpoints the source of the error of idealism, an error which appears to apply to Hayek:

> The very impressiveness of mankind's mental achievements, however, has obscured the fundamental significance of labour. Furthermore, the separation of planning for labour from the labour itself . . . contributed to the rise of an *idealistic world outlook, one that explains people's actions as arising out of thoughts instead of their needs.*
>
> (Quoted in Woolfson, 1982, 77, emphasis added)

The transcendental subject that appears to structure the object in Hayek's social science is, however, in one fundamental aspect different from its counterpart in Kant's schema. The difference turns on Hayek's ability to draw upon cognitive psychology[8] to explain the operation of the mind, where Kant had only metaphysical speculation. This implies that the entire issue of cognitive psychology (implicitly) underpins most of the discussion of Hayek's subjective-idealist epistemology.

Hayek II ends up, then, with what I shall refer to as an 'augmented Kantian epistemology'. Kant's notion of the pure concepts of the understanding, which synthesise the manifold thereby making cognition possible, is replaced with a system of classification. Whilst the former are inexplicable in scientific terms, the latter are based firmly upon the neurological/physiological mechanisms of the nervous system.[9] Hayek substituted sensory psychology for Kant's metaphysical speculation, whilst maintaining the same basic cognitive framework. The idealism remains subjective irrespective of the mechanism that synthesises or classifies, because it is only by this active subjective mechanism that the object is constituted. In other words, the transcendental subject remains at the heart of Hayek's philosophy; only the nature of the cognitive apparatus is changed.

Social ontology

It appears, then, that one can draw the same conclusion for social science as was drawn for natural science. Paraphrasing Bhaskar (p. 28) one might say that the social world becomes a construction of the human mind or, in its modern versions, of the scientific community, the social world is the product of man. That Hayek feels at home in a world of purely ideal social material is because, for him, nothing other than this kind of material matters for understanding social action. And nothing else matters because agents create their own conditions for action. The fact, then, that Hayek opts to focus upon the concepts or ideas held by agents and not upon real social material is derived quite consistently from his subjective idealism, whereby agents construct the ideal social material that constitutes their world.

Hayek's ontological position in social science is, however, different from that in natural science. In the latter he admits only of events given in experience and is quite clearly defined as an empirical realist. In the former, by contrast, he extends the possible objects of knowledge from events given in sense experience to include conceptions. Unlike such entities as atoms and magnetic fields, Hayek is not using conceptions as fictional, theoretical constructs: he takes them as real, as the building blocks of society, as the basic data for social science. Adding another type of existent to events, however, makes inappropriate the ascription empirical realist (in the Humean tradition). I suggest therefore that his ontology be referred to as an 'augmented' empirical-realist one, one that permits not only of events, but also of the conceptions (i.e. ideas, attitudes, beliefs, etc) held by agents.

CONCLUSION

Whilst Hayek virtually cedes *natural* science to positivism, the possibilities opened up by recognition of the role of the active subjective mind and the ideas generated by it cannot be prevented from encroaching upon the practice of *social* science, engendering, in the process, a partial break with positivism. In social science Hayek partially breaks with positivism, something that manifests itself in economics as a break with the mainstream. However, the general epistemological and ontological positions adopted mean that general knowledge can only be obtained on the presumption that events given in sense experience occur in the form of constant conjunctions. Hence in both natural and (implicitly) in social science, Hayek retains, along with positivism, the notion of Humean law. As the next chapter will demonstrate, Hayek's ambivalent action to positivism has implications for his adopted method.

4

THE METHODOLOGY UNDERLYING HAYEK II's SOCIO-ECONOMIC THEORY

Investigation of Hayek's philosophical position reveals the exaggerated emphasis he places on subjective conceptions formed by agents and presumed to be constitutive of the social world. This emphasis, influenced by other aspects of the philosophical synthesis he adopts, extends into, and informs, his methodological approach. The aim of this chapter is to elaborate upon the nature of this method.[1]

SUBJECTIVISM

This section illustrates how, via successive small developments in thinking, the correct insights of subjectivism can become overstated and thereby misleading – particularly if the subscribed-to epistemology is subjective idealism. Subjectivism developed out of the neo-Kantian philosophy of Dilthey and Weber, who stressed the need for understanding, or *verstehen*, as opposed to explaining, or *erklären*, in social science. Since Hayek does not define it, I use Rubinstein's concise definition of the subjectivist method:

> The aim of the social sciences, according to the subjectivist, is to make sense of human conduct by seeing the point . . . [S]ubjectivism considers the interpretive understanding of the ideas of social actors to comprise the heart of social science. This programme takes the form of two related goals: (1) the motivational understanding of action, and (2) an explication of the common-sense cultural beliefs of social actors.
>
> (Rubinstein, 1981, 15 and 62)

Bacharach pushes the notion a little farther towards a more extreme subjectivism by claiming that one key proposition of the approach is that:

> the workings of the economic system depend upon the 'intentional mental states' or 'propositional attitudes' of economic agents – their beliefs, their hopes, fears, evaluations.
>
> (Bacharach, 1989, 129)

Hayek's valid insight is that social science has to be concerned precisely with that which natural science attempts to get away from, that is, the initial perceptions lay agents have of the external world. Entities such as hammers, barometers, land, commodities, food, money, and so on cannot be defined solely in physical terms, but also in terms of the views people hold about them. From this perspective, social scientists need to understand what the humans concerned believe themselves to be doing. In other words, the conscious conceptions agents hold about the external world are not something to be got rid of, as in the natural sciences, but *constitute the basic data of social sciences.*

HERMENEUTIC FOUNDATIONALISM

Lawson (1994c, 138) has claimed that Hayek adopts what the former refers to as 'hermeneutic foundationalism'.[2] One way of coming to understand what hermeneutic foundationalism involves is to conceive of it as extreme subjectivism. It takes the key and correct insight of the subjectivist perspective, then proceeds to overstate the case.

Sayer (1992, 35) defines hermeneutics as 'The discipline or science concerned with the interpretation of meaning'. He goes on to exemplify what hermeneutics implies:

> It is sometimes said of someone that they 'read' a social situation well or badly. This is a revealing definition, for the understanding to which we refer, sometimes termed 'verstehen', is rather like that used in and obtained from reading a book. We do not understand a book . . . by observing and analysing the shape of the words or the frequency of their occurrence, but by interpreting their meaning. To this reading we always bring interpretive skills and some kind of pre-understanding of what the text might be about.
>
> (Ibid.)

The key, correct insight of hermeneutics, then, is the recognition of the ubiquity of interpretation at various stages in natural and social scientific inquiry. Hermeneutic foundationalism results from overstating this insight, by extending subjective interpretation to the point where it becomes subjective construction. In social science, subjective interpretation when overstated leads to a conception of the social world, not merely dependent upon, but fully determined or exhausted by, the (private or social) conceptions held by agents. As Hayek puts it: 'So far as human actions are concerned, the things *are* what the acting people think they are' (1942a, 278). Lawson (1994c, 138–9) sums up this perspective as follows:

> In other words, in addition to highlighting the concept dependent nature of social life, Hayek, most of the time at least, argues as if social life is concept determined, as if it is exhausted by individual conceptions and attitudes . . . Society is then conceptual in nature.

Philosophical roots of hermeneutic foundationalism

Hayek's adoption of hermeneutic foundationalism is, I suggest, a manifestation at the level of social science of his synthesised philosophical position.[3] As noted in the previous chapter, Hayek rejects the physical object as constituting part of the subject matter for social science, and then, in a slippage between the physical and the social domains, he also loses the real social object. Losing real social material does not, of course, mean that social ontology is banished, since the existence of entities of one kind or another must always be presupposed. In Hayek's case, the idealist component (of subjective idealism) expands the domain of the ideal, meaning that agents' conceptions fill the vacuum left by the disappearance of the real social object, whilst the subjectivist component supplies the origin of the ideas – the cognitively active mind of the subject. As Hamlyn (1987, 16) puts it: 'Once given the thought that we have direct access only to the mental, it is an easy step to the thesis that the mental constitutes in some form the only reality.'

As the previous chapter illustrated, Hayek merely succeeds in collapsing the object into ideas about the object, a manifestation at the social scientific level of the subjective-idealist claim that the object is constituted by the transcendental subject. The belief that the social world is subjectively constituted, or concept-determined, leads to a series of other methodological themes which will be explored over the remainder of the chapter.

THE ACTIONS OF AGENTS ARE MOTIVATED BY IDEAS

Whilst a physical stimulus can be described in physical terms, this is inadequate for the purposes of *social* science, since it would involve ignoring knowledge about the way it is perceived and therefore acted upon by humans. As the previous chapter makes clear, Hayek argues that the *only* thing that matters, as far as what humans actually do, is the consciously held knowledge that they believe to be correct and subsequently act upon. The task of the social scientist therefore is not to question the validity of these beliefs or conceptions, but to understand what agents themselves believe, and subsequently to trace out the actions that follow.[4] Only in this way, when the social scientist has a full grasp of the conceptions held by agents, will the former be in a position to understand social action.

Note that it is the *reflected* or *conscious* conceptions that form the basis for action and therefore form the data for social science. As Hayek puts it: 'The social sciences . . . are concerned with man's conscious or reflected action' (1942a, 277). This is significant, since it means that he cannot (yet) countenance a notion of human action that emanates from *unconsciously* held conceptions or tacitly held knowledge. Specifically, tacitly followed social rules are not yet on Hayek's agenda.

Two types of ideas

Hayek takes care to point out that focusing on the conceptions or ideas obliges us to make a two-fold distinction regarding such ideas. The special difficulty afflicting social science is that:

> ideas appear in two capacities . . . as part of their object and as ideas about their object . . . [It] is necessary to draw a distinction between those ideas which are constitutive of the phenomena we want to explain and the ideas which . . . the very people whose actions we have to explain may have formed about these phenomena. [The latter kind of ideas] are not the cause of, but theories about, the social structures.
>
> (Hayek, 1942a, 285)

Hayek observes a distinction between the ideas which motivate agents' action and popular theories which these self-same agents may have regarding the 'whole' or 'economic system' of which these agents' actions are the constituent elements. The first kind of ideas he refers to as motivating or constitutive opinions; the second kind he refers to as speculative or explanatory views. To avoid confusion, Hayek refers to the former as *constitutive ideas*, the latter as *popular theories*.

The danger, according to Hayek, of confusing these two kinds of ideas is shown by the 'popular mind's' formulation of such collectives as 'society', 'the economic system', 'capitalism' and 'imperialism'. Social scientists must regard these collectives as popular theories which they must not mistake for facts. Agents come to form popular theories about their world. Changes in agents' constitutive ideas about a certain good may lead to a change in its price, but this is to be distinguished from any popular theory these agents may hold about why the price altered (a popular value theory perhaps). These popular theories are only of interest to the social scientist (unlike constitutive ideas) in the sense that they need to be revised and improved, i.e. re-classified.

THE NATURE OF SOCIAL WHOLES

It follows as a consequence of Hayek's conception of the social world as being constituted by the aggregate of individual agents conceptions, that social wholes are atomistically constituted. Moreover, the recognition of two kinds of ideas, particularly in this instance popular theories, complicates matters. The following question must be answered: What is the nature of social wholes?

Hayek rejects any investigation of social phenomena that begins by taking, as data, the various popular theories such as 'society' as being 'methodological collectivism', an offshoot of scientism. This approach:

> treats social phenomena not as something of which the human mind is a part and the principles of whose organisations we can construct from

> the familiar parts, but as if they were objects directly perceived by us as wholes.
>
> (Hayek, 1943, 42)

Such wholes are no more than constructions of the popular mind, popular theories which serve to explain the connection between some of the individual phenomena which agents perceive. To treat these as the building blocks of theory is to fall victim to what A. Whitehead described as the 'fallacy of misplaced concreteness' (quoted in Hayek, 1943, 43). Hayek is absolutely adamant that these social wholes have no existence.

Social wholes, then, have no existence apart from the popular theory by which they are constituted; that is, apart from the mental process whereby connections between events perceived in sense experience are forged. As Lawson (1995a) puts it, on Hayek's understanding, social wholes 'must be conceived of as having no existence independently of their investigation'. If 'to exist is to be perceived', and wholes cannot be perceived, then they cannot exist, except as mental constructs, aids to thinking.

A social whole for Hayek, then, is merely the aggregate of the individuals and their conceptions that constitute it. There can be no social structures if by this term we mean something that exists at a societal level but is unidentified by a selection of agents, since such structures cannot exist for them and so cannot be admissible to science.

THE GOAL OF SOCIAL SCIENCE, 1: UNDERSTANDING

Lawson (1995a) has pointed out that, on Hayek's account of social science, understanding is not merely one goal amongst many, it is the *only* goal that social science can attain:

> neither human conceptions nor actions are matters to be *explained* or further analyzed in social science, but *merely* items to be grasped or understood . . . [S]ocial science is restricted to understanding.

Two interesting points follow from Lawson's observation. First, whilst I think it is correct, it is an observation based exclusively on Hayek (1942a and 1943). If, however, we explore Hayek (1955), illuminatingly entitled 'Degrees of Explanation', we find Hayek no longer overwhelmingly concerned with understanding but with what he misleadingly refers to as *explanation*. However, by explanation Hayek means nothing more than prediction – a well-known positivist position. This leads to the second point. Lawson's overall thesis (a thesis to which I also subscribe) that Hayek does not break completely with positivism is strengthened by this foray into explanation as prediction. Recognising this progression in Hayek's work between 1942 and 1955, I shall proceed by elaborating upon what Hayek misleadingly takes to be (a) understanding, and (b) explanation; noting the damaging implications that follow.

Explanation, Hayek claims, reduces to the question of why individual agents perceive the world in the manner they do given that (a) they often (correctly) perceive a similar world in similar terms, and (b) they are often not only incorrect in their perception, but they are often all systematically incorrect. Such explanation, he asserts, 'if it can be done at all . . . is the task of psychology' (1942a, 288). Thus, the social scientist as distinct from the psychologist does not ask: Why does agent X perceive object Y as Z?, but rather: What are the consequences that follow from agent X perceiving object Y as Z?[5]

Making explanation redundant follows from hermeneutic foundationalism whereby social structures are ruled out. Without the latter, Hayek cannot countenance the possibility that agents' actions are not simply reducible to matters of psychology, but are matters of their interaction with real social structures. Unable adequately to theorise the *conditions for action*, he can only consider the *understanding* of agents and the *consequences that follow*.

This has further implications for the issue of prediction. From Hayek II's perspective, the possibility of prediction depends entirely on the possibility of explaining agents' psychology. Prediction is only possible if the 'laws of the macrocosm' could be derived from 'knowledge of the microcosm' (1942a, 290). But, since the microcosm is a system of fantastic complexity, intimate knowledge of it is simply far beyond the capacity of humans to attain, rendering prediction an implausible goal. It is also interesting to note here that the question of prediction for Hayek is not a matter of principle, but of practicalities. In effect Hayek is not rejecting the possibility that the macrocosm can, in principle, be reduced to the microcosm, but accepting that the paucity of knowledge available is the only barrier.

There is another reason why any meaningful notion of explanation is impossible on Hayek's understanding of *social* science, a reason that becomes evident when we consider his notion of explanation in *natural* science and how the latter influences the former. It was noted in the previous chapter that coming to know the object requires the recording of constant conjunction of events given in sense experience. The apprehension of event regularities is required in order to come to know the object and to classify it as such and such, since it appears to act in the same way under certain conditions. 'Coming to know' rests upon the constancy of events; it is synonymous with classifying and thereby (from Hayek's perspective) with explaining.

Social phenomena, however, being thoroughly subjective, are different. Social phenomena constitute not a regular arrangement or order of physical properties; rather, they are 'an order in which things behave in the same way *because they mean the same thing to man*' (Hayek, 1942a, 288, emphasis added). It appears that social scientists have to 'regard as alike and unlike, what appears to the acting man' and not take as our units 'only what Science shows to be alike or unlike' (ibid.). What Hayek is driving at here seems to be the claim that the complex nature of the social system appears to rule out the possibility of event regularities being recorded, making it impossible to classify a social object and thereby impossible to explain.

But, if the conscious conceptions of agents are not phenomena to be explained, then we might well ask: Once we have accessed them, what ought we to do with them? The answer, it appears, is that they are to be assembled or arranged to form theoretical elaborations about the consequences for action that follow upon them. For example, the theory of rent is composed out of the subjective conceptions of agents towards land – in conjunction with other conceptual devices such as the theory of factor substitution. It appears that the task of the economist is to recover the meaning locked into agents' conceptions in order to trace out the (intended and unintended) consequences that follow. As Hayek notes:

> It is important to observe . . . that the various types of individual beliefs or attitudes are not themselves the object of explanation, but merely the elements from which we build up the structure of possible relationships between individuals . . . For the social sciences, the types of conscious action are data and all they have to do with regard to these data is to arrange them in such an orderly fashion that they can be effectively used for their task.
>
> (Hayek, 1942a, 288)

THE GOAL OF SOCIAL SCIENCE, 2: EXPLANATION

In 1955, Hayek's recognition of the goal of social science as understanding is augmented by the further goal of (what Hayek claims is) explanation.[6] His understanding of explanation is, as I shall show, not merely incorrect, it is also a manifestation of his failure to break completely with positivism. I shall make the argument in four stages. First, I show his understanding of natural scientific law to be Humean.[7] Second, I show that he understands that, since society is a complex phenomenon, constant conjunctions of events are not manifest in the social world. This leads to the third point, whereby he reduces the tolerances of scientific laws for the social realm. Finally, I show that he presumes explanation to be synonymous with prediction.[8]

I suspect that the reason Hayek never specifies what he understands by scientific law is simply because he does not see it as controversial. In the 1940s and 1950s, the hegemony of positivism which, as noted in the previous chapters, adheres to the notion of scientific law as Humean is never challenged.[9] Where Hayek differs from the positivists in economics is in his opposition to its illicit extension to social science.

Throughout the period 1942–1960, Hayek continually uses phrases such as 'the regularities existing in the physical world' (1952, 2–3); 'stress on laws, i.e. on the discovery of regularities' (1955, 42), 'explanatory patterns', 'certain typical constellations of physical events – specific patterns' (ibid., 6). The closest he gets to describing a law is the following comment:

> Most people would probably accept some such definition of 'law' as that a 'scientific law' is the rule by which two phenomena are connected with each other according to the principle of causality. . . [a]n ordinary law . . . describes . . . a relation between cause and effect.
>
> (Hayek, 1961, 41)

Whilst it is true that in most of these places Hayek is attempting to argue that these event regularities or constant conjunctions of events cannot occur in the social world, there are two far more important implicit presumptions lurking here that will be brought out in the next few pages. The first is that regular patterns *do* exist in the natural world; the second is that they form the basis of scientific law.

According to Hayek, a theory is constituted by a combination of statements taken from a 'store of accepted statements', which include 'conditional statements', 'hypotheses', 'rules' or 'laws'. A simple form of a conditional statement is, he suggests, 'if *u* and *v* and *w* then *z*' (1955, 5–8). Conditional statements therefore are, in my notation, of the 'Whenever event *X* then event *Y*' format, and hence Humean.

Whilst Hayek mentions the complex nature of the social world in 1942a (290), in 1955 he begins to elaborate upon it in more depth:

> [In complex systems] we shall not be in a position to discover new natural laws . . . which would enable us to arrive at new predictions . . . There is no guarantee that we shall ever be able, physically or conceptually, to handle phenomena of any degree of complexity . . .
>
> (Hayek, 1955, 9; see also 3–4)

The complex nature of social phenomena makes it impossible to demonstrate the link between events and thereby establish any laws. 'If we already knew the relevant laws', Hayek argues, we could predict that whenever a series of causes occurred ($x_1, x_2, x_3 \ldots x_n$), a series of effects ($y_1, y_2, y_3 \ldots y_n$) would follow (1955, 8). However, these laws are typically not known, and in reality one may observe only that (for example,) if causes (x_1, x_2, x_3 and x_4) occur, the effects, say, (y_1 and y_2), or (y_1 and y_3) or (Y_2 and y_3) or some such, would follow.

Complexity, then, makes itself felt in the form of a problem of knowledge or, rather, lack of it. Complexity makes it impossible to specify the conditions under which an alleged law may be observed in its operation. Hayek, then, does not argue that laws are *not* constituted by constant conjunctions of events. On the contrary, he thinks that they *are* and therefore adopts a Humean notion of law. He simply does not think that they can be *discovered* in the social world because of its complexity.

He then transfers this misunderstanding to social science, leading to the situation whereby he does not know what to substitute these laws with in the social world. He knows that the social world is orderly in some sense, but is at a loss as to what theoretical device to employ to understand it. The net result is that he virtually gives up on the quest of uncovering laws in the social world, writing:

> It would appear that the search for the discovery of laws is not an appropriate hall-mark of scientific procedure but merely a characteristic of the theories of simple phenomena . . . and that in the field of complex phenomena [i.e. social science] the term 'law' as well as the concepts of cause and effect are not applicable without such modification as to deprive them of their ordinary meaning.
>
> (Hayek, 1961, 42)

Unable to proffer a notion of law other than one based upon constant conjunctions, and knowing that what one might call 'perfect' constant conjunctions do not exist in the complex social world, Hayek is in an awkward bind. In effect he does not reject constant conjunctions of events as the basis for law, he simply revises the ubiquity of the conjunction, and hence the efficacy of scientific law, downwards and in inverse proportion to the level of complexity of the system in which they manifest. Constant conjunctions still underpin scientific laws, but in complex phenomena they are difficult to ascertain and operate within loose tolerances.

Hayek then goes on to claim that since this is the situation facing social scientists, the methods of natural science cannot be borrowed, and he advocates a new method, namely 'explanation of the principle' (1955, 11), involving 'pattern predictions' (1961, 27). The object of the scientific exercise appears to be to ascertain whether or not the knowledge of properties of elements, forces and mechanisms we do possess can explain the set of observed events under investigation. Explanation, then, or the formation of explanatory patterns, is given high priority. It appears that the task of science is to obtain something called the 'principle at work':

> [S]o long as our expectations derived from the model are not contradicted, there is good reason to regard the model as exhibiting the principle at work in the more complex phenomena.
>
> (Hayek, 1955, 15)

Here the conditional statements mentioned above come in. Hayek presumes that models explain the 'principle at work', because the principle is contained in the conditional statements. Scientists do not evaluate each element of the theory, nor each conditional statement individually; they are taken as a raft, which, if it proves seaworthy, gives some comfort that the components are in some sense adequate. The raft's adequacy appears to depend upon its ability to establish predictions on some definition. The sense in which Hayek uses the term prediction in this context is extremely important. Prediction, on Hayek's understanding involves the following points:

1 Prediction refers not to an individual event but to phenomena of a certain class.
2 Prediction refers not to unique magnitudes, but to a range within which the predicted magnitude will fall. Limitations of measurement make this true of all sciences.
3 Whilst scientists tend to favour 'positive' predictions, i.e. of what will occur, 'negative' predictions may be 'exceedingly useful' (Hayek, 1955, 10). The difference between them is merely one of degree.

Hayek refers to predictions of this kind as 'pattern predictions'. Whilst he leaves us in no doubt that he is interested in explanation, he also leaves us in no doubt that (pattern) prediction is implicated in explanation. Now the conditional statements which constitute the theory, based as they are on the 'Whenever *X* then *Y*' format, clearly contain a predictive component, but Hayek goes further, claiming that they have an explanatory component in that they reveal an explanation of the 'principle at work'. The question that springs to mind, however, is: What are the grounds for this explanatory content? The answer he supplies is based upon an illicit conflation whereby 'explanation and prediction are merely two aspects of the same process' (1955, 9).

This claim to be advancing a notion of explanation is, however, only as good as the concept of 'explanation' which it uses. And here Hayek's understanding of explanation is that it is synonymous with prediction. His understanding of these phenomena is as follows:

- *Prediction*: We know a set of facts, we use rules to derive what follows upon them.
- *Explanation*: We know a set of facts, we use rules to derive what precedes them.

I shall not expand upon the argument against this notion of explanation as prediction, except to note the problem that Hempel (a well-known proponent of the notion) himself acknowledged. Consider the following covering-law model:

Koplic spots are an early sign of measles	(covering law)
Patient *i* has Koplic spots at time *t*	(initial condition)
Patient *i* will develop measles at time $t + 1$	(conclusion)

Such a mode of deduction might prove extremely (instrumentally) useful for a doctor, but it does not constitute an *explanation*. Koplic spots do not *explain* measles – unless we accept an extremely emaciated notion of what constitutes an explanation. A more satisfactory explanation of measles would require the postulation of, for example, a virus that governs the Koplic spots and the disease.

Explanation of the principle requires pattern predictions, which require conditional statements, which turn out to be Humean laws operating with loose tolerances, which in turn permit the construction of normal predictions. It appears that Hayek's attempt to treat explanation as the goal of social science collapses into prediction, and prediction collapses into the ubiquity of constant conjunctions of events. Worse still, Hayek knows that such constant conjunctions do not exist in the complex social world, yet has nothing to replace them with.

This result is, I suggest, a direct result of Hayek's synthesised philosophical position. An ontology that allows no more than the events of experience encourages the search for generalised knowledge as the search for constant conjunctions between these events. An ontology of conceptions encourages the belief that the world is concept-determined, that is, conceptual in nature. Bereft of an ontological category of (materially) causal real (as opposed to ideal) social structure, Hayek cannot even conceive of the possibility that agents' actions are explicable in terms of their interaction with these structures. Unable to theorise the *conditions for action*, he can only consider the *consequences of action* which are given in the events of experience. He has therefore to accept a notion of explanation as based upon (an in some sense watered-down version of) a constant conjunction between these events.

METHODOLOGICAL INDIVIDUALISM AND THE COMPOSITIVE METHOD

Defining methodological individualism is notoriously difficult,[10] and Hayek does not advance a definition of this method. According to Lachmann (1969, 94), methodological individualism is backward-looking in that 'we shall not be satisfied with any type of explanation of social phenomena which does not lead us ultimately to a human plan'. According to Hodgson (1988, 67), it is a 'method of theory building which starts from given elements and builds up a picture of institutions and social wholes'. I suggest that Hayek's methodological individualism is an amalgam of these two notions. That is, it focuses upon agents' subjective beliefs (and desires) as the cause of action, and requires society to be built from some kind of certain building blocks.

Understanding Hayek's version of methodological individualism is assisted by an understanding of (a) his social ontology, and (b) his commitment to extreme subjectivism. His social ontology suggests that the world is conceptual in nature, that is, it consists entirely of conceptions, ideas, and so on. This supplies the building blocks. His subjectivism suggests that 'only what people know or believe enters as a motive into their conscious action' (1942a, 284). This builds human purpose into those building blocks.

Hayek appears to be claiming that, since the social world is, ontically speaking, built up from agents' conceptions, an understanding of it has to begin with these conceptions. As he puts it:

> the specific subjectivist approach of the social sciences starts . . . from our knowledge of the *inside* of these social complexes, the knowledge of the individual attitudes which form the elements of their structure . . .
>
> (Hayek, 1943, 43, emphasis added)

Because of the subjective nature of the subject matter, Hayek argues, social science must start its scientific process with the constitutive ideas of individual agents, aggregating, constituting or composing them to 'produce the complex phenomena'. In the social sciences, according to Hayek, one learns to differentiate the wholes from the multiformity by systematically fitting together all the parts which have familiar properties:

> The social sciences, thus, do not deal with 'given' wholes, but their task is to constitute these wholes by constructing models from the familiar events.
>
> (Hayek, 1943, 44)

The very need to 'start from the concepts which guide individuals' behaviour' is inexorably linked to Hayek's philosophical synthesis, and tethers Hayek to a methodological individualist position. It could not be otherwise. If the social world is constituted solely by individuals' conceptions, then the starting point cannot be other than these individual conceptions. There are, for Hayek, as has been shown above, no social structures acting with (material) causality on agents; there are only agents, who, in their acting, create what Hayek (incorrectly) calls 'structures'. This 'one way street' between agents and structures, i.e. the presumption that agents create structures via their cognitive activity, and the rejection of the influence of structures upon agents' action places Hayek firmly in the voluntarist tradition – of which more in Chapter 6.

SUBJECTIVISED POSITIVISM

Hayek's subjectivism is evident in his critique of scientism, the latter being merely the extension of positivism to social science. Subjectivism and positivism, then, appear to be diametrically opposed. It may therefore come as a surprise to discover that Lawson conceives of Hayek as retaining aspects of positivism. How can an extreme subjectivist simultaneously maintain aspects of positivism? Lawson (1995a) explains the issue as follows:

> Hayek's starting point clearly is a mixture of positivist themes and subjectivist insights. In consequence, although not strictly inevitable, it is perhaps not surprising that what is achieved is not a transcendence of positivism, but essentially a re-working of it within a subjectivist mode. In fact, the 'objective facts' of positivist natural science are not so

much banished as displaced onto the human subject – presenting a move sideways rather than forwards.

Whilst Hayek's subjectivism encourages a break from positivism, the discussion of explanation as prediction, the use of convenient fictions in model-building and the retention of the notion of Humean law noted above indicate an inability to make the break a clean one. Further investigation suggests that Hayek succeeds not so much in breaking from positivism, but rather in reworking some of its themes within a subjectivist mode. Lawson refers to this as a kind of *subjectivised positivism*.

Positivism, at least as used here, presumes that events given in sense experience are self-evident, transparent and incorrigible. These events both constitute and exhaust the range of knowable objects, thereby reducing the physical world to sense experience. Each event is perceived as, and transformed into, a fact as a discrete, unique, temporal and spatial episode that reports or registers the occurrence of that event occurring in the external world. Brute facts given in sense experience as events form the data of natural science.

'Transformed into a subjectivist key', as Lawson puts it, positivism becomes what he refers to as 'subjectivised'. This transformation has three components which I shall outline, then comment upon:

1 The social science analogue of the brute facts of natural science are brute social conceptions, ideas, attitudes, and so on held by agents.
2 These brute social conceptions are taken to be incorrigible, that is self-evident, transparent and constitutive of social objects.
3 Because social material is reduced to conceptions held by agents, social scientists have merely passively to record them.

The claims made for these three components appear, at first glance, to deny the centrality of the role of subjective creativity in Hayek's social science – and thereby, of course, the claim that Hayek's hermeneutic foundationalism is a manifestation of subjective idealism. How, we might ask, can *actively* and *subjectively formed conceptions* (i.e. constitutive ideas, not popular theories) be 'brute', 'incorrigible' and 'passively recorded'?

These conceptions are 'brute' because they are the *only* admissible data for science. Recall that (a) the domain that exists independently of its identification by the agent under investigation, and (b) anything identified by the observing scientist yet not identified by this agent, is ruled out of the problem field for social study.

These conceptions are 'incorrigible' because they are the subjectively formed conceptions of agents, and these conceptions (unproblematically) form the building blocks of social science.[11] Agents hold conceptions, social scientists access these conceptions and utilise them in theory construction. The notion of incorrigibility cannot gain a foothold. As I noted in the previous chapter, the notion that agents' conceptions might be incorrect raises problems for (extreme) subjectivism. To be incorrect implies the existence of a mind-independent domain which is incorrectly apprehended in thought. Since consideration of the properties of mind-independent, external entities is deemed unnecessary for social science, then all that remains within this theoretical universe are conceptions. In this case, conceptions cannot be anything other than 'incorrigible'. 'To be a fallibilist about knowledge', according to Bhaskar (1978, 43) 'is to be a realist about things.' And when the things in question are social structures, Hayek is a subjective idealist.

These conceptions are 'passively recorded', by the *observing social scientist*, not by the agent who has actively and subjectively created them. Here we need to be extremely clear about the different roles played by the agent and the scientist in the process of social science. First, conceptions are actively and subjectively created by the agent; and second, these conceptions are recovered and recorded by the scientist. Scientists, it appears, passively record the brute conceptions actively formed and held by agents.

It is quite correct, then, to follow Lawson and claim that the brute facts of positivism are reworked and substituted by the brute conceptions of subjectivised positivism. However, whilst Lawson argues that this reworking of positivism is not 'strictly inevitable', I would put matters more strongly and argue that such an outcome is virtually irresistible, given Hayek II's philosophical presuppositions.

Knowledge of the reality that is socially constructed by agents is given to the observing social scientist as events in sense experience. If particular knowledge is of the events of experience, then general or scientific knowledge must be of the constant patterns these events reveal. Such constant patterns are the only form of generalisations possible, and take the form of Humean laws[12] – even if (as Hayek implies) they are thought to operate with loose tolerances.

It would be remarkable as well as inconsistent if, for example, Hayek II advocated a description of scientific law as the expression of powers and tendencies of an object attributable to it being the kind of thing that it is; that is, as for example, an expression of Lockean powers, Aristotelian essences or Hegelian contradictions. It comes therefore as no surprise when, in 1955, Hayek attempts to elaborate upon explanation, he merely falls back upon a watered-down version of Humean law.

CONCLUSION

Implicit in Hayek's work is the idea that social science ought to begin from ontology, that is, from the nature of the social world, and then (and only then) devise a method by which to investigate it. This is in stark contrast to the positivist-inspired orthodox economics that begins with a method presumed to be applicable to all aspects of social life. Unfortunately, however, his synthesised philosophical position encourages him to grasp the nature of the social world using the wrong ontological categories (for example, he treats social structures as mind constructions), which means that his adopted method does not permit him to uncover the true nature of this world. He can get (metaphorically speaking) no deeper beneath the domain of the empirical and actual than the domain of the conceptual. The domain of the deep where real social material can be conceived of eludes him. He is therefore trapped in a world consisting entirely of conceptions, and this informs all aspects of his method.

Hayek II, then, adopts a subjectivised positivist method. This has two major implications for his economic thinking. The first implication is constructive, in that it enables him to reformulate key aspects of mainstream economic theory, notably on knowledge, equilibrium and agency – these aspects will be the subject of Chapter 5. The second implication is limiting, in that it arrests the development of his ideas on one key issue: the existence of social structure – this will be the subject of Chapters 7 and 8.

5

THE IMPLICATIONS OF HAYEK II's PHILOSOPHY AND METHOD FOR HIS SOCIO-ECONOMIC THEORY

The philosophical and methodological positions that Hayek II adopts are in many respects inconsistent with, and thereby bring him into conflict with, the positivism that underpins the kind of substantive economics he is doing in the period up to 1936. It causes him to re-examine some of the basic building blocks of economic theory, most notably in the area of knowledge. Once Hayek recognises that the presumptions made by mainstream economists about knowledge are fundamentally erroneous, it casts doubt on other issues, primarily equilibrium, the notion of agency as *Homo economicus*, and creates ambiguity in his understanding of the telecom system.

Criticising the conventional wisdom makes it incumbent upon Hayek to proffer alternatives. And yet at this point in time, he has not worked them out. Many of the new insights that emerge via the critique cannot be welded into a coherent, unified theory. These shortcomings are no accident, for two reasons.

The first reason is a philosophical one in that the philosophical and methodological positions Hayek adopts make it virtually impossible (possible only at the expense of inconsistency) for Hayek to conceive of real social material such as social rules of conduct. The second reason is a substantive one in that the discovery, communication and storage of knowledge by and between agents now plays the central role in Hayek's economics, but he is also aware that knowledge is not homogeneous and in certain forms lies beyond the ability of the telecom system to discover, communicate and store it single-handedly (Hayek, 1936, 50). The dilemma for Hayek is that at this point in his intellectual development he can conceive of no institution other than the telecom system that might facilitate the discovery, communication and storage of knowledge. What he does *not* (as yet) have is a notion of social structure irreducible to agents' conceptions in general, and social rules of conduct in particular, to act as the institution that will articulate with the telecom system.

This chapter highlights the implications for economic theory that follow upon the philosophical position elaborated in the previous three chapters. It elaborates upon Hayek's break with neoclassical theory *vis-à-vis* knowledge, equilibrium and agency, and comments upon his (occasional) exaggerated claims about the telecom system.

KNOWLEDGE

Hayek's displacement of positivism and subsequent adoption of subjective idealism is inextricably linked to his economic thinking in the form of a concern with *knowledge*. Weimer even goes so far as to claim that 'Hayek is at all times an epistemologist, especially when doing technical economics' (1982, 263). For Hayek, the way knowledge is discovered, communicated and stored by and between agents and across time is central to the understanding of how economic actions are co-ordinated – and some semblance of order thereby established. He is quite unambiguous about this:

> Clearly there is here a problem of the Division of Knowledge which is quite analogous to, and as least as important as, the problem of the division of labour.
>
> (Hayek, 1936, 49)

In 'Economics and Knowledge' (1936), Hayek discloses a complete break with the mainstream assumption that knowledge is objective and possessed in full by agents and observing economists – encapsulated in the expression 'given data'. Instead, he emphasises that knowledge of 'objective facts' is subjectively held or interpreted, dispersed or fragmented (so that no one mind can possess it all), possessed by agents in varying quantities and qualities, and subject to continual change (see 1936, 36–52). In other words, knowledge, whilst subjectively held, is about some objective entities such as available technologies, consumers' tastes, agents' endowments, plus a range of facts given to agents or at least '*believed to exist*', including facts relating to the intentions of other agents.[1] This gives rise to two related, yet distinct questions. First,

> the central question of all social science [is]: How can the combination of fragments of knowledge existing in different minds bring about results which, if they were to be brought about deliberately, would require a knowledge on the part of the directing mind which no single person can possess.
>
> (Ibid., 52)

Second,

> the question why the data in the subjective sense of the term should ever come to correspond to the objective data is one of the main problems we have to answer.
>
> (Ibid., 39)

The first question involves the communication of knowledge and opens up the issue of the institutions that facilitate this communication. The second problem gives the communication problem a subjectivist twist, and inquires into why, if knowledge is subjectively held by an individual agent, it might ever come to correspond exactly to the objective world. This inquiry extends, presumably, into why different agents possessing different subjective knowledge should ever come to view the objective world in similar terms – although this is not addressed until 1942.

Both of Hayek's 1942 papers develop the subjectivist themes that were evident in 1936. Whilst he is not concerned here with discussing structures and mechanisms of communication, he clearly has in mind a subjectivist understanding of knowledge that is quite incapable of being treated by the positivist methods of mainstream theory. He attempts an answer to the 1936 question of why the subjectively held views of agents corresponds to the objective world, suggesting that it is due to all agents possessing similar minds.[2]

In 1945 Hayek turns to the theme of communication of knowledge:

> The economic problem . . . is a problem of how to secure the best use of resources known to any of the members of society, for ends whose relative importance only these individuals know.
>
> (Hayek, 1945, 520)

Once Hayek begins to question the formalist, positivist method used by mainstream economists to deal with (or perhaps avoid dealing adequately with) knowledge, he has to consider not only what constitutes knowledge, but also the institutions that facilitate its discovery, communication and storage. At this point, however, he faces a dilemma: he knows how knowledge is *not* discovered, communicated and stored but not how it *is*. He knows that the telecom system by itself cannot facilitate the discovery, communication and storage of the quality and quantity of knowledge necessary for some measure of effective economic co-ordination, but prior to 1960 he has no idea of what other institutions might perform these functions. He has a series of insights which, whilst valid, do not constitute a theory.

This leads to a tension that runs throughout his work, but is far more serious in his work prior to 1960. Unable to offer a systematic alternative to the telecom system, yet unwilling to rely exclusively on mainstream theory, Hayek is caught between a rock and a hard place. He borrows heavily (too heavily at times, as will become clear below) from mainstream price theory on one hand, and has a series of insights that contradict this theory on the other. I shall proceed by elaborating upon his insights at this point, allowing for his ideas on price theory to be returned to later in the chapter when his exaggerated and ambiguous views on the telecom system will be elaborated.

Hayek II's individualistic approach to social science alerts him to the heterogeneity of society, and thereby to the recognition that different agents in different situations and environments possess different quantities and qualities of knowledge; they are able, through different means, to discover, communicate and store knowledge, and cope with varying states of ignorance in different ways. If it can be established that a large part of the knowledge that is actually discovered, communicated and stored within the socio-economy, does not require the medium of the telecom system, then two implications follow.

First, it will tend to undermine Hayek's exaggerated claims on the role and efficacy of the telecom system, since much knowledge is discovered, communicated and stored by other institutions. Second, Hayek's recognition of the limited role of the telecom system encourages him to investigate other institutions that might facilitate the discovery, communication and storage of knowledge. As will become clear in later chapters, his investigations eventually lead him to social rules of conduct.

These implications may appear to amount to no more than a rather trivial point. A critic might reply: 'Of course Hayek knows the telecom system cannot facilitate the discovery, communication and storage of all types of knowledge, but this is not his remit. He is only concerned with how the telecom system might cope with sufficient knowledge to facilitate the mutual co-ordination of economic activity of numerous individual agents.' This trivialisation would, however, miss the point.

The point is this: as Hayek's work develops beyond 1960, other institutions, most importantly social rules of conduct, come to play as important a role in facilitating the discovery, communication and storage of knowledge and thereby bringing about economic order, as the telecom system itself plays. This implies that the system of rules and the telecom system are both implicated in the discovery, communication and storage of knowledge. If one wishes to ascertain exactly how these two systems articulate, then it is necessary to understand exactly what it is the telecom system can and cannot do, as a prelude to understanding what function the system of social rules needs to perform if socio-economic co-ordination is to occur.

My intention in the following sub-sections, therefore, is to demonstrate explicitly and in a systematic fashion, what Hayek demonstrates implicitly and in an unsystematic fashion. The result will be to show exactly what the telecom system can and cannot do, and expose some of the residues of neoclassical thinking Hayek cannot quite leave behind.

This demonstration will be undertaken by identifying what might be called different *agent–knowledge relationships*. Whilst Hayek never laid out these relations as systematically as presented here, I suggest this series can quite easily be assembled from frequent comments which punctuate Hayek's work from 1936 onwards.[3]

Agents and their own minds

In his 1936 paper, Hayek discusses the matter of individual (as distinct from societal) equilibrium, conceiving this as a possibility because agents come to learn 'what commodities can be used and under what conditions they are actually obtained and used' (1936, 50). Once they know what is available, that is, know the 'subjective data', they can set about initiating a plan of action to bring about some desired result. So, before choices can be made, agents have to gain knowledge of what is available, and this itself is a qualitative process that does not require, or at best occurs prior to the intervention of the telecom system.

Agents live in a knowledge- (or information-) soaked environment where messages about available products and services are continually communicated to all members, but with each individual agent knowing only a small fraction of the totality. Producers do not know in the sense that they are not 'given' the lowest cost of production. Nor do they know the 'wishes and desires of the consumers, including the kind of goods and services which they demand and the prices they are willing to pay' (Hayek, 1946, 96; see also Hayek, 1967a, 314). This has to be discovered.

If the data have to be discovered, it would appear that agents are initially ignorant and that one task of the market is to overcome this state. This discovery cannot be a process that is handled exclusively (if at all) by the telecom system:

> Their knowledge of the alternatives before them is the result of what happens on the market, of such activities as advertising etc., and the *whole organisation of the market* serves mainly the need of spreading the information on which the buyer is to act.
>
> (Hayek, 1946, 96, emphasis added)

Hayek's reference to the 'whole organisation of the market' is extremely important. It indicates that he is aware that there are institutions other than the telecom system that facilitate the discovery, communication and storage of knowledge and in this case assist in the initial formation of the 'subjective data'. However, for Hayek, whilst the telecom system is but one of a number of institutions that facilitate the discovery, communication and storage of knowledge, it is far and away the most important of them. Moreover, since prior to 1960 Hayek has no understanding of real social structures, he cannot argue that the 'whole organisation of the market' comprises not only the telecom system, but also social rules.

Agents and their immediate environment

In 1945 Hayek coined the phrase 'knowledge of the circumstances of time and place'. Arguably, each entrepreneur has to draw upon an extensive range of knowledge available in the immediate environment, and the method of obtaining it, as will become clear, is not via the telecom system. Since this will be expanded upon in Chapter 7, I shall not elaborate here. Suffice it to say that much of this 'knowledge of circumstances' bypasses the telecom system.

Agents and knowledge of the future

Streams of ever-changing objective phenomena lead to knowledge being continually updated, discovered, communicated, utilised in the formation of expectations and plans and subsequently used as a guide to action. Agents must act on continually changing data:

> If . . . the economic problem is mainly one of rapid adaption to changes in the particular circumstances of time and place, it would seem to follow that the ultimate decisions must be left to the people who are familiar with these circumstances, who know directly of relevant changes and of the resources immediately available to meet them.
> (Hayek, 1945, 524; see also 523)

Whilst in such a changing environment there might be a case for leaving decision-making to individuals with a finger on the pulse, this does not overcome the fact that even the most informed individual cannot foresee the future. Knowledge in this context shades off into radical ignorance – the term being used here to refer to uncertainty, that is, to a state of affairs not open to probability theory as elaborated by Keynes, Shackle and Knight (Lawson, 1988). And yet, whilst the future is fundamentally unknown, Hayek recognises that agents actually do manage to formulate expectations of the actions of others which are, typically, correct within certain limits, otherwise society would not display the degree of order that it does. The crucial question is, of course: How do they do it?

Agents are capable of initiating action in this context *not* because they obtain knowledge about particular future circumstances – since it is unknowable. Instead, as Hayek makes explicit after 1960, they follow a set of social rules of conduct which allow them to cope with uncertainty. The point being made here is that following these rules does not necessarily require the services of the telecom system – although the converse is not true, that is, using the telecom system does necessarily require the services of rules. To know that an agreement to enter into a partnership at some future date will be honoured because one knows the rules governing the keeping of promises, does not require the telecom system.

There are however two possibilities where the telecom system might be useful in assisting agents to cope with an uncertain future. First, there are the (limited) possibilities raised by futures markets. Second, there is the possibility that current prices act as guides to future prices: a 'fairly constant framework of known facts', as Hayek refers to them (1976, 125). In these cases the telecom system is acting to communicate knowledge across a temporal divide. However, the extent to which the telecom system can perform this task depends upon the extent of futures markets and, perhaps more importantly, the rapidity of socio-economic change – something which, according to Rizzo, Hayek glosses over (Rizzo, 1990).

Interaction between agents

A special part of agents' knowledge of the objective world appertains to the range of knowledge held by others. Ebling (1986, 42) puts this succinctly as follows:

> Since the success of each individual's plans is dependent to some extent upon the actions of others, each of their knowledge sets have to include expectations concerning the plans and intentions of others . . . [T]he knowledge sets of the respective actors have to overlap.

Formation of expectations and plans to undertake a course of action require that each agent takes into account the range of knowledge held by others. Some form of knowledge communication between agents must occur, or socio-economic interaction could not take place. This opens a Pandora's box: a whole network of relations opens up whereby the data for one agent's expectations and plans are the expectations and plans of a series of others. This is enough to create an enormous communication problem: how is one agent to gain access to the expectations and plans of a multitude of others? It is exacerbated by Hayek's subjectivism whereby what each individual knows is subjective.

In some cases, an entrepreneur may act upon knowledge obtained directly, for example, the trade press might reveal that a certain branch of industry has become unprofitable (or alternatively, highly profitable). Entrepreneurs will be monitoring the developments of other market participants quite closely and will form their own expectations and plans and take actions accordingly. Once again, expectations, plans and actions are not processed in the telecom system.

Monitoring the developments of other market participants requires far more than merely noticing price movements or even comparative profit rates. It requires (amongst other things) knowledge of a network of personal relationships. Hayek laments the complete exclusion from general equilibrium theory of all notions of personal relationships between parties, and goes on to explain its function:

> In actual life, the fact that our inadequate knowledge of the available commodities or services is made up for by our experiences with the persons or firms supplying them – that competition is in large measure competition for reputation or good will – is one of the most important facts which enables us to solve our daily problems. The function of competition here is to teach us who will serve us well . . .
>
> (Hayek, 1946, 97)

In instances like this when personal relationships are necessary in discovering how to get a thing done in the most efficient manner, the kind of knowledge discovered and communicated is not of a kind that can be discovered and communicated by the telecom system.

It is significant to note here that Hayek is not claiming that it is the function of the telecom system *per se* to solve our daily knowledge problems – although it might of course be implicated at a later stage. This is a 'function of competition', a function for what he refers to as 'the whole organisation of the market' (1945, 96).

It is often the case that the relationship between agents extends to co-operation between independent firms, either via cartel or vertical co-operation. In these instances, each firm engages in extensive and face-to-face knowledge exchanges, where the telecom system plays no role – at least in communicating knowledge.

Agents and the remote environment

Although most things that happen in the world might have an effect on agents' decisions, agents do not need to know about everything in order to integrate their actions with those of others. Agents appear to have a rather limited spectrum of phenomena of which they need to be aware in order to form expectations, plans and subsequently initiate relatively co-ordinated actions. They do not need to be aware of phenomena which are, for all practical purposes, of no concern to them. Some of what they do need to be aware of, however, can be acquired via the telecom system. The extent of the knowledge acquired from the telecom system, then, turns on the *relative importance* of certain phenomena. As Hayek puts matters:

> It does not matter for [an agent] why at the particular moment more screws of one size than another are wanted . . . or particular machine tools have for the moment become difficult to acquire. All that is significant . . . is how much more or less difficult to procure they have become . . .
>
> (Hayek, 1945, 525)

This is the point of Hayek's famous tin mine example (1945, 526). In such situations, according to Hayek, no local knowledge of the extraction process is necessary for the users of tin; all that is necessary is that price signals be taken into account. Here the telecom system appears in its most adequate form.[4] There are, however, two main problems with this argument.

First, Hayek never manages to state what exactly constitutes this 'relative knowledge' (1936, 50) and the possibility always exists that, whatever it is, it is insufficient for agents to base their expectations, plans and subsequent actions upon. There is nothing to prevent 'relative knowledge' being so limited (qualitatively and quantitatively) that actions cannot even be relatively co-ordinated. Second, consider an entrepreneur faced with a change in the price of, say, tin. Is it true that all the knowledge necessary for a relatively successful economic action will be contained in the price signal? The question has only to be asked to see that it has to be answered in the negative. This scenario is referred to as being characterised by 'noisy prices' (Thomsen, 1992, 33). In this scenario, prices do not contain all the knowledge that the entrepreneur requires, and, knowing this, he will have to engage in a variety of knowledge-discovering processes. He will have to discover whether or not the price is due to a tin shortage or due perhaps to some political factor; discover whether or not the price rise is likely to be temporary; discover knowledge about the availability and suitability of close substitutes for tin, other manufacturing processes, acceptable changes to the product, other products, and so on. Discovery of this type of directly accessible knowledge does not occur via the telecom system.

Whilst this section has demonstrated Hayek's (relatively underdeveloped) recognition that the telecom system appears quite frequently to be bypassed, there is one cautionary point that needs to be made. An entrepreneur for example, may obtain knowledge by a variety of means other than price signals, but once he has it, he will act upon it. This action then becomes embodied in a price signal and thereby communicated to some other agent. Paraphrasing Jack High (1986, 115–19), it is as if the entrepreneur did not merely notice that the supply and demand curves have shifted, but actually shifted them. Thus knowledge, whilst not being obtained via the telecom system, nevertheless ends up entering the telecom system at a later stage.

That prices convey knowledge is indisputable. The point is that by themselves they cannot cope with society's knowledge requirements. As L. Lachmann puts it:

> Here knowledge derived from price messages becomes problematical; it does not cease to be knowledge, but does not tell us the whole story . . . In a world of continuous change, prices are no longer in all circumstances a safe guide to action . . .
>
> (Quoted in Ebling, 1986, 45)

It appears, then, that Hayek's philosophical preoccupation with epistemological matters surfaces in his substantive work in the guise of a preoccupation with knowledge. It does not end here. As the next section will demonstrate, Hayek's recognition of the subjective, heterogeneous and fragmented nature of knowledge encourages his rejection of the mainstream notion of equilibrium.

EQUILIBRIUM

Perhaps the best way to understand what is entailed in Hayek's search for a notion of socio-economic order is to understand what it does not entail. It does not entail a search for a definition of an end state, an equilibrium. That this has to be stated boldly is testament to the fact that a straw poll amongst mainstream economists would probably indicate that the quest for an elaboration of order, initiated by Adam Smith, is synonymous with the quest for an elaboration of General Equilibrium. Take F. Hahn, for example, who writes:

> A. Smith . . . first realised the need to explain why this kind of social arrangement does not lead to chaos . . . Smith not only posed an obviously important question, but also started us off on the road to answering it. General Equilibrium theory as classically stated by Arrow and Debreu . . . is near the end of this road.
>
> (Quoted in Addleston, 1986, 6)

Thinkers such as Hahn clearly see the task confronting neoclassical economics as that of *finishing what Smith started two hundred years ago* (Hahn, 1982). By this they appear to mean establishing all the conditions necessary to demonstrate the existence and perhaps more importantly the stability of equilibrium – or equilibria. For such thinkers, this is what order means. Order and equilibrium are synonymous: they are both organising principles. In fact Hahn writes that in economics, equilibrium is the 'central organising idea' (Hahn, 1973, 1).

It is not accidental that thinkers such as Hahn and Hayek in his pre-1936 period who accept positivism (at least in the form that underlies mathematical economics) equate equilibrium with order; in fact it follows from their ontological position. As noted in Chapter 2, the ontological position underpinning positivism, namely empirical realism, permits only of events given in sense experience. Now, if events are all that is available to sense experience, then they must form the basis for scientific knowledge. Scientific generalisations then turn on the possibility of ascertaining constant patterns of events/actions. The question of order reduces to that of whether or not some patterns of events/actions are consistent or compatible with others. *The analysis is located entirely within the domains of the empirical and actual.*[5]

By 1936, however, Hayek emphatically disagrees with this positivist vision. For him, the notion of order is irreducible to the notion of equilibrium; in fact, he comes to view the latter as more of a hindrance to economics than a help. Butos (1985, 341) neatly captures the development of Hayek's ideas of equilibrium as follows:

> Hayek's mild discomfort with equilibrium theory is evident (though not prominent) in his work of the early 1930s. Thereafter his uneasiness appears to strengthen and by 1937 in 'Economics and Knowledge' the disquietude assumes definite contours.

Hayek's 'mild discomfort' with equilibrium theory extends far beyond 1937 – in part, it drives the search for an alternative conception (order), which he eventually establishes in the 1960s. However, since it is in the 1936–46 period that Hayek breaks with neoclassical theory over the notion of equilibrium, the following section discusses the key changes and ambiguities in Hayek's understanding of equilibrium in this period.[6]

Hayek's 1936 paper contains something of a tension in that he wants both to reject and to retain equilibrium – on some definition. For example, in one place Hayek writes of the 'admittedly fictitious state of equilibrium', only to change tack gradually; writing of the 'supposed existence of a tendency towards equilibrium', then 'the real content of the assertion that a tendency towards equilibrium exists', and finally 'the tendency towards equilibrium, which we have reason to believe to exist on empirical grounds'. In conclusion he refers to the 'empirical propositions of which we must make use if the formal apparatus of equilibrium analysis is to serve as an explanation of the real world' (Hayek, 1936, 43–53).

However, having said that Hayek wishes to retain a notion of equilibrium under some description, his description is fundamentally different from the standard Walrasian/Paretian version that still underpins the core of neo-classical theory. The main bone of contention appears to be the subjective and fragmented nature of knowledge.

The tension in this paper might be reduced if one interprets Hayek as differentiating between equilibrium as an admittedly fictitious, but theoretically useful, description of an end state, and the conditions and processes that might be responsible for a tendency towards this state. He offers a description of an end state in terms of the co-ordination of expectations, plans and subsequently actions over time. Societal equilibrium

> exists if the actions of all members of the society over a period are all executions of their respective individual plans on which each decided at the beginning of the period . . . [A] state of equilibrium. . . means only that compatibility exists between the different plans which individuals . . . made for action in time.
>
> (Hayek, 1936, 37, 41)

Descriptions of end states or equilibria aside, what really appears to interest Hayek are the processes underlying this tendency towards equilibrium. And this is what makes the paper so insightful and relevant almost sixty years after it was published.

With this more sophisticated understanding, Hayek then focuses upon the 'process' involved in, and the 'conditions' necessary for, the subjective, fragmented knowledge and intentions of different agents to come 'more and more into agreement' (ibid., 44). What Hayek has in mind here is a trial-and-error process where agents learn from experience and gradually come to bring their own expectations into line with those of others. 'It is', he claims, 'only relative to the knowledge that a person is bound to acquire in the course of carrying out his original plan and its successive alterations that an equilibrium is likely to be reached' (ibid., 51).

Since in this equilibrium agents do not know everything (i.e. only what is 'relevant'), then they do not know what it is that they do not know. The possibility always remains, therefore, that if they knew one more fact they might be able to alter their plans and improve their position. Knowledge constraints thereby rule out a Pareto-optimal equilibrium.

Hayek, then, firmly rejects the notion of equilibrium in the neoclassical Walrasian/Paretian sense, a rejection grounded in a refusal to share the unreal assumptions about knowledge. Such 'equilibrium analysis', he concludes, has 'little to say about institutions such as the press, the purpose of which is to communicate knowledge . . . and the role played by such institutions as advertising' (ibid., 53).[7]

It is far more difficult, however, to state exactly what notion of equilibrium (if any) Hayek II does eventually accept. Whilst proffering an alternative description of an end state as a fictitious theoretical device, his main aim seems to be the elaboration of real-world conditions and processes necessary to induce agents to acquire knowledge via learning. Acquisition of new relevant knowledge gradually changes subjectively held knowledge, bringing agents' expectations more and more into line, and thereby bringing about a tendency towards equilibrium – even though this end state may never be reached. Hayek does not therefore abandon equilibrium, he merely wants to square it with the recognition that knowledge is a subjective phenomenon. Caldwell (1988, 530) might have the correct interpretation of Hayek's 1936 paper *vis-à-vis* equilibrium by observing that:

> Hayek the economist was, of course concerned very much with finding a definition of equilibrium. But it was as a subjectivist that Hayek encountered a new and vitally important problem . . . If one associates a tendency towards equilibrium with the co-ordination of plans, how might such a tendency be brought about in a world of subjective knowledge? What could lead the subjective knowledge of agents into conformance with objective reality? . . . No, it was not the existence of co-ordination by markets that troubled Hayek. It was how to use equilibrium theory to demonstrate the existence of the tendency.

In chapter 2 of *The Pure Theory of Capital* (1941), Hayek is explicitly concerned with methodological questions surrounding the concept of equilibrium. He is fully cognizant that economic analysis contains two moments: that of describing the qualitative relations between the real structure of production that results from agents plans, that is, an end state; and that of explaining the forces that might bring about such a state, that is, a process. He displays concern that the goal of 'explanation' as a scientific goal is lost in the desire to define equilibrium end states. However, his notion of a 'kind of causal explanation of the processes in time' (1941, 17), as noted in the previous chapter, is synonymous with a deductive process. He is seeking the deduction of one event/action from another event/action; the only thing he adds is that this must take account of historical time.

He then explores the versions of equilibrium analysis that have been floated, and rejects them. He notes that stationary equilibrium simply ignores the processes that are at work, by assuming that all that has to happen has happened. However, the concept of temporary equilibrium is no more adequate since it presumes that there are intervals of comparative rest, where the competitive process has (temporarily) ended. It presumes that economic (in this case investment) activity occurs in discontinuous spurts, rather than being dispersed over a more or less continuous temporal span.

At this point, with equilibrium analysis severely discredited, we await Hayek's delivery of the *coup de grâce* – a complete rejection of equilibrium. This, however, does not materialise. Instead, he changes the methodological approach to equilibrium itself. To be more precise, he drops the pretence that equilibrium refers to the real world:

> I am inclined to believe that these attempts to give the equilibrium concept a realistic interpretation (the legitimacy of which remains in any case somewhat doubtful) have deprived us of an at least equally important use, which the concept will serve if we frankly recognise its purely fictitious character.
>
> (Hayek, 1941, 21)

Hayek advances an argument to justify the notion of equilibrium when it is clearly a 'fictitious state', an 'intellectual tool', which acts as a 'kind of foil' (ibid., 23) with which one can predict the direction in which entrepreneurs will have to revise their plans when faced with frustrated expectations. This appears to be a manifestation of the transcendental-idealist philosophy of science noted in Chapter 2, and is usually associated with his thoughts on natural science, whereby putatively fictional conceptual constructs are allowed into theoretical elaboration.

There appears to be, then, a change in tack. From being conceived of as an empirically existing tendency in 1936, equilibrium becomes a (fictitious) methodological device:

> the extension of the equilibrium concept provides the bridge from equilibrium analysis to the explanation in terms of causal sequences, since it is designed to elucidate the factors which will compel entrepreneurs to change their plans . . .
>
> (Hayek, 1941, 23)

Hayek has thus arrived at the following position. Economics must explain the competitive process at work, not just define an end state. Defining end states is not redundant, however, provided two requirements are observed. First, the equilibrium end state is the dynamic, competitive one he advocates, and second, no 'specious reality' (ibid., 28) is claimed for it, that is, it is treated as a convenient fiction. This allows a bridge to be built between the explanation of causal sequences and equilibrium analysis. By this he appears to mean that one can retain equilibrium as an organising principle, an end state whereby all expectations and plans are compatible over time, then elaborate upon the direction of the causal sequence that an entrepreneur will undertake, should events deviate from expectations. He then adds a cautionary footnote indicating that this elaboration will 'no longer be so simple' (ibid., 23) if more than a single deviation of event from expectations is considered. This of course seriously weakens the entire theoretical efficacy claimed for the 'bridge'.

On the last two pages of the chapter, however, Hayek throws a spanner in the works. After arguing at length that the equilibrium state is a convenient fiction, and that it is justified as a theoretical tool, a foil, he then lapses back to his 1936 position to justify the use of his equilibrium conception. Justification follows from the empirical claim that real-world conditions do approximate towards equilibrium 'to some extent' (ibid., 27).

Thus he ends up with two contradictory justifications. He has a purely formal, logical justification in terms of a foil, and another in terms of an empirical tendency. Yet the argument for retaining some version of equilibrium is rooted in the claim that the 'purely fictitious character' of equilibrium is recognised. Competitive equilibrium, then, is simultaneously both fictitious and real. We are therefore left asking: Is Hayek's competitive equilibrium state a theoretical device or an empirical tendency?

Hayek's 1945 paper has little to say explicitly about equilibrium. It ends with his reiterating the point that equilibrium analysis is no more than a preliminary process to the study of the main problem, and that care must be taken to ensure that reality[8] and theory are not conflated (1945, 530).

In his essay entitled 'The Meaning of Competition', drafted in 1946, Hayek again criticises the technical, formal treatment of equilibrium and perfect competition. His main point is that the outcome of market activity ought not to be measured against some fictitious ideal equilibrium resulting when competition is perfect, but against what would be the case where real competition is absent (ibid., 99, 100, 105). Commenting upon this, Rizzo (1990, 24) observes that 'Hayek is not comfortable in basing the normative case for the competitive process on the optimality features of perfectly competitive equilibrium.'

Summarising these papers, we might conclude that although in the late 1930s and 1940s Hayek rejects the narrow, technical concept of equilibrium in its Walrasian/Paretian versions, he remains rather ambiguous as to what he really believes the notion of equilibrium to imply and how it ought to be used. Whilst it is quite clear that equilibrium, for Hayek, consists in the compatibility of plans over time, he is also clear that this scenario never actually materialises although there is a tendency towards it. Rizzo (1990, 26) appears to have a point when he claims that the Hayek of the 1940s still retained the notion of equilibrium as a 'near competitive benchmark'. Hayek cannot quite break from the idea that the economy approximates to equilibrium on some definition and he tries to establish such a definition. This understanding appears to coexist with the idea that equilibrium is a convenient theoretical fiction.[9]

AGENCY

To my knowledge, Hayek does not explicitly discuss that optimising, calculating, utilitarian entity that is generally referred to as *Homo economicus*. However, once he recognises disequilibrium, disequilibrium prices, changes in the data, learning, and so on, the concept of *Homo economicus* is difficult to sustain. *Homo economicus* cannot do anything that is not already preprogrammed by the economist into his (*sic*) behaviour. *Homo economicus* acts but neither discovers nor creates. As Buchanan put it – with a definite Hayekian ring:

> The entity that acts, and behaves, does so in accordance with the patterns imposed by the postulates of the theoretical science. The actor is, so to speak, programmed to behave in direct response to stimuli. (Buchanan, 1969a, 50)

In addition, Hayek II's subjectivism militates against any possibility that he accepts *Homo economicus*. His 1942 papers and his 1952 book, *The Sensory Order*, reject the behaviouralist premise upon which *Homo economicus* is based.

Hargreaves-Heap's (1989, ch. 1) categorisation might be useful in charting the path of Hayek's thinking *vis-à-vis* agency. Hargreaves-Heap suggests three classes of rationality: instrumental, procedural and expressive. At this point is it possible to claim that Hayek II abandoned the instrumental rationality of optimising, calculating *Homo economicus*, without having anything to substitute for it. It is not until the 1960s that he develops a notion of procedural rationality and humans as rule-following agents.

This, however, leaves Hayek's economics without a theory of human agency. It appears that Hayek's deepening insights have run ahead of the theoretical apparatus at his disposal. The problem for Hayek II, and possibly the reason why he does not spell out his objection to *Homo economicus*, is that at this point in time he has very little with which to replace it. If agents are neither instrumentally rational nor totally capricious, but undertake relatively stable, systematic behaviour on some definition, then what is the source of this stability?

Part of the reason for this problem lies with his ontological position that denies the existence of real social structures such as rules. This in turn encourages a methodological individualism which leaves agents as self-contained atoms who initiate action on some unknown principle. If behaviouralism is rejected, and rule-following is not yet accepted, then there is simply no principle at work guiding human actions.

THE TELECOMMUNICATIONS SYSTEM OF THE PRICE MECHANISM

As we demonstrated above, Hayek is concerned with the discovery, communication and storage of knowledge, and the institutions that facilitate this.

However, despite the fact that he is aware that knowledge is discovered, communicated and stored via institutions other than the telecom system, these other institutions, by comparison, receive virtually no discussion.

Moreover, when he does give attention to these other institutions, he treats them as something separate from the telecom system. It is extremely important to recognise that Hayek equates the telecom system with the price mechanism, and nothing more. The telecom system does not equate to the market or to competition; it is a mechanism that operates in the market and permits competition. In fact, when Hayek wants to indicate that there are more institutions that facilitate the discovery, communication and storage of knowledge than just the telecom system, (for example, advertising) he uses terms such as 'the whole organisation of the market' (Hayek, 1945, 96). As he puts it:

> We must look at the price system as such a mechanism for communicating information if we want to understand its real function . . . The most important fact about this system is the economy of knowledge with which it operates . . . It is more than a metaphor to describe the price system as a . . . system of telecommunications.
>
> (Hayek, 1945, 527–8)

Furthermore, whilst Hayek II's philosophical position allows him to conceive of institutions that facilitate the discovery, communication and storage of knowledge that are *consciously* utilised by agents (i.e. telecom system, advertising, personal contact, and so on) it does not allow him to conceive of institutions that are *unconsciously* utilised by agents. He cannot therefore conceive of social structures such as social rules of conduct, which are both necessary for the discovery, communication and storage of knowledge in their own right, and which supply the social fabric within which the telecom system is embedded. This is taken up again at the end of this chapter.

I shall argue that Hayek's claims *vis-à-vis* the *role* (meaning the extent to which it facilitates the discovery, communication and storage of knowledge) and *efficacy* of the telecom system are often both ambiguous and exaggerated. The ambiguity lies in the fact (noted above) that whilst in places he understands that the telecom system cannot exclusively fulfil all of the system's knowledge discovery, communication and storage requirements, in other places he appears to claim that it can. This latter claim results in exaggeration and, on occasion, a curious flirtation with mainstream economics.[10]

Boehm (1989) argues convincingly that various mainstream interpreters (Koopmans, Arrow, Dasgupta, Stiglitz) have merely interpreted Hayek as holding the notion that prices are a vehicle for communicating perfect information. Thomsen (1992) argues something similar to Boehm but goes into more depth on the economics of information to establish exactly where this perspective differs from Hayek.

According to Boehm, these theorists ignore numerous warnings and caveats made by Hayek and translated Hayek's unfamiliar concepts into the familiar concepts of mainstream economics, thereby thoroughly misunderstanding what role the telecom system plays in Hayek's scheme of things. Whilst not completely disagreeing with Boehm, one might ask: Is there no smoke without fire? Is Hayek really so unambiguous that any such (mis)interpretation is an *obvious* mistake? It is my contention that Hayek himself does not fully understand – or if he does, then he does not fully elucidate – the role and efficacy of the telecom system. The ensuing ambiguity displayed by Hayek allows mainstream thinkers to interpret him in their own terms. The next sub-section will consider Hayek's exaggerated claims for the telecom system. When this is taken together with his recognition that the telecom system cannot meet the system's needs *vis-à-vis* the discovery, communication and storage of knowledge by itself (as discussed in the previous section), his ambiguity becomes evident.

Hayek's exaggeration of the role and efficacy of the telecom system

It is quite easy and perhaps not even contentious to assemble a series of quotations to illustrate Hayek's exaggeration of the role and efficacy of the price mechanism.[11] I merely provide the clearest example.[12] In 1978 Hayek drew upon what Butler calls the 'catallactics of substitution' (1983, 49, fn.11) which is no less than the stuff of General Equilibrium (GE) theory. In the following passage[13] Hayek is attempting to demonstrate how the forces of competition will bring about an efficient allocation of resources:

> Almost any product can be produced by a great many different quantitative combinations of the various factors of production, and which of them will be the least costly . . . is indicated by the relative prices of these factors . . . The prices at which producers can buy different factors will tell each which quantities of any two of them cost the same because they bring elsewhere the same marginal return; and the producer will thereby be induced to adjust the relative amounts of any pair of factors that such quantities of them will make the same marginal contributions to output as will cost the same amount of money. If this is done, and the marginal rates of substitution between any two factors have become the same in all uses, the market has reached the horizon of catallactic possibilities. The general result will be the maximisation of output . . . described as Pareto-optima . . . The combination in fact produced will be determined by the relative strength of the demand for different goods – which in turn depends upon the distribution of incomes . . .
>
> (Hayek, 1978, 118–19)

Eatwell and Milgate (1994), albeit in an extremely selective reading of Hayek, choose to focus on the scant (but nevertheless existing) occasions when Hayek descends into what is in effect GE theory. Their criticism is aimed at Hayek's use of neoclassical price theory and therefore perfect competition; Hayek both wants to reject it and yet needs it.

In what may perhaps be an over-zealous attempt to demonstrate how the market order secures the maximisation of output, Hayek is forced to draw (implicitly of course) upon GE theory. This line of argument works if and only if the panoply of axioms and assumptions of perfect competition (which includes assumptions of perfect knowledge) are utilised – whether Hayek chooses to recognise it or not. We do not have to share Eatwell and Milgate's extremely selective reading of Hayek to agree with them when they write:

> without perfect competition Hayek is left only with the proposition that competition will tend to establish a set of prices. How the magnitudes of those prices are determined, and how they interact with the determination of quantities, cannot be deduced from the process of competition described by Hayek . . .
>
> The contradictions . . . might be solved in two ways – either in abandoning his characterisation of competition altogether, and accepting perfect competition as an integral part of the theory of price; or by preserving the insights which he has into the nature of capitalistic competition, and abandoning the neoclassical theory of value.
>
> (Ibid.)

Hayek wants to maintain the neoclassical parable that a particular set of prices will ensure that costs are minimised and output maximised via factor substitution at the margin. Such a parable is however only (if at all) defensible on the basis of perfect competition, which he knows is a fiction. Since one of Hayek's strengths is his understanding of the real competitive process, it is nonsensical to suspend belief on this merely to utilise neoclassical value theory.

At this point, a thinker sympathetic to Hayek's notion of the market might be tempted to argue that Hayek did not arrive at his understanding of the market via the logical or formal route of GE theory, but more likely via the 'Paris gets fed' route. In other words, via the 'common-sense' observation that markets do work, no matter how poorly – even if this does not constitute a 'proof'.[14]

We can accept this argument and still respond that without neoclassical theory and the device of perfect competition upon which it relies, Hayek can do no more than assert that competition will establish a set of non-arbitrary prices and output will be maximised. This argument only serves to make Hayek's understanding of competition and prices even more contradictory.

Hayek wants to have his cake and eat it. He wants a 'common-sense' understanding of competition and a 'common-sense' notion of price formation, and at the same time to reject perfect competition as an offence to that common sense. He wishes to claim on the one hand that although the results of competition would, within fairly wide margins, be indeterminate, the market would still bring about a set of prices which correspond roughly to costs, whilst knowing on the other hand that:

> correspondence between prices and marginal costs is to be expected only to the degree that elasticities of demand for the individual commodities approach the conditions assumed by the theory of perfect competition or that elasticities of substitution between different commodities approach infinity.
>
> (Hayek, 1946, 100)

Without GE theory, why commodity prices ought to reflect lowest costs; how their magnitudes are determined; why output will be maximised; and upon what basis factor substitution occurs, and so on, all remain unstated. This is not lost on Boehm, who writes that 'Hayek does not come up with – and this is a serious omission – an account of price formation' (Boehm, 1989, 207).[15] It may well be that a subjectivist like Hayek II or, as will be shown, a (quasi)realist like Hayek III could have an alternative theory of prices. However, unless he states this alternative, and as long as he falls back on the neoclassical version, we are forced to agree with Eatwell and Milgate.

Hayek's exaggerated and ambiguous role for the telecom system is illuminated in order to highlight the differential impact it has upon his work in the two periods under discussion. For Hayek II, without a developed understanding of social rules of conduct as institutions that facilitate the discovery, communication and storage of knowledge, exaggeration is inevitable. In the work of Hayek III, by contrast, exaggeration is merely an anachronism, since, armed with an understanding of the institutions that facilitate the discovery, communication and storage of knowledge in the form of social rules he does not have to exaggerate the role and efficacy of the telecom system: he conceives of an articulation between the telecom system and the system of rules of conduct.

CONCLUSION

Sometime between 1936 and 1945 Hayek's (partial) break with positivism encourages a break with mainstream notions of knowledge, equilibrium and agency. Hayek's illusions about the ability of the telecom system obviate the need to develop any other real alternative institutions to handle knowledge. As long as Hayek finds the telecom system a 'marvel' (1945, 527) there is no compelling need to search for other institutions. Yet this merely results in a quandary: he knows how economists ought not to approach knowledge, equilibrium and agency, but he does not yet know how they ought to. This lacuna reveals the problem with his philosophical position.

Hayek II's augmented empirical-realist ontology now permits not only events given in sense experience but also agents' conceptions. Breaking from the classical empiricist ontology, whereby reality is revealed in events, leaves Hayek recognising that there is more to knowledge than what is given in 'objective facts' (1936); more to socio-economic order than the co-ordination of actions based upon these 'facts', i.e. there is a process at work; and more to agency than stimulus responses at the level of the empirical. He is searching beneath the domain of the empirical, as it were. However, at this point in time, the only other entities that he can conceive of are conceptions as revealed in his hermeneutic foundationalism.

Under hermeneutic foundationalism there is no notion of social structures that exist and act to a significant extent independently of agents' identification or classification of them. On the contrary, social structures are reducible to and exist solely in virtue of the conceptions held by agents. They do not act as a (material) cause at all. There is, for Hayek II then, no domain of the deep that can sustain an elaboration of the conditions for action perceived at the level of the empirical.

Hayek is thus impaled on a fork of his own making. The theoretical devices he needs for his substantive economics are ruled out of bounds by the philosophical position he adopts. In retrospect, it is quite clear that if he is to develop the institution of social rules, he has to abandon this untenable philosophical position. By 1960 he successfully abandons this position and adopts a quasi-transcendental realist alternative. This, however, is the subject matter of the next chapter.

6

HAYEK III's QUASI-TRANSCENDENTAL REALIST PHILOSOPHY

The previous chapters have established that Hayek II adopts a philosophical position consisting of a subjective-idealist epistemology, synthesised with an augmented (for social science) empirical-realist ontology consisting of events given in sense experience and conceptions. This encourages a methodological position of subjectivised positivism.

These positions in philosophy and methodology act as a double-edged sword on Hayek's economic thinking. On the one hand they fuel the break with mainstream treatment of knowledge, equilibrium and agency, and subsequent development of these insights causes inconsistencies *vis-à-vis* his claims about the role and efficacy of the telecom system. On the other hand they prevent the development of the phenomenon that proves to be the key to radically transforming his socio-economic theory, namely real social structures in the form of social rules of conduct.

With hindsight, it is evident that by 1960 Hayek does make this transformation in socio-economic theory, by developing his thoughts on social rules of conduct – and also, significantly, on knowledge and ignorance. This is only possible through the abandonment of large sections of his pre-1960 philosophical and methodological position and the adoption of something approaching a transcendental-realist alternative. If the term 'something approaching' appears to be less than rigorous, it is because Hayek neither succeeds entirely in abandoning his previous position nor in adopting entirely the new one. I shall refer to his post-1960 philosophical position, therefore, as *quasi-transcendental realist*.

Whilst the aim of this chapter is to elaborate upon Hayek's mature philosophical position, it is perhaps useful to set out the limits of this elaboration. I shall attempt neither a complete exposition of the transcendental realist perspective and all that it entails, nor a complete discussion of all the areas where Hayek fails to adopt it entirely. Rather, I shall concentrate upon those aspects of the transcendental-realist perspective that Hayek does adopt and that are relevant in understanding Hayek's mature notion of socio-economic order.[1]

In effect, I shall set out a stylised version of Hayek's (quasi-transcendental realist) philosophical position and note the implications this has for his method and socio-economic theory. Whilst some of the claims contained in this stylised version will be little more than assertions, subsequent chapters will argue this to be a valid interpretation of Hayek's post-1960 work.

It is perhaps worth noting that a debate is emerging on the question of Hayek's alleged shift to philosophical realism. As philosophical realism has gained ground among (a small number of heterodox) economists, some have used it to explore the basic philosophical or methodological underpinnings of certain schools of thought or even of particular economists. The Austrian School, long noted for its different methodological approach, has attracted attention from realists such as Maki (1990a and b), Smith (1986, 1990a and b), Lawson (1994c and 1995a) and Peacock (1993). Whilst Maki and Smith have considered Hayek's work under the heading of Austrians in general, Lawson and Peacock have recently investigated Hayek in particular. One common theme of investigation appears to be as follows: since Austrians in general and Hayek in particular are philosophically and methodologically distinct from mainstream economists, are they realists under some description and if so, what kind of realists? This chapter is intended, amongst other things, as a contribution to this debate.[2]

TRANSCENDENTAL REALISM

If the subjective-idealist epistemology and empirical-realist ontology are the result of the 'epistemological turn' taken by post-enlightenment philosophers, transcendental realism might be conceived of as the result of a recent 'ontological turn' – or perhaps more accurately *re*turn.[3] In other words, whilst empiricist philosophy prioritises epistemological questions such as: How can one know what exists? (and variants on this question), transcendental realism prioritises ontological questions such as: What is the nature of existence?

Whilst Hayek II's augmented empirical realist ontology conceives of the world as constituted by events/actions given in sense experience and conceptions formulated by agents, a transcendental realist ontology extends this to include (metaphorically) deep structures, mechanisms, rules, powers, relations, and so on. It is significant that these additional existents (to avoid continual repetition I shall refer to them simply as deep structures) exist independently of one's perception of them. Whilst it is, true that real social material such as social structures (unlike physical material) cannot exist independently of *all* perceptions of them, they nevertheless exist independently of any one person's particular perception of them. If, however, social material can exist independently of a particular agent's perception or identification of it, then for that agent it has an *objective* existence – and cannot therefore be ruled out of the field of inquiry. This runs counter to the subjective-idealist claim that social material is constituted in the cognitive activity of the transcendental subject. It also runs counter to the empirical-realist claim that experience, an epistemological category, is the basic device used in defining the real world, which is an ontological task.

The possibility of identifying and differentiating between a domain where entities are experienced empirically and a domain where the structures that generate these events are operative, encourages the view that there is more than one domain of reality. We could say that reality is *layered*.

Layered ontology

Bhaskar (1978) stablishes the possibility of a layered ontology via an inquiry into the practice of science, with particular emphasis upon notions of scientific law.[4] As I noted in Chapter 2, empirical realism adheres to a view of scientific law referred to as Humean. Such a law is predicated upon the putative existence of a specific pattern observed in the flux of events. When this pattern constitutes an event regularity, or a constant conjunction of events, styled 'Whenever event *X*, then event *Y*', a Humean law is said to exist.

Bhaskar (1978) makes two key observations from this understanding of scientific law, identifies certain problems, then draws the implications for ontology. First, virtually all the constant conjunctions of events that are of interest to science (astronomy appears to be the exception) do not occur spontaneously, but only in experimental situations. The point of experiment is to 'close the system' by creating a particular set of conditions that will isolate the causal mechanism under scrutiny from all those that are not under scrutiny. The causal mechanism of interest is then allowed to operate unimpeded and the results, the constant conjunctions, recorded. Hence, the Humean law is more accurately styled as: 'Whenever event *X*, then event *Y*, *under conditions* Z'. Second, the results obtained from experimental situations where conditions *Z* exist (i.e. in closed systems) are often successfully applied outside experimental situations (i.e. in open systems).

Two problems follow. First, if Humean law is based upon a constant conjunction of events, and such constant conjunctions are, typically, not found outside closed systems, then one must conclude that outside closed systems there are no laws. Second, if Humean law is based upon a constant conjunction of events, and such constant conjunctions are, typically, not found in open systems, then the question of what governs events in open systems is left not only unanswered, but also unaddressed. Moreover, it leaves without any valid explanation the observation that the results obtained from closed systems are often successfully applied in open systems.

These problems can be avoided by abandoning the Humean notion of law. If constant conjunctions of events are, typically, not found in open systems whence Humean law cannot govern or explain them, then (presuming that events are not simply a chaotic flux with no rhyme or reason) something else must govern and explain them. The governing law cannot be predicated upon a constant conjunction of events, because whatever it is that does govern events continues to do so even when the events do not manifest in constant conjunctions. The mechanism (gravity) that governs the fall of the autumn leaf does not cease to govern when the leaf fails to conform to any empirical regularity – i.e. when the leaf is acted upon by a series of other (possibly counteracting) mechanisms such as aerodynamic and thermodynamic mechanisms. This has implications for ontology. There appears to be an ontological domain where events actually occur, a domain where they are experienced empirically, and a domain where the mechanisms and structures that govern these events are operative.

Although the discussion has been couched in terms of natural science, it can readily be extended into social science by making the following claims about human agency. If human agency is real, then (a) human agents could always have acted otherwise, and (b) human action must make a difference to the social world. The implication arising from (a) and (b) is that the social world is open. The conclusions derived from an investigation of the practice of natural science, therefore, hold for social science. The social world constitutes an open system, and the social ontology is (partly) layered. The layered ontology of transcendental realism is schematically presented by Lawson (1994a) in Figure 6.1.

The layers range from the surface domain of the empirical where events/actions are given in sense experience, via the domain of the actual where these events/actions actually occur, to the subterranean domain of the (metaphoric) deep, where the structures which govern and cause these events/actions reside.[5] The best way of understanding what this layered ontology entails is via an example:

- One might perceive motorists stopping when confronted by a red traffic light (domain of the empirical).
- Most motorists actually do stop when confronted by a red traffic light (domain of the actual).
- There are 'deep structures' such as the rules of the highway code that causally govern this actuality – and which may not be directly perceivable (domain of the, metaphorically speaking, deep).

These domains are, typically, *unsynchronised* or *out of phase with one another*. For example, although most of the time most motorists are perceived to stop when confronted by a red traffic light, on occasion some actually do not. This deviant action occurs irrespective of whether or not it is perceived, and despite the fact that the rules of the highway code persist throughout.

Being out of phase means that phenomena existing at the level of the deep, for example, rules of the highway, act *transfactually*: that is, they continue to causally govern motoring behaviour even when they do not manifest at the level of the actual or empirical, i.e. when motorists do not stop, and are perceived not to stop, when confronted by a red traffic light. These rules do not

Domain	*Entity*
Empirical	Experience Perception Impression
Actual	Events Actions
'Deep'	Structures Mechanisms Rules Powers Relations

Note: I use the terms 'structures' and 'deep structures' generically to connote all the phenomena of domain of the deep; for example, rules are deep structures. The term 'deep' is a metaphor.
Source: Lawson (1994a)

Figure 6.1 A layered ontology

cease to govern motoring behaviour when they are not followed with perfect regularity.

Transfactuality implies that non-directly perceivable structures might persist in governing actions/events given in sense experience, but these events/actions will not, typically, be regular, that is, not constantly conjoined. This is because other, countervailing, causally governing structures (for example, high alcohol level in the blood stream) might also be governing the behaviour of the motorist. The actual resultant events/actions given in sense experience, then, depend upon the interplay of a range of transfactual, causally governing, deep structures. Moreover, because of this interplay, the resultant events/actions are, typically, non-regular, non-constantly conjoined.[6]

Without constancy in the conjunctions of events/actions, the empirical-realist project of using Humean law(s) to deduce consequences from initial axioms buttressed by assumptions is untenable. Such lack of event regularity, by contrast, is no handicap to transcendental-realist inquiry, because such inquiry is not directed at the domains of the empirical and actual, and thereby with the discovery of event regularities but at the domain of the deep.

The (social or physical) entities that constitute reality, on the transcendental realist ontology, then, are both structured and intransitive. They are structured in the sense that they are irreducible to each other. Deep structures are irreducible to the events/actions of experience or to the subjective conceptions held by agents, so that such structures can be neither solely empirical nor solely conceptual in nature. Put another way (and in complete contrast to Hayek II's position), reality consists of more than what is experienced and more than what agents conceive it to be.

The entities that constitute reality are intransitive, or exist in the intransitive domain, in the sense that they exist and act independently of their identification. Women, for example, will continue to be allocated to secondary positions in the labour market because of the deep structures in the form of male–female relations, irrespective of whether the latter are perceived by agents or not. Moreover, women's secondary position is not something that is merely believed or thought to exist, i.e. unlike God or fairies, it is a *real* social conception, not an *ideal* social conception.[7]

However, if transcendental realism privileges ontology over epistemology, it is important not to commit the obverse mistake of empiricist philosophy, and collapse the epistemic into the ontic (i.e. commit the *ontic fallacy*). Epistemology must be taken seriously. If the claim to an intransitive domain is an ontological claim about the nature of objects, then there must exist an epistemological domain where these objects are considered, grasped or reflected upon in thought. This domain is referred to as the transitive domain, where transitive objects such as facts, observations, conjectures, and so on exist.

There is, then, an intransitive domain where objects exist and a transitive domain where these objects are considered in thought. Recognising this division explains how science has continually created changing knowledge of (often relatively) unchanging objects.

HAYEK III's QUASI-TRANSCENDENTAL REALISM

Around 1960 Hayek abandons his previous philosophical position and adopts quasi-transcendental realism. Rather than examine the myriad of philosophical changes that Hayek undergoes, I shall identify only those aspects that are crucial to understanding his work on socio-economic order.

Hayek II's subjective-idealist epistemology encourages an augmented empirical-realist ontology that admits not only of events/actions given in sense experience, but also conceptions. When, therefore, Hayek II commits the epistemic fallacy, he commits a slightly different version of it. Instead of collapsing the intransitive into the transitive, that is, collapsing being into knowledge of being, Hayek II makes being synonymous with the construction in thought of being. In the case of what Hayek misleadingly refers to as social 'structure', for example, there is no object that can be collapsed into knowledge of it, only an object as knowledge. The object exists only in virtue of, that is, it is exhausted or fully determined by, the conceptions held by agents. Hayek cannot, in other words, even get an intransitive–transitive division going, therefore he cannot collapse one into the other. Just as Hayek II's ontology has to be described as augmented empirical realism, I suggest that he commits an *augmented* epistemic fallacy. He collapses being not into *knowledge* of being (which would be a sceptical position), but into the (constructed) *thought* of being (which is a subjective-idealist position).

In the 1960s, however, as Lawson observes, a shift in language occurs as conceptions, i.e. 'opinions', 'beliefs', 'ideas', 'attitudes', are replaced by 'rules that govern action', 'rules people obey' and so on (Lawson, 1994c, 151). This is not simply a semantic change, but reflects a change in the categories which Hayek uses to explain the social world. At one point Hayek notes the existence of

> a sort of connection between the knowledge that *rules exist in the objective* world and a disinclination to deviate from the rules commonly followed in action, and therefore also between the belief that events follow rules and the feeling that *one 'ought' to observe rules in one's conduct.*
>
> (Hayek, 1967b, 79, emphasis added)

This comment, along with many others in this paper, make it quite clear that Hayek now presumes rules to be social structures that have a real existence and are no longer treated as merely conceptual in nature. Social rules of conduct are now an example of *real* social structures. Moreover, rules exist apart from the events/actions they govern.

With the recognition of social structures in the form of social rules of conduct, Hayek's ontology is given a boost (augmented further) to include not only events/actions and conceptions, but also deep structures – in the form of social rules. These entities now exist and act independently of their identification and cease to be concept-*determined*. There is, subsequently, nothing standing in the way of Hayek adopting a layered ontology and sustaining the intransitive domain.

At this point, subjective idealism and hermeneutic foundationalism are abandoned at a stroke, and Hayek is left with the correct insight that this position encourages, namely the hermeneutic position (no longer foundationalist) that the social world is concept-*dependent*. Moreover, if social structures are no longer merely what agents conceive them to be, they need not be considered as inert, that is, they can now be considered as having (material) causal efficacy in the sense that they are real and make a difference to action.

Hayek can now conceive of the events/actions of experience being both ontologically distinct from, and out of phase with, the structures that govern them. As the passage noted above illustrates (and as we shall develop in Chapter 8), Hayek treats rules as distinct from events/actions. Thus, whilst he notes that rules lead to relatively regular patterns of events/actions, these regularities are not perfect. Rules exist transfactually, that is, they exist continually, irrespective of the effects they produce. This underlies Hayek's claim that rules are abstract, general and prescriptive. They advise on how one ought to act; they do not and cannot force agents to act in a certain way. According to Lawson, the recognition that the world is separated from knowledge of it

> encourages serious consideration (or perhaps follows from a vision in Hayek's beliefs about) the manner in which social objects are in fact known. Specifically, discursive, tacit and unconscious levels of knowing are now entertained.
>
> (Lawson, 1994c, 152)

Hayek II's work focuses upon the subjective and fragmented nature of knowledge, but ignores tacitness. The problem he identifies is essentially one of how fragmented knowledge is communicated by the only institution that he has at this point in time, the telecom system. Hayek III's work, by contrast, whilst not ignoring the communication of fragmented knowledge, adds tacitness to the scenario. Here, much of what agents know is tacit, and refractory to being discovered, communicated and stored via the telecom system. Moreover, an important part of this stock of tacitly held knowledge is embodied in social rules of conduct.

Once Hayek breaks from the notion that agents' conceptions constitute the social world, it becomes possible not only that agents know things tacitly, but also that there is a range of things that they do not know; that is, he has to recognise and deal with ignorance.

When the recognition that social structures are no longer reduced to agents' conceptions but are now objective entities is coupled with the possibility of agents knowing these structures only tacitly or partially (i.e. in the sense that they know 'how'), the possibility exists that they may not be known (i.e. in the sense that they do not know 'that') by agents who draw upon them. Not only the structures that agents draw upon, but also their own actions facilitated by them, may be 'opaque to themselves' (Lawson, 1994c, 142). In this case, the 'compositive method', which focuses upon creating social phenomena from the conceptions held by agents, becomes problematic. If agents do not discursively know and/or adequately conceptualise the structures that facilitate their action, then society cannot be composed out of these conceptions alone.

With social structures now irreducible to agents' conceptions, existing independently of knowledge and, therefore, having a real input into human action, that is, making a difference to agents' actions, Hayek can now switch the task of science from merely tracing the (intended and unintended) consequences of action to the investigation of the conditions of that action. This leads Hayek to the conclusion that human beings are essentially rule-following animals, and to the notion that human agents are *procedurally*, as opposed to *instrumentally*, *rational*. Underpinning this new notion of agency is Hayek's cognitive psychology – of which more in Chapter 8.

If there is more to society than the consciously formed conceptions of agents, then phenomena that do not originate in the mind of the transcendental subject become a subject for investigation. Put simply, once Hayek recognises that agents cannot take any kind of social action without having a network of rules of conduct to draw upon, then the focus of attention ceases to be the individual and becomes the unity of individual and structures. As Hayek puts it:

> the overall order of actions in a group is more than the total of regularities observable in the actions of individuals and cannot be reduced to them.
>
> (Hayek, 1967b, 71)

The reason for this is because

> the existence of those relations which are essential for the existence of the whole cannot be accounted for wholly by the interaction of the parts but only by their interaction with an outside world both of the individual parts and the whole.
>
> (Ibid.)

Individuals not only interact with one another, they interact with rules. In fact, interaction with one another presupposes that they draw upon the rules which exist independently of any one of them. The socio-economic order exists as a unity of individuals and rules. This makes it *impossible* to break the socio-economic order down into ultimate constituent parts. The socio-economic order or whole is an unbreakable unity of individuals and rules.[8]

The following quote from Hayek with its definite transcendental-realist ring, indicates just how close he comes to the latter perspective at times:

> Rule . . . means a propensity or disposition to act or not to act in a certain manner, which will manifest itself in what we call a practice or custom. As such it will be one of the determinants of action which, however, need not show itself in every single action, but may prevail in most instances. Any such rule will always operate in combination and often in competition with other rules or dispositions and with particular impulses; and whether a rule will prevail . . . will depend upon the strength of the propensity it describes and of the other dispositions or impulses operating at the same time.
>
> (Hayek, 1973, 75)

Since Hayek appears to treat social rules of conduct as deep structures governing the events of experience, one can claim that he adopts the layered ontology characteristic of transcendental realism. There are, then, grounds for ascribing to Hayek the label quasi-transcendental realist, although there is something more to add here. Bhaskar develops transcendental realism in the mid-1970s primarily from a critique of the positivist-grounded philosophies of natural science. But as an essentially ontological thesis, it has resonances in the social science which he begins to explore soon after. The development and extension of transcendental realism into social science produced what is now referred to as *critical* realism (Bhaskar, 1989b, 190). Henceforth, I shall use transcendental realism as a *generic* term and critical realism to refer specifically to *social* science.

One of the most important developments of critical realism is the Transformational Model of Social Activity (TMSA). Not only is it an important development in social theory, it is important for this thesis as Hayek appears to adopt something approaching it. I shall elaborate upon the TMSA as set out by Bhaskar (1989a, ch. 1) in the rest of this chapter, then return to it in Chapter 10 when I shall claim Hayek adopts a transformational conception of spontaneous socio-economic order.

THE TRANSFORMATIONAL MODEL OF SOCIAL ACTIVITY (TMSA)

At the heart of social theory lies a fundamental question in social ontology, namely: What is society? Whilst traditionally most commentators recognise that society consists of people or agents and (in some sense) structures, the debate centres upon the way they interact. With the TMSA, Bhaskar enjoins this debate and lays out the critical-realist social ontology.

His starting point, that is, the raw material for his theoretical elaborations, is the traditional positions in social ontology of which there are three. In true Aristotelian (dialectic) fashion, he proceeds to identify and retain the correct parts of these traditional ontologies, synthesising them to form a new position.

From the reificationist[9] position presented by Durkheim, Bhaskar retains the notion that external structural elements exert constraint upon agents. From the voluntarist[10] position presented by Weber he retains the notion that social material is concept-dependent, that is, depends upon the intentional and meaningful behaviour of individuals. From the 'dialectical'[11] position presented by Berger, he retains the notion that the other two positions are reductionist, and that the solution lies in elaborating the way structures and agents interact. The task of social theorists, then, is to find a way of avoiding the Scylla and Charbydis of reification and voluntarism, whilst elaborating a *meaningful* interaction or relation between agents and structures.

When, for example, a person begins work for the first time, she discovers a set of social structures in the form of rule-governed practices already in existence such as clocking on, working at a set pace, and so on. These practices, which must be followed at least to some extent in order that working activity is possible, exist independently of or externally to each employee. Recognition of these social structures as external, causal phenomena prevents the error of voluntarism, that is, the error of presupposing that these practices are simply created or invented by the individuals involved. Recognition that the workforce must have some idea or reason (even if it is the wrong one) why they do the things they do, and that if they cease to act purposively such practices would disappear, prevents the error of reifying such structures.

The point to take is that agents do not create society by creating the social structures that constitute it; society pre-exists them. Moreover, society continues to exist only because agents produce and transform those aspects that they may encounter in their social actions. Every action performed requires the pre-existence of some social structures which agents draw upon in order to initiate that action.

For example, the industrial production of goods and services requires an industrial relations system; communicating requires a medium, for example, language; driving requires a highway code; making a profit requires the ownership of capital and labour, and so on. This ensemble of social structures, according to Bhaskar, simply *is* society. He notes that:

> if society is always already made then any concrete human practice . . . can only modify it; and the totality of such acts sustain it . . . Society stands to the individuals then, as something that they never make, but that only exists in virtue of their activity.
>
> (Bhaskar, 1989a, 34)

Nothing happens out of nothing, as it were. The social material that exists does so in virtue of the fact that it is continually reproduced and transformed in the act of production. Social material is both a condition and an outcome of human action. Agents do not create structures *ab initio*, they *re*create, *re*produce or *transform* them via their activities. Production (which captures many aspects of human productive activity) is therefore simultaneously reproduction and transformation, and it is in this way that structures continue to endure. Bhaskar calls this the TMSA and exemplifies it by employing the Aristotelian metaphor of a sculptor fashioning a product out of the material and tools available. The sculptor cannot do other than work with given tools and on given materials that are reproduced and transformed via production:

> [P]eople do not create society. For it always pre-exists them and is a necessary condition for their activity. Rather society must be regarded as an ensemble of structures, practices and conventions which individuals produce and transform, but which would not exist unless they

> did so. Society does not exist independently of human activity (the error of reification). But it is not the product of it (the error of voluntarism).
>
> (Ibid., 36)

By separating societies and human agents categorically, Bhaskar is able to differentiate properties possessed by societies from those possessed by the agents upon which the former depend for continued existence. Human agents have intentionality but societies do not. Agents acting consciously, unconsciously reproduce the structures which govern their actions in daily life. People do not marry with the conscious aim of reproducing the nuclear family, yet this is nevertheless an unintended consequence of, as well as a necessary condition for, their activity.

Of significance, here, is the insight that while social structures are necessary for action, that is, they facilitate action, they do not determine it. The rules of grammar, as structures, limit speech acts but they do not determine what is said. Social conventions may put pressure on people to marry but they do not determine whom they should marry. By using this conception Bhaskar is able to maintain an active role for human agency whilst at the same time avoiding the error of voluntarism and retaining constraining (and enabling) structures:

> Society may thus be conceived as an articulated ensemble of relatively independent and enduring generative structures . . . [S]ocial structures exist only in virtue of the acts they govern, they do not exist independently of the conceptions that the agents possess of what they are doing . . . that is, of some theory of these activities.
>
> (Ibid., 38)

A SWITCH IN THE MODE OF THEORISING

With the layered and transformative ontology given by the TMSA, the emphasis of socio-economic investigation switches (ontologically speaking) from the fused domains of the empirical and actual to the domain of the deep. Investigation ceases to be (solely or even primarily) the definition of final outcomes given as the events/actions of experience, and becomes an investigation into the deep structures and mechanisms that make the final outcome possible. This is due to the recognition that the events/actions given in sense experience that constitute the final outcome are (a) merely the starting point for investigation, (b) are not regularly conjoined, (c) are governed in part by underlying mechanisms and structures, which are (d) typically out of phase with these events or actions.

With the recognition that the deduction of consequences in terms of events/action from axioms and assumptions via Humean law is untenable, and the further recognition that something must govern the events/actions of experience, the mode of theorising switches. Consequences of actions cannot be deduced, but conditions for that action can be uncovered. The deep structures that act with transfactual necessity to govern the events/actions given in sense experience can be uncovered and their operation explained. Hence the domain of the deep is where investigation must focus. As Bhaskar puts matters:

> Looked at in this way [TMSA] . . . the task of the various social sciences [is] to lay out the structural conditions for various conscious human actions – for example, what economic processes must take place for Christmas shopping to be possible – but they do not describe the latter.
> (Bhaskar, 1989a, 36)

Metaphorically speaking, the task of science is not to move (horizontally) between actions/events, trying to ascertain or generate constant conjunctions, but to move (vertically) from events/actions to the deep structures that govern them. Economics, from the transcendental-realist perspective, then, does not proceed by using Humean law(s) to deduce consequences from initial axioms buttressed by assumptions; rather, it proceeds by inquiring into and explaining the conditions (in the form of deep structures) necessary for socio-economic action.[12] Illumination and explanation supplant prediction.

As will become clear in the final chapter, the TMSA is perhaps the most important concept in understanding Hayek's notion of spontaneous socio-economic order. With it, Hayek can finally break from a focus upon events/actions given in experience and the fused domains of the empirical and actual and consider orderly behaviour as grounded in, but out of phase with, underlying deep structures. The nature of order is understood without the need for regularity of agents' action.

CONCLUSION: ONTOLOGY AND IMPLICATIONS OF HAYEK I, II AND III

This chapter has begun to illustrate Hayek's shift away from his earlier philosophical position and his adoption of quasi-transcendental realism. After laying out a stylised version of transcendental realism, at least on those aspects that Hayek approaches, a number of implications for Hayek's socio-economic theory were introduced. These will be elaborated upon throughout the remaining chapters.

At this point, sufficient philosophical elaboration has been done to lay out the basic structure underlying the development of Hayek's notion of order. The following brief schema depicts the thread running through the remainder of the book.

Whilst I did not elaborate upon the point, it appears that prior to 1936 Hayek's adherence to 'narrow technical economics' (1962, 91) is compatible with his positivism, and thereby with his implicit adoption of an empirical realist ontology of events. Thus the search for order reduces to the search for equilibrium, and this reduces to compatibility of events/actions between agents.[13] Moreover, since positivism allows for the use of theoretical and possibly fictional constructs, all the devices used by mainstream economics are permitted – for example, perfect knowledge, equilibrium, and so on. Hayek I, then, like other positivist economists, attempts to investigate the compatibility of actions that appear to constitute socio-economic order in the guise of equilibrium.

Hayek II breaks partially from positivism only to adopt subjective idealism. As with most non-realist positions, the emphasis on epistemology generates an implicit ontology. In the case of Hayek II he adopts an augmented empirical-realist ontology that permits not only of events/actions given in experience, but also agents' conceptions. Whilst this allows Hayek II to break with many aspects of mainstream theory, particularly in terms of knowledge and equilibrium, it has the drawback that it prevents him from saying a great deal in terms of socio-economic order.

If the social world is conceptual in nature, the only task open to economists is to understand the way in which agents perceive their world. Explanation of social action in terms of an elaboration of the conditions for action are impossible when the conditions for action are merely the creation of agents' cognitive activity. Moreover, whilst Hayek II now rejects equilibrium as a concept that presupposes a system of event regularities, he has no alternative conception to replace it with. He can go (metaphorically) deeper, that is, beneath the events/actions of experience, *but only as far as the concepts, attitudes, ideas and opinions that he takes as social 'structure'*. His inability to conceive of real social structures prevents him from developing an alternative notion of socio-economic order to equilibrium.

Hayek III adopts a quasi-transcendental realist philosophy, the subjective-idealist epistemology evaporates, and he adopts an ontology of events/actions, conceptions and, most importantly, deep structures in the form of social rules of conduct. At this point he can proffer an alternative to equilibrium by going beneath the events/actions, but this time to the real structures that govern these events. He develops something approaching the TMSA, to end up with a sophisticated social theory that allows him to combine the themes of knowledge (kinds), ignorance, rules and the telecom system in his elaboration of the market process or catallaxy.

7

KNOWLEDGE, IGNORANCE AND SOCIAL RULES OF CONDUCT

> Man prides himself on the increase in his knowledge. But, as a result of what he has himself created, the limitations of his conscious knowledge and therefore of the range of ignorance significant for his conscious actions have constantly increased . . . The more civilised we become, the more relatively ignorant must each individual be of the facts on which the working of his civilisation becomes. The very division of knowledge increases the necessary ignorance of the individual of most of this knowledge.
>
> (Hayek, 1960, 26)

The shift in philosophical position that occurs around 1960 opens up new directions in which Hayek's thought can travel. This chapter pursues two of these directions, namely kinds of ignorance and knowledge. Whilst we shall not discuss philosophical issues, the point to bear in mind continually is that Hayek's development of the themes of ignorance and knowledge is facilitated by *an ontology that allows for real social structures (in the form of social rules of conduct) to exist independently of their identification*.

The chapter consists of three parts. The first elaborates upon Hayek's notion of ignorance. The second part explores his notion of knowledge, noting especially that knowledge is divided into knowing 'how' and knowing 'that', with the former raising the possibility that agents might know things tacitly. The third part brings ignorance and knowledge together again to probe deeper into the nature of social rules as devices for coping with ignorance.

IGNORANCE

Ignorance implies far more than the mere absence of knowledge; there are various states and/or potential states of ignorance. Whilst, as Hayek knows full well, many of these states are, typically, overcome by agents, any investigation of the mechanisms that enable agents to overcome them requires an understanding of what it is they are overcoming. The term 'ignorance' requires further clarification.

One state of ignorance, which might be termed 'common-sense ignorance', refers to a situation where an agent does not possess requisite knowledge, although this state of ignorance can be overcome within a reasonable time period and at reasonable cost. Another state of ignorance can be termed 'radical ignorance'. This extends to situations where agents are ignorant of the future and, by extension, of the unintended consequences of their actions. This radical ignorance cannot be overcome at all, only coped with.

Close to the radically ignorant state are several (interesting) scenarios. Ignorance might stem from the tacitness of knowledge. Because (as will become clear later) much knowledge is tacit and non-discursive, it is often resistant to being transmitted from one agent to another. We might, for example, know how to operate a particular machine, yet be completely unable to state how we do it, and therefore, *in a special sense* be ignorant.[1] Whilst there may be ways of accessing what one knows (for example, careful observation) this will (typically) not be easy, making ignorance, if not radical, then virtually so.

Much knowledge, whilst not strictly non-tacit, is what might be called semi-tacit, held in the unconscious mind, and accessed only under certain conditions that bring it to the fore. In the absence of these conditions, agents are neither conscious of this knowledge nor do they advertise it, implying not only that others remain ignorant of this knowledge but also that there are no means by which it can be overcome.

Ignorance might be conceived of as stemming from the sheer amount of knowledge that would be needed to initiate a particular action. As Hayek continually argues, a central planner would be totally ignorant of the amount of facts necessary to co-ordinate successful action. Whilst this is due to ignorance of the unintended consequences of actions and to the tacitness and semi-tacitness of knowledge, it is compounded by the sheer volume of facts that would be necessary. Not only central planners, but also market-players face this problem; their precise level of ignorance depends upon their spatio-temporal location, and the quality and quantity of knowledge they seek.

Whilst ignorance becomes important in Hayek's work, it is the radical and virtually radical kind that is of crucial importance. I shall, as a consequence, use the term radical ignorance to include the virtually radical kind.

The development of Hayek's understanding of ignorance

Whilst prior to 1960, Hayek II is not explicit about ignorance, from 1960 onwards there appears to be more emphasis placed upon the different forms that (knowledge and) ignorance may take. One of the most significant forms becomes radical ignorance. This is not merely accidental. The philosophical position adopted by Hayek II ensures that all that falls within the interest field of the social scientist are agents' conceptions, and of course, *agents can neither be ignorant, nor possess only tacit or semi-conscious knowledge of their own conceptions*. Whilst the agents in Hayek II's theory are not instrumentally rational, they are fully conscious of the social world they inhabit. It is only after 1960, that is, once Hayek allows for the existence of real social entities such as rules that exist independently of their identification, that the possibility arises that agents may be ignorant of them.

Hayek's broadening view of knowledge and ignorance appears to make him increasingly aware of the fact that, on occasion, radical ignorance implies that knowledge can never be obtained. And if it cannot be obtained, it cannot be communicated and used as a guide to action. However, after 1960, he can sustain the possibility that agents can *remain* ignorant in a special sense and yet still manage to initiate action, via social rules of conduct.

In 1960 Hayek refers to the Socratic maxim that the recognition of ignorance is the beginning of wisdom (p. 22) and one year later he reminds us (in an anti-constructivist manner) that 'it is high time that we take ignorance more seriously'(1961, 39). Hayek bemoans the fact that whilst knowledge has received great attention from scholars down the ages, ignorance has (with notable exceptions) received scant attention. This theme was first advanced in 1960 (ch. 2), in 1970b, and again in 1973 (ch. 1).

Summarising the content of these texts one may argue that, for Hayek, knowledge has traditionally been discussed in the form of the power of human reason, achieving, perhaps, its fullest expression in French Rationalist philosophy of the seventeenth century. Hayek feels that this 'Age of Reason' has misled subsequent generations of thinkers by glossing over the role of ignorance, with unfortunate political and intellectual consequences. The political consequences, according to Hayek, are unfortunate in that some believe that human reason has created society, and that therefore humans can change it at will, resulting in revolutionary politics. The intellectual consequences are unfortunate in that humans cannot understand the workings of the market mechanism or the social structures in which the market is embedded, since, Hayek claims, ignorance lies at their root. If these thinkers do not recognise radical ignorance, then they are led to overstate their ability to understand and thereby intervene either to assist the market, or to replace it with another mechanism. By the mid-1980s, reflecting on his life's work, Hayek writes:

> I've come to believe that both the aim of the market order and therefore the object of explanation . . . is to cope with the inevitable ignorance of everybody of most of the particular facts which determine that order.
>
> (Hayek, 1983, 19)

It would appear then, that the philosophical changes that occur after 1960 introduce the possibility of conceiving of ignorance. Hand in hand with this go the substantive changes in terms of social theory (social rules) that allow

Hayek to accommodate radical ignorance. Whilst the following comment by Barry is correct, it is only correct *vis-à-vis* Hayek's post-1960 work:

> Underlying all Hayek's social philosophy is a theory of knowledge. The most significant feature of this theory is Hayek's emphasis on man's ignorance.
>
> (Barry, 1979, 9)

KNOWLEDGE

Butos gives a neat summary of what knowledge entails in Hayek's work:

> the kind of knowledge which Hayek has in mind is far broader than that typically incorporated into economic models. In addition to prices, quantities and price expectations, it also refers to all sorts of detailed, practical knowledge available to individuals as well as knowledge of general rules of behaviour, traditions, and social customs that may be largely tacit.
>
> (Butos, 1985, 340)

Any notion of order that is more than a formal description of the conditions necessary for equilibrium must explain how agents initiate actions that are relatively spatio-temporally co-ordinated[2] with one another under the really existing situation of incomplete knowledge. As was demonstrated in Chapter 5, Hayek reasons that actions may be co-ordinated if plans are co-ordinated, which depends upon the co-ordination of expectations, which in turn is based upon agents having access to knowledge (in one form or another, and not necessarily directly or consciously) of what others are doing or intend to do.

The recognition of the limited knowledge available to agents opens up certain possibilities. Under certain circumstances, certain agents may possess extremely limited knowledge, or even no knowledge at all; that is, they might be ignorant.[3] Whilst it is one thing to investigate how agents co-ordinate their actions on the basis of communicating knowledge, however limited, it is quite another to investigate how agents co-ordinate their actions when they are ignorant. It appears, then, that not only knowledge but also ignorance needs to be understood in far greater detail.

Kinds of knowledge

Popular use of the term 'knowledge' tends to obliterate the fact that it is not homogeneous.[4] There are different kinds of knowledge, and it is possible to 'know' in different ways. Moreover, sometimes agents possess a lot of knowledge, sometimes a little and sometimes none – at least none of the requisite kind. Furthermore, different kinds of knowledge are handled by different institutions.[5] These will all be elaborated upon below. Hayek tends to use the phrase 'knowledge of the particular circumstances of time and place' as a generic term encompassing different kinds of knowledge. Whilst in this period Hayek is (implicitly) aware of these differences, his tendency to run them together blinds him to the importance of one particular kind – tacit knowledge.

It is important to understand that before the 1960s Hayek's understanding of tacit knowledge is at best rudimentary. In 1936 (50, fn. 1) he illustrates his awareness of the distinction between knowledge as a skill and as the possession of a set of facts, but he makes nothing of it. In 1945, he recognises knowledge as embedded in rules, practices, habits and institutions (p. 528), and his quote from Whitehead that 'civilisation advances by extending the number of important operations which we can perform without thinking about them', shows his awareness of tacit knowledge. In 1952 (p. 39), Hayek first registers his awareness of Ryle's distinction between 'knowing how' and 'knowing that', although Polanyi is not mentioned until 1962.

It is, however, not until 1960 (ch. 2, esp. 25, fn. 4) and more importantly 1962 that Hayek really begins to make use of Polanyi's and Ryle's work. Prior to 1960, then, and although he shows some recognition of tacit knowledge, it plays no part in his discussion of the discovery, communication and storage of knowledge. In his 1962 paper, Hayek cites language-speakers, bicycle-riders, carpenters, skiers and billiard-players as examples of agents being ignorant in terms of knowing 'that' whilst applying knowledge 'how'. The implication here is that there is a range of phenomena that each of these agents cannot articulate and, more importantly, do not and cannot know, but this does not prevent them from acting.

Knowledge of the particular circumstances of time and place

Hayek makes great use of the notion of 'the knowledge of the particular circumstances of time and place' possessed by 'the man on the spot' (1945, 524), although there is a lot packed into this short, dense phrase. This section sets out the different kinds of knowledge that appear to be buried within this 'knowledge of circumstances' in order to emphasise the distinctiveness of tacit knowledge.

First, given that Hayek is aware of advertising, personal contact, and so on, it would be impossible to imagine that his reference to 'knowledge of the facts of his [agents'] immediate surroundings' (ibid., 525) did not include knowledge embodied within a range of formal institutions. This kind of knowledge that is independent of the knower is referred to by Popper as 'knowledge without a knowing subject' (Popper, 1972, 115). It is embodied in formal institutions such as education/training, stock market reports, technical specifications, market research, operations research, libraries, press agencies, advertising, and all kinds of media, especially trade newsletters. Ioannides notes something similar, referring to localised or 'technical knowledge' defined as:

> all information that a person has acquired through a teaching process . . . and is therefore . . . alienable in the sense that it can be transferred from one individual to another.
>
> (Ioannides, 1992, 36–7)

Second, some 'knowledge of circumstances' is already available to the agent at any spatio-temporal location. Drawing upon Hayek's examples, it could be knowledge of the immediate environment (for example, the under-exploitation of a surplus stock or knowledge of half-empty tramp steamers). It could be knowledge held by other agents (knowledge *with* a knowing subject) and embodied in personal relationships (for example, between an entrepreneur and a supplier of a particular product or an arbitrage opportunity). Hayek's reference to a trader's unwillingness to make public how and where to obtain cheaper wares reveals that some 'knowledge of circumstances' is 'observable' and 'tangible' (Hayek, 1988, 89).

Judging by these examples, Hayek appears to have in mind not tacit, unconsciously held, inarticulable knowledge, but non-tacit, consciously held and articulable knowledge. If an entrepreneur knows of a half-empty tramp steamer, then he knows this consciously and can articulate it.

I shall refer to the two foregoing types of knowledge as *non-tacit local knowledge*. If non-tacit local knowledge is, in part, what Hayek has in mind, then it is likely that he is aware of three important points about such knowledge:

1 It is *indirectly* accessible. Agents do not initially or directly possess it, they can gain access to this type of knowledge, although it may be as simple as consulting a library, or as difficult as engaging in market research.
2 It is communicated and stored by formal institutions such as libraries or news media, not by the telecom system. When one possesses non-tacit local knowledge, one possesses knowledge 'that' – something which will become clear in the next section.
3 It is alienable or transferable, in that this kind of knowledge is independent of the knower. When non-tacit local knowledge is possessed, it is possessed consciously, in that agents know what they know, can articulate it, and therefore communicate it. It is discursive knowledge.

Third, and in complete contrast to non-tacit local knowledge, some 'knowledge of circumstances' is tacitly held. The term 'tacit' is usually used to mean that something is understood without being stated, which does not necessarily mean that it could not be stated. The emphasis of the term is on the way that something is known, rather than on the ability to state it. Tacitness might, but does not necessarily, imply inarticulability. We might, for example, possess tacit knowledge in the form of knowing how to ride a bicycle, and be either able or unable to state the reasons why this feat is possible. Articulability depends upon the context, and nothing can be said *a priori*.

Where in 1945 Hayek's examples refer to substantive knowledge of particular states of affairs such as half-empty tramp steamers, by 1960 the focus changes. What he refers to as 'expert knowledge' possessed for example by the entrepreneur 'is not substantive knowledge but merely knowledge of where to look and how to find the needed information' (1960, 25). By 1988 Hayek is even clearer:

> there is a difference between following rules of conduct, on the one hand and knowledge about something on the other (a difference . . . between 'knowing how' and 'knowing that' . . . The habit of following rules . . . ought to be seen . . . as a skill to fit oneself into, or align oneself with a pattern of whose very existence one may be barely aware and of whose ramifications one has scarcely any knowledge.
>
> (Hayek, 1988, 78)

Hayek notes further that:

> so much knowledge of particular circumstances is unarticulated, and hardly even articulable (for example an entrepreneur's hunch that a new product might be successful) that it would prove impossible to make it public.
>
> (Ibid., 89)

Glossing the differences between Hayek's work before and after 1960 leads to a failure to recognise the importance of tacit knowledge, inarticulability and the differentiation between knowledge 'how' and 'that' in his developed work. The importance of tacit knowledge, then, is as follows:

1 It is *directly* accessible. Agents do not need to gain access to it, they already possess it ('in the stacks of their minds', as Bacharach puts it), on the presumption that they are socialised adults who, after a learning process, have mastered the art of living in a society and following social rules. They already know 'how'.
2 It is not communicated and stored by formal institutions, but embodied in society's informal institutional network, the key one being social rules of action.
3 It is inalienable or non-transferable in that this kind of knowledge is quite dependent on the knower. The agent who knows how to follow the rule need not, and typically does not, know a range of facts that are embodied in the rule itself. When agents know tacitly, they tend to know non-discursively – I shall elaborate more on this in a moment.

The importance of making these distinctions is to throw tacit knowledge into relief, to establish that it is qualitatively different from non-tacit local knowledge. The non-tacit local knowledge that a tramp steamer is operating half-empty is qualitatively different to the tacit knowledge of a web of social rules of action that the entrepreneur draws upon in order precisely to acquire knowledge about the steamer.[6]

For Hayek, the inquiry into tacit knowledge and tacitly followed rules does not stop with physical acts such as riding a bicycle or speaking a language. Here Hayek goes not only beyond his own work in *The Sensory Order* (1952), but also beyond thinkers like Polanyi and Ryle, who are primarily concerned with physiological actions. He also goes beyond thinkers such as Peters who see rules as useful in acts like road-crossing (Peters, 1959, ch. 1). Hayek extends the scope of inquiry to include social activities or processes such as work activity, traditions, institutions or social rules. It is in his extension of tacit knowledge to these latter domains that Hayek's originality lies.[7]

For Hayek, agents are able to 'go on', that is, to initiate successful social action, because they know 'how' to follow social rules. Moreover, they need not consciously follow rules:

> So long as individuals act in accordance with rules it is not necessary that they be consciously aware of the rules. It is enough they *know how* to act in accordance with the rules without *knowing that* the rules are such and such in articulated terms.
>
> (Hayek, 1973, 99)

If, however, agents 'go on' by following social rules, a question is thrown up: What are the characteristics or properties of social rules that allow them to fulfil their function? This is an inquiry into the nature of social rules, into what they are and how they perform their function. The short answer is that social rules are the embodiment of social knowledge.

THE NATURE OF SOCIAL RULES: THE EMBODIMENT OF KNOWLEDGE

Whilst knowledge must be of something, it can only exist and be communicable provided it has a bodily form, vehicle or receptacle in which to reside or become embodied. This receptacle could be, for example, the mind, a newspaper, a book, a weather bulletin or even a social rule. The two receptacles that interest Hayek are undoubtedly the mind and social rules. Since the mind is the subject of the next chapter, attention is focused here upon social rules. In one place Hayek writes:

> In such spontaneous formations [as a market society] is embodied a perception of the general laws that govern nature. With this cumulative embodiment of experience in tools and forms of action will emerge a growth of explicit knowledge, of formulated generic rules that can be communicated by language from person to person.
>
> (Hayek, 1960, 33)

Whilst Hayek uses the term 'embodied' only very occasionally (for example, 1973, 119; 1960, 157), the sentiment is echoed in numerous passages especially in 1960 (chs 2 and 3), 1973 (ch. 1) and 1983 (19–20). Hayek describes an historical, evolutionary process of trial and error whereby agents discover new rules or modify existing ones, using them as a basis for action. Successful action results in the rule being selected, whilst unsuccessful action results in the rule being de-selected. Irrespective of the merits of Hayek's evolutionary approach (which is itself currently being debated in Austrian circles[8]), the point is that after a process of trial and error, certain rules come to be drawn upon because they facilitate successful action, and by being drawn upon they endure.

It is important to understand that the reason rules can perform this function is because they embody the collected wisdom of the society. As Hayek puts it:

> Like all general purpose tools, rules serve because they . . . help to make the members of the society . . . more effective in pursuit of their aims . . . The knowledge that has given them [rules] their shape . . . is knowledge of the occurrence of certain problem situations.
>
> (Hayek, 1973, 21)

> [By] guiding the actions of individuals by rules . . . it is possible to make use of knowledge which nobody possesses as a whole.
>
> (Ibid., 49)

> Most knowledge . . . is obtained . . . in the continuous process of sifting a learnt tradition . . . The tradition is the product of a process of selection . . . which without anyone knowing or intending it, assisted in the proliferation of those who followed them . . . The process of selection that shaped custom and morality could take account of more factual circumstances than individuals could perceive, and in consequence tradition is in some respects superior to, or 'wiser' than human reason.
>
> (Hayek, 1988, 75)

The idea that rules embody knowledge is not unique to Hayek; institutionalist economists have long known of what one leading thinker calls the 'informational function of institutions' (Hodgson, 1993). Hayek's rules are a species of institution:

> Institutions establish and produce a set of rules and behavioural norms. These are fixed in part by habit, but also typically by tacit or legally supported social acceptance or conformity. These rules and norms are not necessarily inviolable, but the point is that they help agents seek to estimate the potential actions of others. The critical point is that both routines and formal institutions, by establishing more or less fixed patterns of human action, actually supply information to other agents

> ... [They] enable decision and action by providing more or less reliable information regarding the likely actions of others.
>
> (Hodgson, 1993, 10)

> Habits, routines and institutions have a stable and inert quality and tend to sustain and thus 'pass on' their characteristics through time ... [they] thus preserve knowledge, particularly tacit knowledge in relation to skills, and act through time as their transmission belt.
>
> (Ibid., 7; see also Hodgson, 1988, ch. 6)

Whilst an investigation of the similarities between Hodgson's characterisation of institutions and Hayek's social rules of conduct might be interesting, it is tangential to this thesis. The point to note is that institutions and rules possess a knowledge or informational function. They are able to perform this function because the knowledge or information generated by past (relatively successful) actions and thereby found to be useful, resides, is embodied or embedded in the institutions or rules that agents currently follow.[9]

The paradox of ignorance

According to Hayek, social rules are the embodiment of society's collected wisdom, and agents who know 'how' to follow them are thereby, typically, enabled to undertake relatively successful action. But where exactly does (a) knowledge 'that', i.e. knowledge of a range of facts, and (b) ignorance, fit into this analysis? When agents know 'how' but not 'that', they are able to act yet at the same time are ignorant in a sense. They are *simultaneously, and paradoxically, knowledgeable and ignorant.*

There are two ways to solve the paradox. The first is to claim that there is no paradox, thereby curtailing the investigation. The second encourages a closer look into the phenomenon of ignorance and leads to a far deeper understanding of what social rules of conduct really are and how they actually function.

Consider first the claim that there is no paradox. We could claim that agents are always knowledgeable and never ignorant in the sense that they, typically, always know ('how') which social rules to follow. Social rules allow agents access to knowledge 'how'. Now this is of course true. If agents did not have knowledge of rules, they could not initiate social action. So in this sense they are knowledgeable and not ignorant.

This, however, is only half the story, and as such, it leaves too much unsaid, particularly with respect to ignorance. What, on this view, is it that agents are ignorant of? Whilst agents have knowledge of some things, some facts, some knowledge ('that'), there is a range of other things that they do not know. Claiming that agents are not ignorant because they know 'how' simply brushes to one side the question of what it is that they are ignorant of, dismissing in the process the entire phenomenon of ignorance, something which Hayek is keen to suggest ought not to be done. Moreover, if the investigation rests content with claiming that there is no paradox, it can never uncover just how it is that rules are able to perform their function. The investigation stops before it has really begun.

The other way of solving the paradox requires that we state exactly what is meant by the words 'do not know', in Hayek's statement that we have a 'capacity to follow rules which we do not know' (Hayek, 1962, 45). Agents, it appears, are ignorant of something. The question is: what is the nature of their ignorance?

Hayek's concern is not with superficial matters, such as where agents are ignorant in the sense that they cannot name the rule or even advance some rudimentary commentary about what following it entails or why they follow the ones they do. Rather, Hayek advances three more fundamental impediments to agents knowing social rules.

First, agents are ignorant of the range of knowledge ('that'), in the sense that they are ignorant of a multitude of particular facts that would be necessary to engage in some form of instrumentally rational optimisation calculation (Hayek, 1973, 13, 30). In this case, however, not knowing is not insurmountable, that is, ignorance is not radical. Here rules are what Nyiri (1988, 23) refers to as 'a practical abbreviation' whereby knowledge 'could in principle, though perhaps only with a loss of convenience, be communicated in a purely discursive fashion'.

Second, part of what it means not to know rules is bound up with the fact that, typically, lay agents cannot foresee the (alleged) benefits that accrue to society at large by certain rules being followed. Agents follow rules handed down in the form of tradition which they could not possibly know in the sense of knowing the entire evolutionary history that led to the formation of such rules. Hayek therefore describes the term 'extended order' as concerning

> that which far surpasses the reach of our understanding, wishes and purpose, and our sense perceptions, and that which incorporates and generates knowledge which no individual brain, or any single organisation could possess or invent.
>
> (Hayek, 1988, 72)

Thus can Hayek write of the 'submission to undesigned rules and conventions whose significance and importance we largely do not understand' (1962, 63).

Third, the totality of knowledge that exists within the socio-economic system cannot be gathered together in one place and known by one agent because this knowledge is not only dispersed, but also is only known socially. For example, whilst some individuals know a lot about various aspects of car manufacture, no one individual knows how to produce cars in all the intricacies. This involves more than a division of labour and knowledge, it suggests that the knowledge of how to make a car is embodied in the institutional structure of a car plant, and only at that level of aggregation.[10]

It is arguably something like this that Hayek is getting at in his application to the social world of Goedel's theorem. Eriksson manages a succinct interpretation, when he observes:

> spontaneous orders . . . have information processing capacities that are unreachable to any individual . . . The only institution that has this capacity is the institution itself, and it cannot be used in a self reflective way.
>
> (Eriksson, 1993, 20)

That is, the totality of knowledge that exists in the socio-economic system, exists in the institutions that comprise the system, includes that which is tacitly locked into agents' minds. In this case, the totality of knowledge can never be accessed by any system (such as a human agent or agents) which is smaller than itself.

Knowledge of the type discussed in the second and third points above is what Nyiri refers to as 'practical knowledge that could in no sense be dissolved into knowledge of a propositional sort . . . a bedrock upon which all knowledge rests' (Nyiri, 1988, 23).

Hayek, it appears, is claiming that it is knowledge 'that', in all its diverse forms that agents are ignorant of. However, it is quite clear that ignorance of this kind does not prevent agents from acting, since they know 'how' to follow rules.

To suggest, then, that agents following rules know 'how' but not 'that' implies that rules obviate the need to know 'that'. If one 'knows how', one does not need to 'know that'. Adopting rules, according to Hayek, 'saves us the trouble of considering certain questions every time they arise' (Hayek, 1967a, 40). Rules 'serve to abbreviate the list of circumstances which we need to take into account in the particular circumstances' (Hayek, 1964, 11).

The proposition that rules obviate the need to access a range of knowledge ('that') can be sustained if it can be shown that rule-following agents are capable of acting in the world, yet possess no more knowledge ('that') after the rule-inspired action than they did before it. We know no more about the laws of mechanics after drawing upon a set of tacit rules and successfully riding a bicycle than we did before this act. Similarly, we know no more about the 'laws' of society after drawing upon a set of social rules and successfully initiating a social act, than we did before. We merely know how to follow a rule – although we may know how to do this a little better.

Consider the cases of radical and non-radical ignorance, the possibilities of obtaining knowledge, and the ability to initiate an action in each case. Being in a state of ignorance might potentially lead to a situation of impotence *vis-à-vis* initiating an action. This situation might be dealt with in two ways:

1 If ignorance is of a non-radical kind, agents might access a formal institution such as a library, change their state from one of ignorance to one of knowledge and change the situation of impotence to one of potence.

2 If ignorance is of a radical kind, learning is quite impossible via access to a formal institution. We can, however, draw upon social rules and in so doing overcome the condition of impotence. The point is that whilst the situation changes to one of potence, the state of ignorance endures.

It is undeniable that after a rule is successfully drawn upon, the agent has been enabled via that rule to carry out an action. In this case, a change has occurred. But the change lies in the capacity to act, not in the stock of knowledge held. The change that occurs in knowledge when agents access social rules is therefore different to that when formal institutions are accessed. Accessing formal institutions increases the agent's stock of knowledge 'that' in a quantitative, additive manner. Rule-following might not increase the agent's stock of knowledge 'that' at all. The nature of the change is qualitative in the sense that the agent is now a more skilful manipulator of knowledge 'how'. This is what Hayek is really getting at when he writes:

> If the law thus serves to enable the individual to act effectively on his own knowledge and *for this purpose* adds to his knowledge, it also embodies knowledge, or the results of past experience, that are utilised so long as men act under these rules. In fact, the collaboration of individuals under common rules rests on a *sort of* division of knowledge.
> (Hayek, 1960, 157, emphasis added)

Hayek obviously does not mean that following a law or rule somehow permits one agent to know the range of facts another agent possesses – of these facts they remain ignorant. What he does mean is that following a rule serves the purpose of allowing agents to know 'what they can expect from others' (Hayek, 1960, 160). Ryle puts matters succinctly: 'knowing a rule . . . *is not like possessing a bit of extra information* but being able to perform an intelligent operation' (Ryle, 1945, 7; emphasis added). Knowing a rule obviates the need to access 'a bit of extra information'. Whilst of course agents who perform a rule-guided action do possess more knowledge in the sense that they are more skilful manipulators of the rule, that is they know 'how' in more depth, the point is that they have not added even one small 'bit' of knowledge 'that' – in any of its forms.

Hayek argues that by drawing upon these rules, agents avail themselves of the collected wisdom of an evolving society, and are thereby enabled to initiate socio-economic activity, although they can never know or articulate this collective wisdom. They are simultaneously knowledgeable and ignorant, although the paradox is now solved by recognising that they possess knowledge 'how', whilst simultaneously being radically ignorant of knowledge 'that'. Thus can Hayek write:

> That such abstract rules are regularly observed in action does not mean that they are known to the individual in the sense that it could communicate them . . . Even when they [people] have acquired the

> power of conscious abstraction, their conscious thinking and acting are probably still guided by a great many such abstract rules which they obey without being able to formulate them.
>
> (Hayek, 1960, 149)

Elsewhere he writes of the 'submission to undesigned rules and conventions whose significance and importance we largely do not understand', adding: 'The appropriateness of our conduct is not necessarily dependent upon our knowing why it is so' (ibid., 63–4).

Circumstances when rules are both necessary and operational

Elaborating upon the difference between types of knowledge and the nature of ignorance allows the formation of a far more in-depth understanding of the nature of rules. Moreover, it illuminates on the one hand the circumstances where rules are *necessary*, and on the other, the circumstances when they may *become operational*. Rules are only (a) *necessary* under circumstances of (virtual) radical ignorance, that is when agents cannot know 'that', and (b) *possible to operationalise* when agents know 'how' to select and follow them.

In other words, recognition of radical ignorance illuminates the need for social rules, whilst recognition of different kinds of knowledge illuminates the way in which they are used. Hayek explains the link between the prevalence of radical ignorance and the rules which facilitate action:

> The need to rely on abstract rules in maintaining a spontaneous order is a consequence of that ignorance and uncertainty . . . and the enforcement of rules . . . will achieve its purpose . . . only if we do not treat them merely as a substitute for knowledge which in the particular case we do not possess.
>
> (Hayek, 1976, 8 and 127)

The real impact of Hayek's claim was only fully brought home to me after reading Ryle and, I presume, this is the source of Hayek's ideas. Ryle is keen to stress that knowing 'how' cannot be reduced to knowing 'that' nor ought it to be conceived of as in any way an inferior form of knowledge. He attacks the adherents of the 'intellectual legend' who postulate

> an internal shadow performance to be the real carrier of the intelligence ordinarily ascribed to the overt act, and think that in this way they explain what makes the overt act a manifestation of intelligence.
>
> (Hayek, 1949, 50)

The internal shadow performance refers to an algorithm or set of regulative propositions which (according to the intellectualist legend) the agent mentally runs through before initiating an action. This is of course precisely what

Homo economicus is presumed to do. Ryle rejects this, claiming rather that doing and thinking about doing form a unity. As he puts matters:

> The wit, when challenged to cite maxims or canons by which he constructs or appreciates jokes, is unable to answer. He knows how to make good jokes and how to detect bad ones, but he cannot tell us or himself any recipes for them. [Agents] do not plan their arguments before making them. Indeed, if they had to plan what to think before thinking it they could never think at all, for this planning would itself be unplanned. Efficient practice precedes the theory of it.
>
> (Ryle, 1949, 30)

Doing and thinking are brought together in the practice of rule-following, a skilled accomplishment that has to be learned via practice. This conception allows Hayek to adopt a sophisticated notion of agency. As noted in Chapter 5, Hayek too rejects the instrumental rationality of *Homo economicus* but cannot capitalise upon this rejection because he has nothing to replace it with. Hayek III's understanding of rules, by contrast, allows him to adopt a theory of agency which may be described as *procedural rationality*. Hargreaves-Heap defines procedural rationality as rooted in a

> tradition in the social sciences that locates the individual in a web of rules and norms which define the expected behaviours associated with a person in that position. It is a vision that portrays the individual as a rule follower, a person who follows norms, recipes or procedures for action . . . It makes the individual irreducibly social in a way not found in the purely instrumental account . . .
>
> (Hargreaves-Heap, 1989, 4)

That agents do not possess an algorithm or a set of regulative propositions which the agent runs through in her head before initiating an action means that *Homo economicus* is thereby rejected as a travesty. Hayek's understanding of cognitive psychology not only confirms the claim that the presuppositions of instrumental rationality held by neoclassical theory is unfounded, but it confirms the alternative conception proffered, namely procedural rationality.

8

RULES AND THE COGNITIVE PSYCHOLOGY UNDERPINNING RULE-FOLLOWING

> Man is as much a rule-following animal as a purpose seeking one. And he is successful ... because his thinking and acting are governed by rules. The problem of conducting himself successfully in a world only partially known to man was thus solved by adhering to rules ...
>
> (Hayek, 1973, 11, 18)

The previous chapter, by focusing upon (kinds of) ignorance and knowledge, established that social rules: are the embodiment of knowledge as society's collected wisdom; facilitate discovery, communication and storage of relevant knowledge when it is possessed; and enable agents to cope with ignorance when it is not possessed. This chapter moves on to consider rules in more depth by proceeding in two directions. First, it places social rules in a more concrete social context to establish what kinds of social rules there are, and the social function they perform. Second, it elaborates upon the cognitive rules that constitute the neural processes whereby agents are enabled to internalise these social rules, thereby explaining how the process of knowing 'how' to follow rules actually works. These themes recognise Hayek's claim that 'thinking and acting are governed by rules' (ibid.) and require a discussion of Hayek's work on cognitive psychology.[1]

SOME PRELIMINARY COMMENTS ON RULES

Prior to 1960, Hayek hardly makes reference to the term 'rule'. In fact he manages to discuss cognitive psychology in *The Sensory Order* (1952) without recourse to this term at all. In *The Constitution of Liberty* (1960), he begins to use it, but without any suffix. In 1962 he adds a suffix and uses the phrase 'rules of *action*'. By 1967 he replaces this phrase with 'rules of *conduct*', and continues to use it in all his later works. I suggest that there is more to this than just semantics.

Judging by the sub-title of his 1967 paper: 'The Interplay between Rules of Individual Conduct and the Socio-economic Order of Actions', Hayek now clearly differentiates between the rules of conduct that individual agents follow and the overall pattern or order of socio-economic action that might subsequently ensue. Rules of conduct and the actions they facilitate are, therefore, different kinds of things. This has important implications.

Hayek, as a quasi-transcendental realist, accepts a layered ontology whereby events/actions are governed by deep structures and, moreover, the events/actions of experience are typically out of phase with these structures. By differentiating between events/actions (domain of the empirical and actual) and rules of conduct (domain of the deep), Hayek is able to recognise the conditions for orderly or regular behaviour without having to accept that the ensuing actions will be completely or perfectly regular. He can therefore accommodate the fact that regular behaviour on the part of individuals does not automatically lead to an overall socio-economic order in the combined actions of this group of individuals. The switch to the term 'rules of conduct', strongly suggests a cognition of *rules as deep structures* and *actions as the events that are facilitated by these structures.*

Hayek defines rules as follows:

> the term rule is used for a statement by which a regularity of the conduct of individuals can be described, irrespective of whether such a rule is known to the individuals in any other sense than that they normally act in accordance with it.
>
> (Hayek, 1967b, 67)

Boehm (1989), however, points to an ambiguity in Hayek's usage of the term 'rule', noting that:

> Occasionally he [Hayek] conceives of a rule simply as a statement describing regularity of conduct; but usually he means a prescription of a proper course of action.

Arguably, however, the type of rules Hayek has in mind are based upon regularities, whilst simultaneously being prescriptions for action. The regularities Hayek has in mind are not, however, what one might call complete or perfect regularities which would render action a mere epiphenomenon of rules of conduct.[2] For example, a perfect regularity would exist in the case in which every time the price of the factor labour was increased, it would be substituted by another factor. Hayek of course knows full well that this kind of perfectly regular behaviour does not occur in the social world. In fact both his 1955 and 1961 papers discuss this matter at length. However, if it were not for the fact that social activity exhibited *some degree of regular behaviour*, the mind would not be able to recognise it as a form of behaviour. As Hayek himself puts it:

> Questions will arise at first only after our senses have discerned some recurring pattern or order in the events . . .
>
> (Hayek, 1961, 23; see also 1962, 45; 1952, ch. 5 and 176)

In other words, agents can understand the actions of others, and learn to undertake that (or a similar) action themselves, because they can detect the presence of relatively regular behaviour. And this behaviour is relatively regular because, Hayek claims, it is rule-guided. Once so understood, there is, *contra* Boehm, no contradiction on Hayek's part in treating a rule both as a statement of relative regularity *and* a prescription of action.

Hayek (1970b) argues that society knows of three types of rules:

1 Constructivist rules, which are rules which are deliberately created and maintained by humans.
2 Spontaneous, tacitly known and followed, *informal* rules. These are rules which have evolved in human society unconsciously, for instance rules of fair play or of justice. The point to note is that these rules enter into what might be called popular culture, but are not written down or explicitly known.
3 Spontaneous non-tacitly known and followed *formal* rules. These are derived from (2) but have been formally written down, for example, honouring contracts.

The second type of rule, the spontaneous, informal type, is the major preoccupation in Hayek's work, and is the only type I shall consider here. Hayek then goes on to locate different kinds of spontaneous informal rules under three class headings: rules of conduct, rules of perception and meta-conscious rules of the mind. These are all dealt with via his work on cognitive psychology. Whilst these will now be elaborated upon in turn, it is important to understand that they form a unified whole; exposition requires them to be treated separately.

SOCIAL RULES OF CONDUCT

The following discussion, couched as it is in terms of cognitive psychology, should not mislead us into thinking that social rules *originate* in the mind. Social rules of conduct are just that – *social*. Whilst they are, typically, internalised by agents via the (cognitive) learning process, they are not merely in and of the mind. They have an existence independent of any particular agent's identification of them. They are, as Hollis (1987, 145) puts it, 'external to each actor, yet internal to all' who can follow them. As structures, social rules of conduct are not akin to the 'structures' elaborated by Hayek II, where 'structures' (Hayek II does not of course refer to rules), being no more than conceptions, are precisely in the mind, devoid of real (as opposed to ideal) existence.

Moreover, social rules of conduct do not simply restrain action: they typically enable. Even where a rule forbids a certain course of action, the restraint usually increases the success rate of any action that is subsequently taken. The rules of the highway code, for example, enable motorists to drive in a co-ordinated manner without actually predetermining which route is taken. When a particular rule forbids, say, proceeding through a red traffic light, it is merely to enable more drivers to initiate co-ordinated and thereby successful action. Rules of the highway are necessary because every driver is ignorant about the spatio-temporal location of other drivers, and of the expectations, plans and actions of other drivers.

According to Hayek, rules of conduct assist the individual agent in deciding upon a course of action when the action of others must be taken into account. Social rules are an essential constitutive element of society. In any form of society comprising large numbers of people it becomes impossible for one agent to know the precise details of what all other agents intend to do. Yet this does not render humans impotent since they are able draw upon a stock of rules, a 'repertoire of perceptual patterns', as Hayek terms it (1962, 51), which render a substantial part of the behaviour of others relatively predictable.

Hayek extends the work of other philosophers on the question of following rules tacitly from physiological or physical actions to the social domain. He sees no reason 'why for example, the sense of justice should not also consist in such a capacity to follow rules which we do not know in the sense that we can state them' (Hayek, 1962, 45). By 1979, Hayek is far more specific:

> We do not understand how it [our moral system] maintains the order of actions on which the co-ordination of the activities of many millions depend. And since we owe the order of our society to a tradition of rules which we only imperfectly understand, all progress must be based on tradition.
>
> (Hayek, 1979, 167)

Tacitly understood and unconsciously followed rules are often presented in the form of custom or habit. They should not be thought of as referring to particular actions, but as abstract or general guidelines:

> They will often merely determine or limit the range of possibilities within which the choice is made consciously. By eliminating certain kinds of action altogether and providing certain routine ways of achieving the object, they merely restrict the alternatives on which a conscious choice is required.
>
> The moral rules, for example, which have become part of a man's nature will mean that certain conceivable choices will not appear at all among the possibilities between which he chooses . . . [The] rules which guide an individual's action are better seen as determining what he will not do rather than what he will do.
>
> (Hayek, 1962, 56)

Thus, faced with a situation where an agent may stand to gain from dishonesty, rules of 'fair play' may intervene. An agent will know, perhaps without being able to articulate the reasons, that rules of fair play 'ought' to be adhered to.

Rules, when adhered to, serve two purposes. First, anyone who deviates from social rules of conduct is likely to be rejected by the rest of society, or have negative sanctions applied. Second, failure to observe such rules may 'release the most terrifying events' as one enters a world where one cannot orientate oneself towards a range of external objects, events and peoples actions:

> The rules which one knows can be relied upon only so long as one plays the game oneself according to the rules, i.e. keeps within the kind of actions the consequences of which are tolerably predictable. . . . The world is fairly predictable only so long as one adheres to the established procedures, but it becomes frightening when one deviates from them.
>
> (Hayek, 1967b, 80–1)

The second reason for agents adhering to rules carries the weight of the argument. Agents follow rules because they minimise uncertainty and thereby increase their own chances of engaging in successful action. Rules of conduct are a guide to action. According to Butler (1983, 23), rules of action 'give us an instant and unconscious summary of how to act'.

RULES OF PERCEPTION

Hayek makes it quite clear that in addition to those instances where action is guided by rules, that is where the nervous system acts as a 'pattern effector', there are instances where agents are able to recognise or perceive action in others as being guided by rules, that is where the nervous system acts as a 'pattern detector' (Hayek, 1962, 45). According to Hayek, these rules also, typically, exist without the agent being aware of them. 'Rules which we cannot state do not govern only our actions. They also govern our perceptions . . . of other peoples actions' (ibid.).

Hayek adds the notion of rules of perception for the following reason. When discussing purely physiological action (i.e. motor responses), as he does in *The Sensory Order*, he need go no further than to elaborate upon a situation where there is a physical stimulus and a physiological response. When, however, he moves from physiological to social actions (as he does after 1960), there is another dimension to be included. Between stimulus and response there is another phase of cognition, namely perception. Agents have to '*versteh*' (ibid., 58) the meaning of the stimuli they receive before initiating a suitable response. Agents are therefore not only skilled actors, they are skilled perceivers. Not only is learning how to act a skill, learning how to perceive the action of others as action of a certain kind or class is also a skill.

However, since no two situations are identical, whilst agents are able to recognise the action of others as action of a certain class, there is a need to be far more accurate. It is, for example, one thing to recognise that a particular physiological movement is part of the class of actions known as 'waving', quite another to recognise that this in turn is part of the class of actions known as 'greeting someone', and quite another to be able to discern that this as a 'warm' or perhaps a 'cold' greeting.

One may respond to signs such as gestures and facial expressions by seeing them as kinds of thing: sad, happy, aggressive. When someone cries, we may understand that this kind of behaviour is a sign of sadness even though we do not know why. Hayek refers to these phenomena, using Sapir's phrase that such classes of structures of events are 'known by none, and understood by all' (ibid., 45). In other words, meaning has to be imputed to the class of observed actions before a response can be initiated; or before one follows a rule, one must know which is the appropriate one.

Perceiving action in others as rule-guided is quite a complex undertaking, involving the capacity to identify patterns, imitate them, internalise them and transfer action or perception across domains of space and time. Before imitation and therefore action is possible, agents have to identify certain actions, some of which may never before have been observed. However, it is unlikely that phenomena are completely novel; rather, they are likely to resemble something that has been previously experienced:

> The recognition of a correspondence between the patterns made up of different sensory elements . . . presupposes a mechanism of sensory pattern transfer, that is, a mechanism for the transfer of the capacity to discern an abstract order or arrangement from one field to another.
>
> (Hayek, 1962, 49)

By transfer between fields, Hayek means that skills learned with one hand are transferred to the other; monkeys transfer the ability to respond to light signals to sound signals. Patterns learned in one format can be transferred to another so that a pattern is recognised but is of a different format. The fields in this case are areas where an abstract pattern is called upon to make sense of a particular pattern. However, Hayek wants to go further and argue that it is the brain's capacity to classify sensory elements which allows patterns to be recognised as 'one of the same kind' even when it has never been experienced before:

> Whenever the capacity of recognising an abstract rule which the arrangement of these attributes follows has been acquired in one field, the same master mould will apply when the signs for those abstract attributes are evoked by altogether different elements. It is the classification of the structure of relationships between these abstract attributes which constitutes the recognition of patterns as the same or different.
>
> (Hayek, 1962, 50)

The ability to transfer sensory patterns is extremely important, given that humans inhabit an open world where novelty is the normal state of affairs. Under such conditions, it would be impossible to have a specific social rule to cover every eventuality: instead, social rules are abstract and general. The ability to transfer sensory patterns greatly enhances the capacity for the perception of rule-guided action in others, and thereby for rule-guided action oneself. Some completely new pattern of events can be classified then, not because it is governed by a particular rule that already exists, but because the pattern is similar to some previously observed patterns for which an abstract, general rule of action (or more accurately, combination of general rules) already exists.

Agents are able to perceive and classify action that they may never have seen before as conforming to a general rule, and thereby initiate an appropriate action in response because they have an internalised stock of similar general rules. Without the capacity to transfer patterns across fields, agents would be incapable of perceiving any kind of novel behaviour.

THE ARTICULATION BETWEEN RULES OF PERCEPTION AND RULES OF CONDUCT

Hayek appears to have in mind a kind of continual feedback process, whereby rules which guide perception are continually modified by the rules which guide action, and vice versa. The ability to act is therefore a result of an articulation between rules of perception and action; the seat of causality appears to be the entire web or network.

The rules which guide perception are referred to as guiding the sensory (cognitive) elements, whilst the rules which guide action are referred to as guiding the motor elements. Both are of course necessary for social (or for that matter physical) action. However, the pedagogic differentiation of these two kinds of rules should not obscure the fact that these two dimensions are so interrelated that 'we should conceive of the whole rather as one continuous stream' (Hayek, 1962, 58):

> The first step in the successive classification of the stimuli must thus be seen as at the same time the first step in a successive imposition of rules of action, and in the final specification of a particular action as the last step of many chains of successive classifications of stimuli according to the rules to which their arrangement belongs.
>
> (Ibid.)

Meta-conscious rules

Hayek attempts to explain what Weimer (in language reminiscent of critical realism) calls the 'mechanism underlying "higher" cognitive phenomena such as perception and conception', or 'deep conceptual structures (patterns of neural activity)' (Weimer and Palermo, 1982, 265–7). Hayek himself refers variously to 'supra-conscious rules', 'mental processes', 'supra-conscious order', 'supra-conscious matrix' (Hayek, 1962, 60–2), or 'multiple classification by the super-structure' (1968, 45). He writes that:

> [C]onscious . . . thought must . . . be assumed to be directed by rules which in turn cannot be conscious – by a supra-conscious mechanism which operates upon the contents of consciousness . . . [I]n order to be conscious, [mental processes] must be guided by a supra-conscious order . . . [A]ll we can talk . . . and consciously think about presupposes the existence of a framework which determines its meaning, i.e. a *system of rules which operate us* . . .
>
> (Hayek, 1962, 61–2, emphasis added)

> [I]n all our thinking, we are guided (or even *operated*) by rules of which we are not aware . . .
>
> (Hayek, 1964a, 87)

At this point, however, a problem emerges. Are these meta-conscious rules of the mind something different in kind, or merely degree, from the social rules of conduct and the cognitive rules of perception? Two interpretations are possible:

1 Meta-conscious rules of the mind are an extension of rules of conduct and perception, they are not different in kind, only different in degree. Gray (1984, 23) appears to opt for this interpretation.
2 Meta-conscious rules of the mind refer to the neural/physiological structure of the nervous system, and are to this extent different in kind from rules of action and perception. Kukhatas (1989, 53) appears to opt for this interpretation.

In 1977, Hayek debates this issue with Koestler who believes that:

> there is a continuous scale of degrees of awareness, from focally conscious processes through fringe-conscious ones like tying one's shoelaces absentmindedly, and so on down to quite unconscious actions and physiological processes. It is a continuum. [R]ules [are] highly conscious to start with, but now they function unconsciously . . . The rules occupied first the top floor of my mind, and now they have been relegated to the boiler room in the basement.
>
> (Koestler and Smithies, 1969)

Hayek's response is that he does not deny that there are 'learnt rules' (by which presumably he means *consciously* learned rules), such as the rules of chess but that one could not explain learning if there were no additional rules which had not been learned. Koestler 'agrees', adding: 'that which does the knowing cannot be known, that which does the seeing cannot be seen', to which Hayek then 'agrees'. We are left with the impression that they both understand meta-conscious rules as different from rules of conduct and perception in that there appears to be a cut-off point in the hierarchy.

Whilst it must be said that it is difficult to understand exactly what Hayek really does mean on this matter, the interpretation I opt for is as follows. The mind is a hierarchy of classificatory devices. Some stimuli start off consciously classified as a particular rule, then 'descend' to ever-lower levels of consciousness. Other stimuli bypass the stage of consciousness and proceed directly to the lower levels of unconsciousness. It appears, though, that at some point a threshold is crossed where rules of conduct and perception become meta-conscious rules of mind. Once this threshold is crossed, meta-conscious rules become unknowable. A difference in kind has emerged from a difference of degree. Whilst Hayek never put matters in this way, it might not be unreasonable to borrow transcendental-realist terminology and claim that meta-conscious rules are emergent from, but irreducible to rules of action and perception.[3]

The reason for my choice of interpretation lies in the nature of the cognitive process that Hayek elaborates in *The Sensory Order*. If one opts to treat the meta-conscious rules of the mind not as rules at all but as mechanisms, as the neural hardware that govern the internalisation of rules of conduct, then the question of the origin of these mechanisms arises. Hayek never suggests that agents are born with innate classifications; rather he suggests that agents learn how to classify. And they do this by learning to recognise patterns of relatively regular activity via sense experience. They learn the rules that govern phenomena (social or physical) either consciously as one, for example, learns to play a guitar, or unconsciously as one, for example, learns to speak a language. Either way, for Hayek, the rules that govern phenomena eventually become 'hard-wired' into the neural network of the mind. Some rules that govern phenomena are internalised and known consciously, whilst other such rules descend so low into the sub-conscious that they are no longer known consciously. At this point, they cross the threshold and become meta-conscious. They then, in conjunction with other meta-conscious rules, guide the responses of the agent to other external events. The learning of social rules via the process of their becoming 'hard-wired' into the neural network is considered in the next sub-section.[4]

The cognitive process

An event occurring in the external world stimulates the nervous system and triggers an incoming impulse in the neural fibres. On its own this event and stimulus might not be registered in the mind, it might simply be ignored – although this process occurs unconsciously. However, should the event and the subsequent stimulus be repeated with some minimal regularity, something begins to register in the mind.

A neuron begins to acquire a clearly defined place in the web of other neurons, connected by nerve fibres. This neuron location attains a specific functional significance since it is now connected to, yet differentiated from, other neurons and their own particular impulses. Hayek refers to this formation of neural connections via impulses as 'linkages'. Any impulse entering the neural web will follow the linkage, or as he puts it, establish a 'following'.

Each time the same event and subsequent stimulus is experienced, the same following is excited. This means that the impulse travels via the same route, forming the same linkage and establishing the same following. The result is that, these events are classified as the same. As Hayek puts it:

> the mental significance of any impulse (and group of impulses) proceeding anywhere in the central nervous system is determined by the following it evokes through linkages created by former occurrences of these impulses.
>
> (Hayek, 1982a, 290)

The formation of linkages does not yet involve the formation of a mental event that we may be conscious of. 'It is a sort of learning to discriminate which may occur before any discriminations are yet possible' (Hayek, 1952, 104). In effect, the mind is building up a record of past stimuli or, more accurately, of associations or connections between stimuli with which to compare new incoming stimuli. It learns to classify a particular stimulus as action of a certain kind.

As current stimuli are registered and classified in the nervous system, the impulses 'descend' to lower levels of consciousness. The function of these impulses:

> will be less and less to evoke specific responses but increasingly to modify and control behaviour in the light of the whole situation, presented not only by simultaneously arriving other impulses but also by the retained picture of the environment.
>
> (Hayek, 1952, 112)

New impulses will not be acted upon immediately in a stimulus-response manner; this would produce erratic behaviour. Instead, they will be surveyed by the mind to see how they fit into the total picture the agent is gradually building up. Selection, then, of the appropriate response involves not merely responding to one impulse with one action, but drawing upon a record of past associations. Examples could of course be extended to social intercourse.

This record of associations appears to be what Hayek has in mind when he writes of meta-conscious rules of the mind. These rules, then, do not start out as innate mechanisms or hardware, they are the internalisation of external events such as social activity which become 'hard-wired' into the neural network.

Hayek uses analogies of the 'map' articulating with the 'model' to illuminate the articulation that occurs between the record of past associations and fresh stimuli. This enables him to show how the nervous system facilitates humans in navigating their way around the physical and social world.

The map

Hayek employs the analogy of the map to illustrate the relationship between the structure of external events and the structure of neural events (linkages and followings) which they produce. This map will be very imperfect and subject to continual, although not rapid, updating. It will give not a constant, but a slowly varying, picture of the structures which it produces:

> The different maps which will be formed in the different brains will be determined by factors which are sufficiently similar to make those maps similar to each other . . . The mere fact that for each individual the map will be subject to constant changes practically excludes the possibility that . . . the maps of two individuals should be completely identical.
>
> (Hayek, 1952, 110)

The map analogy refers to the neural mechanisms responsible for the classification of older or past impulses, capable of being called into operation by a new impulse, but existing independently of current or fresh impulses. It classifies events into kinds of things which have been significant, but by itself provides no handle on the present environment. It is a relatively static system. It provides the 'categories in terms of which the impulses proceeding at any time are evaluated' (ibid., 115):

> Sense experience therefore presupposes the existence of a sort of accumulated 'knowledge', of an acquired order of the sensory impulses based on their past co-currence; and this knowledge . . . is based on pre-sensory experience.
>
> (Ibid., 166)

The model

As the organism moves around the environment, the map based upon past pre-sensory linkages is inadequate for navigation. Something more is therefore required. Hayek explains this something via the introduction of a new analogy, that of a model. Like the analogy of the map, the analogy of the model refers to the neural mechanisms responsible for the classification of impulses. But, unlike the map, the model deals with fresh impulses. The model is dynamic and augments the map which is (relatively) static.

New experiences are translated into impulses and processed in the nervous system of linkages. Current experiences simply would not be able to be processed at all unless the categories formed by pre-sensory linkages were in place. Pre-sensory experiences determine the forms which sensory experiences may take.

The established linkages of the map often fail to give an adequate account of the current environment in which the organism finds itself, or even of the immediate future (i.e. a wrong prediction). The organism is in a state of conflicting experiences, those of the model conflicting with those of the map. The result is a gradual reclassification of the linkages.

The map and model analogies, then, refer to the hierarchical neural systems that process the streams of stimuli continually entering the nervous system. Some of these (fresh) stimuli are themselves classified, whilst other (older) stimuli, assist in that classification. The combined result is the formation of a mental quality or image – for example, a physical entity, or a social entity such as a social rule. The entire process of classification, then, ultimately facilitates the taking of a physiological or social action (Hayek, 1952, 119).

Agents, typically, have a vast repertoire of rules existing as linkages which they are able to combine to meet unforeseen situations. This temporal aspect is one of the most important tasks of the cognitive process.

EXPECTATIONS

The model of the environment is so dynamic that fresh impulses are not only evaluated against the presentations of the past and current environment, but also presentations of the expected changes in that environment:

> We must therefore conceive of the model as constantly trying out possible developments and determining action in the light of the consequences which from the presentations of such actions would appear to follow from it. . . [C]lassifications . . . by the joint results to be expected . . . [involve] the presentation of the range of expected results by a pattern of impulses essentially in the same manner in which the actual environment is presented by such a pattern . . .
>
> . . . we live as much in a world of expectations as in a world of facts, and most responses to a given stimulus are probably determined only via fairly complex processes of 'trying out' on the model the effects to be expected from the alternative courses of action. The action to stimulus frequently implies an anticipation of the consequences to be expected from it.
>
> (Hayek, 1952, 121; see also 1968a, 48–9)

The use of a model that captures temporality for the organism is two-fold. First, it allows the possibility of thinking through certain courses of action instead of simply taking an action and awaiting the results. If the organism can develop not only the ability to respond to harmful influences but to retain a memory of similar past encounters, its chances of survival are increased. The organism is thus able to learn to act in a certain way whenever certain signals are received. Hayek noted this survival technique elsewhere (1967b, 73).

Second, it allows uncertainty to be minimised. The future becomes relatively more certain in the sense that the mapping and modelling processes permit the agent to construct likely scenarios from known, similar experiences. This does not of course imply that the future will be identical to the past, but that agents use the past as a guide to the future. Something like rule-orientated thinking lies, arguably, behind the following Hayekian comment from Lachmann:

> The future is unknowable, though not unimaginable. Future knowledge cannot be had now, but it can cast its shadow ahead. In each mind, however, the shadow assumes a different shape, hence the divergence of expectations. The formation of expectations is an act of our minds by means of which we try to catch a glimpse of the unknown.
>
> (Lachmann, 1976, 58)

Hayek's work on sensory psychology in general, and on expectations based upon rules in particular, is precisely an attempt to explain what Lachmann refers to as 'an act of our minds'. Ten years later, Lachmann discusses how 'particles of information are continually interpreted in light of existing knowledge possessed by the agent' (Lachmann, 1986, 45–53). Arguably, it is Hayek's work on cognitive psychology that allows Lachmann to deploy this type of argument. Hayek has supplied the theory of operation of the nervous system that Lachmann (necessarily) presupposes (see also Galeotti, 1987, 171).

This chapter has thus far established what kinds of social rules there are and the social function they perform. It has, furthermore, elaborated upon the cognitive rules that constitute the neural processes by which agents internalise social rules, and thereby explained how the process of knowing 'how' to follow rules actually works. There are, however, two more points that need to be cleared up before the final chapters can begin to pull the various strands together. These points are: the degree of abstractness or generality of the rules to which Hayek makes reference; and the role played by the mind in Hayek III's philosophy. These will now be addressed in turn.

SOCIAL RULES VARY IN THE DEGREE OF ABSTRACTNESS OR GENERALITY

Unfortunately, Hayek tends to discuss rules of differing degrees of abstractness or generality[5] in different parts of his work. This makes it difficult to understand the real articulation between rules of different degrees of abstractness, and to grasp the continuity between the different parts of his work. This section will attempt to address these difficulties. In particular it will show that Hayek's work on cognitive psychology ought not to be treated as a digression from his more overtly socio-economic work.

I shall proceed in two stages. First, I shall outline what appear to be three *analytical levels of abstraction* used by Hayek to discuss rules. Second, whilst all the levels form a unity, by concentrating upon those rules that are located at the 'micro' level of analytical abstraction the articulation between all rules will be highlighted.

The three levels of analytical abstraction could be termed: (1) the *macro* socio-economic level; (2) the *micro* socio-economic level;[6] and (3) the *cognitive* level.

1 When operating at the *macro* socio-economic level and discussing spontaneous order *per se*, he tends to draw upon examples such as the rules of private property, justice, honesty, custom, contract and law. This gives the impression that socio-economic order occurs due to a small number of abstract or general rules.
2 When operating at the *micro* socio-economic level and discussing smaller scale interactions, he tends to draw upon examples such as the rules facilitating a doctor treating sick children in an order that will increase efficiency (Hayek, 1979, 4); preventing run-off water damaging a neighbour's property (ibid., 26); speaking a language or playing a game (1962, 43–5).
3 When operating at the *cognitive* level he discusses the rules facilitating sensory psychological activities like recognising a face or learning to perform a task with one hand, then transferring the skill to the other (ibid., 48–9).

Possibly because of the compartmentalised nature of contemporary social science, there is a tendency to approach these three levels of abstraction, and therefore the issues that reside within them, separately. It is, therefore, not difficult to (mis)treat Hayek's work on cognitive psychology as unconnected to his work on socio-economic order; and as a consequence to (mis)treat cognitive issues as unconnected with socio-economic issues. The gap between the cognitive level and the macro level appears so large that the articulation between them becomes extremely difficult to perceive. Once, however, the middle-level, that is the micro level, is introduced, the gap can be bridged, making the articulation easier to perceive. I shall concentrate, therefore, on the micro level and the rules that are located within its ambit.

This thesis has established Hayek's claim that human beings are rule-following animals: they can initiate social action, that is, they can 'go on', only because a range of social rules of conduct are available to be drawn upon. This implies that every second of every minute of every day, and so on, agents are drawing upon the entire hierarchy of social and cognitive rules. If socio-economic order is to occur, even though it is often discussed at the macro socio-economic level, then the whole range of rule-following is necessary for each and every social action.

Heath (1992) has also noticed something akin to this hierarchy of rules, identifying six classes where rules express regularity of behaviour. The first four are discussed at what I have styled the micro socio-economic level, and the last two are discussed at the macro level. Heath goes on to claim that for the purposes of explaining Hayek's social theory, a focus upon rules in the last two levels 'would seem best'. Heath is implying that Hayek's theory is best explained by focusing on rules that occur at the macro socio- economic level. I disagree. Recognition of the entire hierarchy of rules is necessary if we are to understand Hayek's socio-economic theory as an overall project – i.e. one that unites the three levels of analytical abstraction. If this is not understood, then a problem goes unnoticed.

The problem is as follows. Spontaneous socio-economic order requires the relative co-ordination of agents' actions and therefore the relative co-ordination of their plans which, in a market economy require that knowledge is discovered, communicated and stored by a combination of formal institutions, social rules of conduct and the telecom system. When Hayek addresses the issue of socio-economic order, he is actually inquiring into the conditions that make relatively co-ordinated human action possible in a market economy. This in turn leads to an inquiry into the rules they follow in order to be able to use the telecom system or access any other formal institution. As he puts matters:

> The question which is of central importance as much for social theory as for social policy is thus what properties the rules must possess so that the separate actions of the individuals will produce an overall order.
>
> (Hayek, 1973, 45)

Whilst it is not incorrect, it is not very enlightening merely to be told that socio-economic order comes about because agents follow rules of honesty, contract, private property, and so on – i.e. issues located at the macro socio-economic level of abstraction. And this is often all that Hayek does tell us (see 1960, chs 2, 4, 10; 1962; 1976, 123–31; 1979, 153–71; 1988, ch. 1).

The problem is that if Hayek is saying no more than this, then why does he spend so much time discussing issues that are located at the micro and cognitive level of abstraction? Why does he spend so much time discussing the sociology, cognitive psychology and social psychology of rule-following and rule-learning? Why does he go to such lengths to establish that rule-following requires a high level of tacit knowledge? If all that is required for a theoretical understanding of socio-economic order is the recognition that agents follow a small number of well-defined rules, then surely social science becomes far too easy? Social science merely becomes the inquiry into a dozen or so well-defined social rules.

I suggest that, standing back and taking Hayek's work as a whole, he is trying to forge a link between sensory psychology, social psychology, and subjects such as law, sociology and economics.[7] He is trying to establish that acting in the market process is a skilled accomplishment and only occurs by agents drawing continually upon the entire hierarchy of rules. If this is correct, issues located at the micro socio-economic level of abstraction become just as necessary for the investigation of spontaneous socio- economic order as issues located at the macro level.

Unfortunately, however, Hayek does not develop his own insights. Although he has all the ingredients to explain how human beings with particular cognitive apparatus can perform a range of the skilled social actions that are necessary for an overall spontaneous order to emerge, he never quite manages to assemble them.

One person who does attempt to make something of Hayek's ingredients is Ebling (1986). Operating in a Hayekian manner (and concentrating upon issues located at the micro level of abstraction) he explains how agents manage to take sensible action under the really existing conditions characterised by non-perfect price signals. In effect, Ebling fine-tunes Hayek's understanding of the role played by rules, without actually using the term 'rule'.

As with Hayek, Ebling knows that prices 'do not tell us the whole story'. On their own, they are insufficient guides to action. What is required is that agents share the same institutionalised meaning framework, that allows them to interpret social situations in a similar (although not identical) manner and thereby make informed guesses about the actions of others now and in the future. But how does this occur?

Ebling argues that agents form 'images in their minds' or 'ideal types' of behavioural patterns of other agents and institutions, which they can then draw upon to 'size up' or interpret a new or unique situation. The similarities here between Ebling and Hayek are, however, apt to be overlooked by Ebling's use of the term 'ideal types'. This immediately conjures up images of Hayek in the 1940s as a subjective idealist. This is, however, not the case – or at least need not be the case.

Ebling says nothing in his paper to suggest that these 'ideal types' are solely what agents understand them to be. On the contrary, he gives the impression that these ideal types are generalisations formed by agents monitoring a situation and picking out what appear to be the most common features. Thus he writes that 'ideal types' are 'composed of various concrete generalisations concerning behavioural motivations and patterns of actions to be expected from any individual in the particular role' (Ebling, 1986, 48). Agents come to see certain patterns of behaviour as routine, because these patterns really do exist and are learned by agents. Moreover, they make the world a far more predictable place:

> The routinisation of behaviour along typical patterns introduces ranges of knowability about the possible future conduct and motivation of others. It is this that makes societies and economies possible in lieu of a perfect knowledge of each separate individual.
>
> (Ebling, 1986, 49)

I suggest that this be interpreted as agents learning to perceive the actions of others as conforming to a Hayekian pattern, regularity or rule, and identical to social rules of action. Note also that knowledge of ideal types (typically) like that of social rules of conduct is knowledge 'how' rather than knowledge 'that'. It is tacit knowledge.

The entrepreneur, for example, operates in a particular corner of the economy and his knowledge is of a highly specialised nature, built from continual experience. His knowledge consists not only in the non-tacit sense of particular, potential sources of profit (such as knowledge of half-empty tramp steamers), but also in a tacit sense, a web of ideal types relating to all aspects of business in this sector, allowing him to be familiar with typical causes and effects of market occurrences. Entrepreneurs and/or managers, and so on know 'how' to deal, for example, with irate customers, late account-settlers, creditors, militant shop stewards, lazy managers, and so on They know ('how') what is likely to sell and how it needs to be packaged, advertised, and so on, what arbitrage opportunities there are and where they are likely to be found.[8] Even in activities such as using discounted cash flow methods which at face value appear to be the epitome of instrumental rationality, there is space for tacit knowledge as agents intuitively select the rate of interest they feel is appropriate (Dreyfus and Dreyfus, 1987, 162).

Ebling's contribution to an understanding of Hayek's work on rules, then, is that he brings to prominence the myriad of activities that market participants are continually initiating and thereby brings to prominence the myriad of rules they continually draw upon.

By understanding the types of action and the rules that facilitate them that are located at this micro level of analytic abstraction, the gap between the cognitive and the macro levels is bridged. Rules of the mind (cognitive level) facilitate the following of social rules of conduct (micro level) that are apt to be overlooked when the issue under investigation is socio-economic order (macro level). Not only is the articulation between all types of rules now visible, it is easy to see how cognitive rules underpin the entire range of social rules of conduct. The gap between cognitive psychology and macro-socio-economic activity is bridged without committing the fallacy of reducing socio-economic activity to individual psychology. Henceforth, when referring to social rule-following, this is to be understood as comprising the entire range of social rules of conduct.

HAYEK III's PHILOSOPHY AND THE ROLE PLAYED BY THE MIND

We noted in Chapter 3 that Hayek II adopts what I referred to as an augmented Kantian epistemology, due to his refusal to abandon the transcendental subject responsible for structuring the object whilst substituting cognitive psychology for metaphysical speculation. In Chapter 6 we noted that with

Hayek III's adoption of quasi-transcendental realism, the Kantian-inspired subjective idealism (and with it therefore the necessity for a transcendental subject) is abandoned. And yet, as the above discussion on cognitive psychology illustrates, the mind still seems to be playing a central role in Hayek III's work. Does this cast doubt upon the claim that Hayek moves away from Kant and subjective idealism and towards transcendental realism?

Whilst I shall argue in a moment that it does not, note that this view of Hayek III as retaining (at the very least) a Kantian residue in terms of the role of the classifying (Hayek) or synthesising (Kant) mind appears to be dominant. Moreover, there is textual evidence in Hayek himself to support this interpretation. In 1968 he writes:

> I did not mention it in my oral exposition, and therefore will not enlarge here on, the obvious relation of all this to Kant's conception of the categories that govern our thinking – which I rather took for granted.
> (Hayek, 1968b, 45)

Hayek also notes that much of what he writes here 'was already implicitly contained in *The Sensory Order*' (ibid., 36). These comments indicate not only that Hayek III himself sees a continuity between his (Kantian-inspired) work in 1952 and the late 1960s, but also that the latter is related to Kant's metaphysics.

Unfortunately, however, Hayek does not spell out the nature of the relation to Kant's thinking. Simply to see a relation between Kant's categories of understanding and his own classificatory capacity of the neural system does not make Hayek III a Kantian. It would be a mistake to conclude *because* Hayek III writes extensively of the mind as a classificatory system that deals with sense data, that he must conceive of the mind as a (Kantian) system, allowing the transcendental subject to structure the object. Whilst the mind is implicated in both perspectives, there has as yet been no differentiation between the roles that the mind is playing in the work of Hayek II and III. The important question to ask, therefore, is: What role is the mind playing in Hayek III's overall schema of things?

If the role of the mind is considered as part of Hayek's wider considerations, and not just as the subject matter of cognitive psychology, then one finds that whilst it is (obviously) implicated in cognition, it does not perform the same *ontological* role as it did in his previous subjective-idealist-inspired schema.

With Hayek's adoption of a quasi-transcendental-realist ontology, the transcendental subject is no longer required to structure the object. Real social objects and material are now admitted as existing independently of their identification. In the socio-economic world, structures in the form of social rules of conduct exist independently of any one agent's identification of them. They are not conceptual in nature, not concept-determined, or creations of the active Kantian mind. There are, arguably, two main reasons why most commentators fail to notice this point and continue to label Hayek III as a Kantian due to his emphasis on cognitive psychology. The first is due to the failure to discern a chronological shift in both his substantive and ontological commitments, so that commentators feel free to draw textual support from any period in Hayek's work. The second reason stems from the fact that since most commentators do not adopt a transcendental-realist philosophy, they are ultimately unable to transcend the epistemic fallacy, that is, they transpose questions of ontology to questions of epistemology. The result is that some form of Kantian epistemology remains in their own work, making Hayek II's Kantianism seem less problematic.

CONCLUSION

This chapter may appear somewhat disjointed. It has, however, elaborated in a little more depth exactly what social rules of conduct are, the range of actions they cover, the function they perform and the nature of the cognitive processes involved that actually enable human agents to follow rules. The section on cognitive psychology is important in the sense that, whilst it will hardly be mentioned again, the weight of Hayek's entire social theory of agency as rule-following, that is, of agents as procedurally rational, is actually taken by cognitive psychology. Not only does Hayek III have an alternative to *Homo economicus*, he also has a social psychological theory to ground it in, whereas *Homo economicus* is (nearly always) accepted by neoclassical economists as a fiction. The final two chapters pull the apparently disparate threads together.

9

THE ARTICULATION BETWEEN SOCIAL RULES OF CONDUCT AND THE TELE-COMMUNICATIONS SYSTEM

> The 'Ordering Forces' of which we can make use in such instances are the rules governing the behaviour of the elements of which the orders are formed. They determine that each element will respond to the particular circumstances which act on it in a manner which will result in an overall pattern.
>
> (Hayek, 1964b, 460)

Up to this point, the telecom system has been treated as something distinct from the network of social rules of conduct, as existing independently from the latter. The reason for the dichotomy is that this is how Hayek treats matters – at least up until 1960. Recall (Chapter 5) that for Hayek II, the telecom system is simply the price mechanism. When he wants to discuss other institutions that facilitate the discovery, communication and storage of knowledge, he uses phrases such as 'the whole organisation of the market'. There is, however, one such institution that Hayek II does not, and as this book has been at pains to point out, cannot, conceive of: namely social rules of conduct. Moreover, not only can Hayek II not conceive of social rules as facilitating the discovery, communication and storage of knowledge, he cannot conceive of them as part of the social fabric from which society is constructed. That is, Hayek II cannot conceive of the network of prices that constitute the telecom system as embedded in, and performing their 'signalling function' (Hayek, 1978, 170) only because of, the existence of a network of social rules of conduct. Having no social rules of conduct, he cannot possibly conceive of the telecom system articulating with these rules.

After 1960, however, the entire picture changes. The recognition of social rules of conduct means that Hayek III no longer needs to maintain this (implicit) dichotomy. Social rules of conduct become one of the key institutions in his understanding of spontaneous socio-economic order. The telecom system can only function when embedded in the network of social rules of conduct. This means that the telecom system is a different kind of thing from the rule network, but can only function by being part of the latter.

At this point in the argument, then, the dichotomy can and must be discarded. It is misleading in that it suggests an either/or approach to the discovery, communication and storage of knowledge: the discovery, communication and storage of knowledge is facilitated either by rules, or by the telecom system. The corrected approach will reveal the complex articulation between the entire range of rules of conduct, and the network of price signals which constitute the telecom system. O'Driscoll and Rizzo (1985, 106) are aware of this articulation:

> Prices and markets function as part of the social system, not in isolation. A social system generates many kinds of signals and rules besides prices. Unless these other guides are superfluous, it is erroneous to suggest that prices alone are sufficient guides . . . Prices are formed on markets composed of contracts, rules and customs . . . Not prices, but people allocate resources, and flesh and blood human actors depend on all these non-price variables in their decision making.[1]

It is important to comment here on the nature of the telecom system and how the term is used. Prior to 1960, Hayek uses the term 'telecom system' to refer solely to the price mechanism. After 1960 he ceases to use the former term and (usually) adopts the terms price mechanism or price system. Whilst the name is not important, and for consistency I shall continue to use the term telecom system, what Hayek means by it *is* important. Hayek refers to it as the 'signalling function of prices through which people are informed what they ought to do' (1978, 170; see also 1976, 72). He further claims that:

> although the price mechanism is an imperfect guide . . . it is still an indispensable guide . . . if all knowledge and foresight dispersed among many men is to be used.
>
> (Hayek, 1960, 350)

> [I]t is mainly changes in price that bring about the necessary adjustments. This means that, for it [the price system] to function properly, it is not sufficient that the rules of law under which it operates be general rules, but that their content must be such that the market will work tolerably well. The case for a free system is not that any system will work satisfactorily where coercion is confined by general rules, but that under it such rules can be given a form that will enable it to work . . . *[T]he efficiency of the system will depend on the particular content of the rules.*
>
> (Ibid., 229, emphasis added)

> the price and market system is in that sense a system of communication, which passes on (in the form of prices, determined only in the competitive market) the available information that each individual needs to act . . . The price of any one thing tells the user of that thing all she or he *needs to know* about the other users of it, which information

> is needed in order to use it efficiently. What is being communicated by the price is on the one hand, the cost in terms of all other users, who are using the thing for that particular purpose; and on the other hand, the equivalent value people might be prepared to give for the same, in a sense information about the needs of persons the producer doesn't even know about . . .
>
> (Hayek, 1982a, 326–7)

It is quite clear from these comments that Hayek regards the telecom system as a system that utilises the dispersed knowledge or information of a multitude of differentiated agents, by embodying it in the price signal. By monitoring the price signals, and particularly changes in relative prices, agents are able to tap into a range of knowledge that they themselves do not possess, because it is dispersed throughout millions of minds. Moreover, *the telecom system can only perform its signalling function if it is embedded within a suitable network of rules.*

Prices are not rules, but parcels or bits of knowledge or information that can be utilised only within a suitable rule framework. Not being a rule, a price is not a prescription to act such as 'give me £10 and I will give you commodity *X*'. The price is a signal that commodity *X* is (in some sense that I do not wish to elaborate upon) of equal worth to commodity *Y*, and both are worth £10. If relative prices change, then the agent reading the signal gains some knowledge about changes in economic conditions and may take appropriate action.

The exchange of commodity for money might take place if both parties understand the myriad of rules that facilitate transacting, and which range from, for example, the tacitly known rule that this piece of paper is a £10 note, to the rule of honesty that suggests that one ought not to take the commodity and keep the £10. One could say that in the example of exchange, the price signal is the efficient cause and the rule system the material cause.

The previous two chapters explored Hayek's understanding of social rules of conduct, and this chapter has so far elaborated upon his understanding of the telecom system: the task of the rest of this chapter is to elaborate upon the complex articulation between them.

THE ARTICULATION BETWEEN PRICES AND RULES

Whilst Hayek's writing on the telecom system and rules of conduct is extensive, he never succeeds in capitalising upon these themes by linking them satisfactorily. Two shortcomings are evident. First, and not unconnected with his exaggerated claims about the telecom system, the way in which he approaches the interaction of telecom system and social rules tends to treat the latter as inert institutions, whose task is merely to act as a backdrop to the operation of the 'real' knowledge-communicating institution – the telecom system.

Second, when he deals with this interaction, he tends to remain at the macro socio-economic level of abstraction, which was introduced in the previous chapter. He fails, therefore, to emphasise and capitalise upon his own work on those social rules located at the micro level. That is, he fails to capitalise upon the knowledge-communicating potential of the entire hierarchy of rules and fails therefore to elaborate upon the complex articulation between the entire hierarchy of rules and the telecom system.

These shortcomings, however, are easily remedied without having to attribute to Hayek a range of ideas that are not already contained in his work. For example, after discussing the co-ordinating function of rules, he adds:

> The orderliness of social activity shows itself in the fact that the individuals can carry out a consistent plan of action, that at almost every stage, rests on the expectations of certain contributions from his fellows.
> (Hayek, 1960, 160)

All that appears necessary is to make explicit the implicit links between his ideas on the telecom system and the entire hierarchy of rules. It is from these ideas that commentators like Ioannides have begun to piece together a Hayekian perspective on the complex interaction between rules and the telecom system. According to Ioannides (1992, 38):

> The price mechanism is not however the only knowledge-dispersion system in a market society . . . the rules of conduct and the social institutions which have evolved through centuries . . . themselves constitute a knowledge disseminating system. Through them, the knowledge of the legal, political and moral framework of any social activity is conveyed to all market participants.
>
> There is thus a major difference between the information disseminating functions of the price system and those rules and institutions. The knowledge dispersed by the former is of a dynamic nature, in the sense that it leads individuals to a constant revision of their plans. The knowledge dispersed by the latter is stabilising, in the sense that it constantly affirms the stability of the social framework in which individuals act.

Ioannides's recognition that social rules are not only structures that facilitate the discovery, communication and storage of knowledge in their own right, but also that there is an articulation between them and prices, opens up a fruitful line of argument.

The articulation has three key aspects: first, the telecom system stimulates the discovery and acquisition of knowledge; second, the telecom system can only work by being embedded within a network of social rules; third, social rules facilitate the discovery, communication and storage of knowledge in those situations where the telecom system is inoperative. Recognition of the role played by social rules, places them on an equal footing with the telecom system, making the investigation of social rules part of the subject matter of economics.

THE TELECOM SYSTEM AS A STIMULUS TO KNOWLEDGE ACQUISITION

An agent, already in possession of a stock of knowledge is alerted by a price signal, often a price change. At this point the agent in neoclassical theory knows exactly how to act and the consequences are completely deducible from the initial axioms and assumptions. Hayek, by contrast is interested in the processes and mechanisms that are triggered by this price change.

The price signal triggers a process of mental and physical activity whereby expectations, plans and subsequently a course of action are formulated. This process occurs by agents drawing upon the stock of knowledge already in their possession, and by acquiring knowledge of aspects where they are ignorant. These two moments are considered in turn.

Sometimes agents already possess 'knowledge of circumstances', some of which is held non-tacitly. It might be knowledge of the immediate environment (for example, the under-exploitation of a surplus stock or knowledge of half-empty tramp steamers). It might be knowledge held by other agents, and communicated via personal relationships (for example, between an entrepreneur and a supplier of a particular product or an arbitrage opportunity). Such knowledge is held consciously and is articulable.

Sometimes agents already possess 'knowledge of circumstances', some of which is held semi-tacitly. This might refer to a range of facts that are known, in the sense that they are deeply embedded in the unconscious and only recalled from the memory when it is scoured. In this case, such knowledge is knowledge 'that' but, rather like the rules of chess, the agent is not conscious of it. Such facts have been gradually and consciously assembled through a learning process, only to be relegated to some lower level in the hierarchy of mind and brought to consciousness when needs dictate – the result of 'racking one's brain' when faced with a problem.

Sometimes agents are not in possession of the requisite knowledge with which to initiate a course of action, but they might be able to access certain institutions to acquire the knowledge they lack. That they can overcome their (non-radical) ignorance is due to the fact that some knowledge is independent of the knower, i.e. Popper's 'knowledge without a knowing subject', or knowledge embedded in the 'atmosphere' of Marshall's 'industrial districts'. Such knowledge is embodied in institutions such as education/training, stock market reports, technical specifications, market research, operations research, libraries, press agencies, advertising and all kinds of media, especially trade newsletters. When agents access these institutions and therefore come to acquire knowledge, they know in a non-tacit sense. The price change stimulates the agent into accessing these institutions, thereby overcoming his or her ignorance.

It appears, then, that a range of knowledge already available in the system in one form or another is not only activated or brought to life by the telecom system, but a process of knowledge acquisition is stimulated. As Hayek III put matters:

> What [an agent] will need in order to choose successfully among the opportunities known to him are the signals in the form of known prices . . . Given this information, he will be able to use his *knowledge of the circumstances of his environment* to select his immediate aims . . .
>
> (Hayek, 1976, 9; emphasis added)

> Prices direct [agents'] attention to what is worth finding out about market offers for various things and services. This means that the, in some respects, always unique, combinations of individual knowledge and skills, which the market enables them to use, will not merely . . . be such knowledge of facts that they could communicate . . . The knowledge of which I speak rather consists of a capacity to find out particular circumstances . . .
>
> (Hayek, 1968a, 182)

THE TELECOM SYSTEM IS EMBEDDED IN A NETWORK OF RULES

Social rules render intelligible the situation whereby a price change is encountered by facilitating the interpretation of price signals. Without having a repertoire of rules to follow, agents would not know what a price signal is, let alone how to devise a response to it. Price signals may act as the trigger for immediate action but must themselves be interpreted by drawing upon the network of social rules. The articulation between rules and price signals, then, allows agents to decide upon a subsequent course of action. Rules in this sense facilitate the interpretation of knowledge that is embodied in price signals.

How exactly does this allow agents to take sensible action when prices (*pace* mainstream economics) do not contain sufficient knowledge to allow a decision to be made? When a price change is encountered, the entrepreneur draws on a stock of social rules of conduct and must choose the one which he thinks is likely to be best. This by no means implies that the correct decision is chosen; it simply demonstrates how the entrepreneur operates. The stock of rules is extremely large and impossible to catalogue *a priori*, since new situations call forth new connections in the web of rules.

On occasions such as that exemplified in Hayek's famous tin mine case, the recipient of the knowledge in the form of a price signal knows nothing (at least nothing obtainable from the price signal itself) about the circumstances of time and place appertaining to the tin-producing firm – of this range of facts, the recipient remains ignorant. It is if, and only if, the recipient of the price signal is a skilled agent and thereby knows 'how' to interpret the signal, that a suitable and therefore co-ordinating course of action can be initiated. Ebling neatly sums up how prices and ideal types (which I interpret as Hayekian social rules) form a useful unity:

> Market prices are used in conjunction with ideal typification in the minds of actors . . . They give meaning to prices, just as prices assist in deciding which meanings may be relevant to the decision problem in hand . . . And it is the structures of prices within the structures of meanings that create the potential for market co-ordination.
>
> (Ebling, 1986, 52)

RULES AND KNOWLEDGE WHEN THE TELECOM SYSTEM IS INOPERATIVE

Social rules of conduct are institutions that facilitate the discovery, communication and storage of knowledge in their own right. In the situations where the discovery, communication and storage of knowledge is not carried out via the telecom system (see Chapter 5), then some other institutions must be in operation. These could be formal (for example, a library) but of more importance here is the claim that they could also be social rules. Rules, in this sense, step in and facilitate the discovery, communication and storage of knowledge in situations when the telecom system cannot. They do this in two ways.

First, rules are the ever-present condition (and reproduced outcome) facilitating all forms of social interaction in general, and any form of knowledge discovery, communication and storage in particular. It would not be possible to form an expectation or initiate an action without them. Second, as noted above, agents are often radically ignorant, a situation that cannot be overcome by the acquisition of certain facts, i.e. knowledge 'that'. In this scenario, social rules play a central role. For example, agents will be ignorant of a vast range of facts such as whether or not a supplying firm can be trusted to deliver the quality and quantity of a component on time. And whilst such matters can be written into contract and penalty clauses added, the vast majority of such transactions succeed simply because parties honour promises. Following the rules of making and accepting promises is an integral part of business life. What is significant, however, is that following the rule does not overcome the state of ignorance, it merely facilitates the formulation of an appropriate expectation, plan and subsequent action (see Chapter 7).

The key point to note in this elaboration of social rules is that they are an institution that facilitates the discovery, communication and storage of knowledge in their own right. Boehm (1989, 210–11) notes that for Hayek, social institutions should

> be appraised by reference to their conduciveness to generate, store and transmit knowledge. On this account, markets are conceived of as epistemic institutions geared to the production and distribution of socially valuable knowledge.

He then adds:

> What is interesting about Hayek's conception of institutions as carriers of traditional wisdom, as indispensable, highly useful guideposts in our attempts somehow to get by despite our ignorance of our less immediate surroundings . . . is the light it sheds on the co-ordination problem; incomplete, divided knowledge might no longer prove fatal to it.

The kind of rule-following outlined here is so ordinary, so second-nature, that it is apt to be overlooked by economists, particularly those who rest content with the version of *Homo economicus* deploying instrumental rationality on the basis of perfect knowledge and equilibrium prices. Yet without the ability to draw upon a set of social rules and thereby gain access to society's collected wisdom, the amount of knowledge available to any one individual at any one spatio-temporal location would be far too limited to enable a co-ordinating decision to be made. And if one rejects this version, as Hayek does, then an alternative must be postulated.

As we noted in Chapters 7 and 8, Hayek offers a social-psychological theory whereby humans are rule-followers rather than rational calculators. It is the ability to follow social rules, according to Hayek, that enables agents to know 'how' to conduct their socio-economic affairs with a fair chance of being successful:

> Even today, the overwhelming majority of people, including, I am afraid, a good many supposed economists, do not yet understand that . . . in an economic order involving a far ranging division of labour it can no longer be the pursuit of perceived common ends but only abstract rules of conduct . . . [that] tells people what to do to adapt their activities to events of which they have no direct knowledge.
>
> (Hayek, 1978, 162)

The market process, then, is inconceivable without social rules of conduct acting to stimulate the acquisition of knowledge, to interpret price signals and to handle knowledge in situations when the telecom system cannot. This articulation goes a long way to explain how agents acquire and communicate knowledge when they possess it, and cope with ignorance when they do not. Galeotti (1987, 172) sums up Hayek's position, indicating the distance between it and neoclassical theory:

> to have rational choice and action normally theorists either assume perfect knowledge and complete information, or develop a theory of probability to deal with the risk and uncertainty, or a game theory to

face a strategic environment. The first alternative is not very interesting since it is highly unrealistic; the other two alternatives imply a very good computational capacity on the side of the actor, which contrasts with Hayek's theory of the limitation of rationality, and, moreover they rely on the implicit assumption of what is plausible. Hayek's solution rather points to the system of unregulated rules as the source of actual, sensible, expectations, available without straining the actor's limited capacity, and enabling him or her to make rational plans fitting with the others.

ADVANTAGES OF HAYEK'S CONCEPTION

Possessing an understanding of how social rules facilitate the discovery, communication and storage of knowledge, Hayek is able to offer a more sophisticated explanation of some of the problems of the market process discussed recently. A good example of this is given by considering Kirzner's 'Knowledge problem B' (1992, ch. 10).

Here a disequilibrium situation is brought about by a combination of over-pessimism and relative ignorance due to segmented markets. Agents are unaware of opportunities to trade in another market and so refrain from trading. This market is such that if they were aware of it they would trade. Knowledge problem B then results not from unco-ordinated expectations, but from failure to obtain potential gains due to agents' ignorance of them. The problem is not self-correcting because it is not self-revealing via the telecom system. What agents fail to know today, they may continue to fail to know tomorrow; they do not know, and moreover, they do not know that they do not know.

According to Kirzner, the existence of Knowledge Problem B creates an 'incentive for its solution by profit discovery in the activity of the profit alert entrepreneur' (1992, 170). Entrepreneurial alertness then becomes a crucial organising phenomenon. Agents *X* and *Y*, being pessimistically ignorant of one another, simply fail to trade. *X* would actually have been prepared to sell at £3 and *Y* would have been prepared to buy at £10. Both could have made a gain. Along, however, comes entrepreneur *Z*, with knowledge of this situation. He buys from *X* for £4 and sells to *Y* for £9, and thus earns a pure profit. Spurred into action by the lure of a profit opportunity, and guided simply by disequilibrium prices, the alert entrepreneur *Z* discovers knowledge that is actually in the system (i.e. in agent *X* and *Y*'s heads), but it is not in the 'correct' location. Being alerted to this knowledge allows agents' expectations to be co-ordinated. Entrepreneur *Z* is 'switched on by the configuration of market prices, to conjecture, (and try out) hunches' (ibid., 148).

Kirzner is arguing that the telecom system is the *sole* institution by which knowledge problems are overcome by alert entrepreneurs uncovering arbitrage opportunities. In fact the title of the chapter, 'Prices, Knowledge and the

Discovery Process', reveals the thrust of his argument. Kirzner, however, has to turn every situation where a breakdown in communication occurs into an arbitrage opportunity, so that it can be overcome by the co-ordinating mechanism of the telecom system.

Moreover, he is forced to overplay his hand to make the claim (implicitly) that the disequilibrium prices that constitute the telecom system are sufficient to facilitate the discovery, communication and storage of knowledge because he has no other institution to augment it with. He is also forced to overplay his hand on the notion of alertness, because he does not conceive of entrepreneurs as rule-followers. Kirzner's entrepreneur is guided by a kind of instrumental rationality based upon alertness to arbitrage opportunities, whereas Hayek's entrepreneur is guided by procedural rationality, i.e. is a rule-follower. This places Kirzner in the kind of situation that Hayek II is trapped in – and escapes from. Hayek III, by contrast, does not have to overplay his hand, since co-ordination for him is a socio-economic, and not merely a narrowly economic, problem: it is overcome via a range of socio-economic institutions, mechanisms and structures, not just the price signals of the telecom system. Hayek's developed multidisciplinary social science can go into areas that others, which includes other Austrians, cannot go.[2, 3]

10

HAYEK III's TRANSFORMATIONAL CONCEPTION OF SPONTANEOUS SOCIO-ECONOMIC ORDER

> [T]he individual with a particular structure and behaviour owes its existence in this form to a society of a particular structure, because only within such a society has it been advantageous to develop some of its characteristics, while the order of society is in turn the result of these regularities of conduct.
>
> (Hayek, 1976, 76)

The spade-work for this final chapter has already been done. From Chapter 6 onwards, Hayek's mature work has been scrutinised to ascertain three crucial things. First, in terms of philosophy, Hayek III (a) abandons subjective idealism completely; (b) abandons empirical realism to a large degree; and therefore (c) largely abandons the ontologies that these philosophical positions presuppose. In their place he adopts a quasi-transcendental-realist philosophy and ontology.

Second, in terms of method, Hayek III shifts the focus of attention (ontologically speaking) from the fused domains of the empirical and actual to the domain of the deep. With the recognition of deep structures, the focus of attention shifts from using Humean law(s) to deduce consequences (in the form of events/actions) from axioms buttressed by assumptions, towards ascertaining and explaining the structural conditions necessary for such events/actions to occur.

Third, in terms of substantive theory, Hayek develops a set of categories (for example, all kinds of knowledge and ignorance, a range of rules of conduct, rules of the mind, rule-following behaviour, the articulation between social structures in the form of social rules of conduct and the telecom system, and so on) that constitute the theoretical building-blocks for his notion of spontaneous socio-economic order.

Whilst all that is necessary in this final chapter is to assemble these categories, there is one factor that makes such an assembly extremely difficult. This factor is Hayek's rejection of any notion of equilibrium and his adoption of a transformational conception.[1] The former is a well-known principle adopted by various economic theorists, whereas the latter is virtually unknown outside social theory. Hayek's notion of spontaneous socio-economic order is, therefore, not only an economic but also a social theory. It is this combination of (a) the switch from equilibrium to transformation, and (b) the merging of economic and social theory, that complicates the task of assembling the categories.

The foregoing argument does not require Hayek to be conscious of the transformational conception – which, of course, he is not. The advantage of such a conception is that it serves to make explicit what is merely implicit in his work. Attributing a transformational conception to Hayek supplies him with an alternative ordering principle to that of equilibrium.[2]

I shall proceed by briefly outlining the main components of the argument that will unfold over the course of the chapter, before elaborating each one in more depth.

THE ARGUMENT IN SUMMARY

If the various elements that comprise a system fit together to display order, as opposed to chaos, then some *principle of organisation* must be in operation. According to Oliver[3] (1951, 11), if a set of entities is not merely to be a 'heap' but an 'order', then there must be in operation some 'principle of arrangement'. When the system under investigation is a socio-economic system, then the following question needs to be addressed: What is the principle of organisation in operation ensuring that a semblance of order occurs? There appear to be two principles on offer, each one rooted in a philosophical position.

The first principle of organisation, and the one typically adopted by positivist economists, is *equilibrium*. Hahn (1973, 1) uses equilibrium as the 'central organising idea' of neoclassical theory. Since there are far too many notions of equilibrium to deal with individually, I shall make use of the following generic, working definition given by Dow:[4]

> The equilibrium concept is pervasive in economics because it imposes order on complex relationships: it provides a natural point at which to look at the outcome of particular forces. Even if it is the process itself by which the forces are exerted which is the primary interest, *the end point provides a useful benchmark for analysis*.
>
> (Dow, 1985, 112, emphasis added)

Equilibrium, on this working definition, might for example occur when, via market exchange, a particular set of prices is so established that the actions of all agents terminate in a situation that could not be improved upon; or perhaps when the economy generates signals which do not cause agents to change their expectations and therefore their actions. What differentiates the various notions of equilibrium is, for our purposes irrelevant: what unites them, however, is not. All notions share (a) an empirical realist ontology, therefore (b) a similar positivist methodology, and (c) a preoccupation with defining an end state.

The second principle of organisation, and the one adopted by the mature Hayek, is, and this must be emphasised, *radically, fundamentally and qualitatively different* to any mainstream notion of equilibrium. Hayek adopts what I shall refer to as a *transformational (and spontaneous*[5]*) conception of socio-economic order*. This notion (a) presupposes a quasi-critical realist ontology; (b) a quasi-critical realist method; and (c) a preoccupation with processes as opposed to end states. The processes are essentially tied up with the discovery, communication and storage of knowledge and the mechanisms and structures that facilitate this.

This chapter will show that the mature Hayek abandons the concept of equilibrium for a quasi-critical-realist, transformational conception of order, and that the processes involved in this conception are those he describes as constituting the catallaxy. I hope to demonstrate the possibility of something that is, typically, denied by most contemporary economists – namely, that *we can abandon equilibrium without having to fall into analytical anarchy*.

Having briefly outlined the main components of the argument, I shall now proceed to develop the key points in more depth. The next section will show how the ontology of empirical realism encourages the use of equilibrium as the organising principle. The fourth section will show that Hayek's notion of socio-economic order is the antithesis of equilibrium, while the fifth section introduces the transformational model of social action, with its emphasis upon the process of production, reproduction and transformation of socio-economic resources, mechanisms and structures. The penultimate part shows that this process is contained in Hayek's notion of the catallaxy.

ONTOLOGY, METHOD, EQUILIBRIUM AND EMPIRICAL REALISM

The empirical-realist ontology presupposed by positivist economists, contrary to that postulated by critical realists, is not layered, but (metaphorically) flat.[6] Empirical realism recognises, although it fuses, the two domains of the empirical and the actual – but the domain of the deep is not recognised. Since the domain of the deep is not recognised, investigation cannot focus upon this domain and must remain, therefore, within the domains of the empirical and actual. Put another way, investigation must focus upon events/actions given in sense experience. Empirical realist investigation, then, takes events/actions given in sense experience as the particulars of the world and attempts to establish general scientific knowledge by discovering regular patterns in, or constant conjunctions of, these events, i.e. Humean laws. Economic theorising, from the empirical-realist perspective, proceeds by using these Humean laws to deduce consequences from initial axioms buttressed by assumptions.

All economic theory purports to make some valid claim about the way the world really is – even if this requires a tortuous explanation of the correspondence between theory and reality. Statements about events/actions derived in theory must have (or be thought to have) some resonance with the real world, and laws derived in theory are presumed to hold in the real world.

Most economists recognise that the events/actions occurring in the real world are not constantly conjoined. Laws do not hold with perfect regularity. No mainstream economist using, for example, the law of factor substitution would claim that whenever the price of factor L rose, it would be substituted for, *in each and every case*, by factor K. In more general terms, no mainstream economist would actually expect (Humean) laws to hold in reality. What is necessary for theory construction, therefore, i.e. constant conjunctions of events/actions, does not appear to exist in the real world.

What, then, is the positivist economist to do? The fact that reality is not perfectly regular makes it impossible to find any pattern in the flux of events/actions. If on one occasion a rise in wages results in the substitution of capital for labour, and on another occasion results in no change in the ratio of capital to labour, what can be said about the relation between wages and factor employment? Not much.

There are two possible ways out of this dilemma. The first requires the switch in the mode of theorising noted in Chapter 6, from the fused domains of the empirical and actual to the domain of the deep. Knowing that the events of experience are most unlikely to manifest in regular patterns, the critical realist shifts the focus of investigation to underlying structures that give rise to these events/actions. Adhering to a flat ontology, however, the positivist economist simply cannot take this route, and must opt, therefore, for the second possibility, namely, the resort to analytical abstraction.

The positivist deals with the (real) complicating factors that cause the irregularities in events/actions, by spiriting them away via the often completely fictitious use of axioms of human behaviour, assumptions and *ceteris paribus* clauses. The presumption is that a theoretical model is constructed as a 'scaled-down' version of reality as it were, a model that captures not every aspect but, in some, typically, undefined sense, the most important aspects of reality. This procedure is known by critical realists as *closing the system* (see Lawson, 1989a). A closed system is one in which the complicating factors that cause irregularities have been removed (theoretically of course), regular patterns in the flux of events/actions engineered, and Humean law resurrected.[7] Economics can then proceed by using these Humean law(s) to deduce consequences from initial axioms buttressed by assumptions.[8]

Once the economist attempting to construct a theory of order has a series of laws appertaining to the course of action that a particular agent will take in a particular situation, what use are they? Following Loasby (1991, 9), one could argue that 'the co-ordination of economic activities, of course, is what economics is all about' in which case, the task of the economist is to utilise these laws to say something about socio-economic co-ordination between actions and their (intended and unintended) consequences.[9]

Any positivist attempt to conceive of co-ordination between the actions of agents and the consequences of these actions can only focus upon the fused domains of the empirical and actual. In a positivist conception of generalised co-ordination, and hence a conception of socio-economic order, action must be based upon a law (or a combination of laws) such that it is possible to state or predict *ex ante* that if agent A initiates action X, consequence Y follows.

Generalising, it appears that agents $A_1, A_2, A_3 \ldots A_n$ initiate actions $X_1, X_2, X_3 \ldots X_n$ (subject to various constraints), and consequences $Y_1, Y_2, Y_3 \ldots Y_n$) will be known to follow. The task of the economist is to discover, or more accurately with positivist economics, merely to describe, the conditions under which the consequences of these courses of action co-ordinate with one another. This co-ordination might be said to occur when (a) each agent is satisfied with the consequences of their respective courses of action, *and* (b) when the action of any one agent does not hinder the action of others so as to frustrate the objectives of any agent within the system.[10]

The way this is done in Walrasian general equilibrium theory, for example, is to ascertain whether or not, between a set of agents with initial endowments, technology and tastes, there is a particular price and quantity configuration which results in market-clearing. The presumption is that all agents will modify their actions *vis-à-vis* price and quantity until the consequences of their actions co-ordinate with those of everyone else. The resultant configuration is then described as equilibrium. Of significance here is the fact that the focus is not on the *process*[11] whereby actions are modified, but on the consequences that arise from these actions and terminate in some *end state*. In fact the process itself reduces to tatonnement, a well-known fiction, legitimised as an aid to theorising.[12]

It appears, then, that once we are committed to an empirical realist ontology, we are committed to theorising solely in terms of the domains of the empirical and actual, that is, in terms of actions/events. Any co-ordination must be based upon regular patterns in the flux of events/actions. This is, however, precisely the domain where regularity does not exist to be perceived. And since it is impossible to find any pattern in the flux of events/actions, it is impossible to discover Humean laws. In order to cope with this lack of regularity, the system is closed via the construction of a model wherein all complicating factors that might lead to irregularity have been exorcised and Humean law is resurrected – although now in terms of a theoretical model only. The positivist economist attempts to describe, or state, the conditions under which the consequences of agents' actions co-ordinate with one another, at which point overall socio-economic order, in the guise of equilibrium, is said to exist. The principle of organisation is equilibrium, and carries two negative implications:

1 The emphasis is upon end states and not the processes by which these end states allegedly come about or tend to come about.
2 The emphasis is necessarily upon a closed model, not reality.

These negative implications have been unacceptable for Hayek since the mid-1930s. As will become clear below, when Hayek abandons empirical realism and adopts a quasi-critical-realist ontology his notion of socio-economic order simply has no need for the concept of equilibrium and the negative implications it carries.

As a positivist, Hayek I does not question these negative implications. As a subjective idealist, Hayek II questions them but cannot replace them with satisfactory alternatives because, although he recognises something approaching the domain of the deep, the 'structures' he finds there are merely ideal, not real, and therefore incapable of facilitating action – they exist but are inert. It is only when Hayek III adopts a quasi-critical-realist ontology that the possibility exists of advancing an alternative. With this layered, as opposed to flat, ontology, Hayek III's notion of socio-economic order simply has no need for the concept of equilibrium and the negative implications it carries.

Hayek III is, therefore, enabled to provide an account of socio-economic order that is couched in terms of processes as opposed to end states, and these processes are not hypothetical or fictional, not designed to remove phenomena that might give rise to irregular activity: they are real. Once an empirical realist ontology is abandoned, Hayek can shift the focus of economic investigation: he can move beyond the events/actions given in experience, beyond the fused domains of the empirical and actual, to the underlying structures, that is, to the domain of the deep. Lack of perfect regularity between events (i.e. lack of Humean laws) is simply no longer a problem, because the nature or essence of the orderliness is established at the level of the deep. Deep structures act with transfactual necessity and do not therefore become problematic when they do not give rise to event regularity at the level of events.

The claim that Hayek III is enabled to provide an account of socio-economic order that is couched in terms of processes as opposed to end states is strengthened by the observation that these processes are precisely those contained in his explanation of the operation of the catallaxy. Moreover, these processes are of a transformational nature, meaning that Hayek's principle of organisation is transformation.

Before I go on to explain these transformative and catallactic processes, there is one matter *vis-à-vis* equilibrium to be cleared up. Even after 1960, Hayek III does occasionally give the impression that he still has some residual conception of equilibrium, a point that has been picked up by those Austrians who have leanings towards neoclassical theory. Clearing up this matter is a valuable exercise, because it throws light on Hayek's alternative to equilibrium.

ORDER VERSUS EQUILIBRIUM

In 1968 Hayek explicitly abandons the notion of equilibrium for the alternative notion of order:

> Economists usually ascribe the order which competition produces as an equilibrium – a somewhat unfortunate term, because such an equilibrium presupposes that the facts have already been discovered and competition therefore has ceased. The concept of an 'order' which . . . I prefer to that of equilibrium, has the advantage that we can speak about an order being approached to varying degrees, and that order can be preserved throughout a process of change.
>
> (Hayek, 1968a, 184)

He defines order as

> a state of affairs in which a multiplicity of elements of various kinds are so related to each other that we may learn from the acquaintance with some spatial or temporal part of the whole to form correct expectations concerning the rest.
>
> (Hayek, 1973, 36)

The progressive nature of the shift lies in understanding that *order, unlike equilibrium, is not an alternative description of an end state but rather a continual process of reproduction and transformation. Moreover, it is a process with no (temporary or permanent) termination point.*[13]

Thus the search in Hayek's work for an alternative *end state* to the 'full Hayekian equilibrium' (Rizzo, 1990) might be misguided. Spontaneous socio-economic order is not a different conception of equilibrium, it is the rejection of equilibrium and equilibrium economics.

Boetke, Horowitz and Prychitco argue that the nature of the ordering process is an alternative conception that works without reference to any equilibrium construct. They add:

> An evolutionary process is open ended, in that the process does not tend towards any state. Consider what it would mean for human evolution to tend towards a final state. No biologist would ever say that we need to have a fully evolved human to understand the process of evolution.
>
> (Boetke, 1986, 8)

The point to note here is that if no fully evolved human is required to understand or explain the process of evolution, why is a fully evolved, terminated economic model required to understand and explain the processes involved in the establishment of socio- economic order?

It cannot go unremarked, however, that in places, Hayek III gives the impression that, due to the discovery or learning possibilities involved in the market processes, there is a tendency for expectations to converge gradually over time. In one place he writes:

> The correspondence of expectations . . . is brought about by a process of trial and error which must involve constant disappointment. The process of adaption operates, as do the adjustments of any self organising system, by what cybernetics has taught us to call negative feedback: *responses to the differences between the expected and the actual results of actions so that these differences will be reduced. This will produce an increased correspondence of expectations* . . .
>
> (Hayek, 1976, 124–5, emphasis added)

If this is interpreted to mean that negative feedback will generate a learning process and thereby an 'increased correspondence of expectations', then it is hard to ignore the possibility that given enough time and effort, expectations will become so co-ordinated that they terminate in some end state. In other words, if expectations become gradually more co-ordinated, what is to prevent their perfect co-ordination terminating in some end state, some form of equilibrium?[14]

However, once we break with thinking in terms of end states, another possibility opens up. What Hayek has in mind is most definitely not a correspondence or tendency towards an end state on any description. 'Increased correspondence' for Hayek, and this is the important claim, is *relative to the level of correspondence that any other system of socio-economic organisation could achieve*.

I agree therefore with Rizzo's observation that Hayek's 1968a paper marks the site of Hayek's complete break with the notion of equilibrium as a never-attained 'benchmark' and his acceptance of a 'more radically relativistic' conception of order as a more co-ordinated state relative to that attainable in any other social system. I suspect that Hayek would agree with O'Driscoll and Rizzo's (1985, 109–11) observation that:

> A theory of evolved orders is not a theory of optimality or efficiency, precisely because it is a process not an end state theory . . . It is not what competition does to fulfil our expectations that commends it; it is what we would not have expected it to do that commends it.

As Hayek himself puts matters:

> The discovery procedure which we call competition aims at the closest approach we can achieve by any means known to us to a somewhat more modest aim which is nevertheless highly important: namely a state of affairs in which all that is in fact produced is produced at the lowest possible costs . . . Only because the market induces every individual to use his unique knowledge of particular opportunities and possibilities . . . can an overall order be achieved that uses in its totality the dispersed knowledge which is not accessible as a whole to anyone.
>
> (Hayek, 1967d, 91)

The notion, then, of order and a tendency towards order is fundamentally different from the notion of equilibrium and a tendency towards equilibrium. Hayek long ago abandoned any thoughts of end states, and to look for an alternative 'Hayekian equilibrium' is to miss the point: no alternative exists. The tendency is not actually towards any end state, but is a tendency to co-ordinate expectations better than any alternative socio-economic system. We could well imagine Hayek saying something like: 'a tendency towards the co-ordination of the consequences of actions, i.e. order generated by a market-based socio-economy, is stronger than the tendency towards order generated by a planned economy.'

His defence of capitalism, that is, his claim to the superiority of the market-based socio-economy over any alternative forms, then, does not turn on the theoretical capacity to 'prove' or describe a unique or stable equilibrium. It turns on the power of the explanation of how and why a market-based socio-economy makes use of the totality of dispersed knowledge to co-ordinate actions and consequences, and thereby bring about socio-economic order, better than any hitherto known alternative.

With all lingering doubts about Hayek's use of equilibrium dispelled, it is time to turn to the question of just how we could, drawing upon Hayek's work, suggest an alternative principle of organisation, namely a transformational one. This will be the subject of the next sections. I shall begin with a fairly abstract elaboration and move gradually towards the concrete.

ONTOLOGY, METHOD, TRANSFORMATION AND CRITICAL REALISM

It should be clear by now that Hayek's notion of socio-economic order refers to a process. I shall discuss this process at both a higher and lower level of abstraction. The transformational model of social activity (TMSA) supplies the analytical framework for the higher level; whilst the process Hayek describes as the catallaxy is outlined at the lower, that is, the more concrete, level. The higher level will be the focus of this section, the lower level the focus of the following section.

Hayek's quasi-transcendental realism extends into social science in the form of a quasi-critical realism, where he elaborates a quasi-TMSA. The term 'quasi' in this sense means 'something approaching', and implies that Hayek does not actually adopt the entire social ontology of the TMSA. Again, as with quasi-transcendental realism, I shall not (except for one example) elaborate upon those aspects where Hayek fails to adopt the TMSA.

Figure 10.1 may assist in bringing together some of the categories developed thus far; it adds one or two more that will be introduced as the chapter unfolds.

The essence of the TMSA, as outlined in Chapter 6, rests upon a particular understanding of the critical-realist ontology. Not only is the ontology

Agency	Intentional action Procedural rationality Cognitive apparatus that facilitates rule-following
Resource	Knowledge
Mechanisms	Formal knowledge-handling agencies Telecom system
Structures	Social rules of conduct

Figure 10.1 The components constituting Hayek's quasi-TMSA

layered, it is also transformational. Being, in this case social being, is understood to be transformational in nature. What does this mean? It means that the social material that exists (resources, mechanisms, structures) does so in virtue of the fact that it is never produced *ab initio* by the action of agents, but is always *re*produced and often transformed in the act of production. Social material is both a condition for, and an outcome of, socio-economic action.

According to the stylised Hayekian quasi-TMSA presented here, society is the ensemble of resources mechanisms and structures. These elements are, however, not merely thrown together in a heap; there is a principle of organisation in operation, and that principle is transformation. These elements are the ever-present condition of, and continually reproduced outcome of, human agency.

Agents motivated by the desire to bring about an intended outcome and in possession of resources employ or engage mechanisms, draw upon structures, initiate courses of action and try to bring about intended consequences. Agents are only able to initiate such action because they are able to employ mechanisms and draw upon structures. In the absence of these mechanisms their actions would, typically, be insufficient to bring about their intended consequences. In the absence of these structures, no action at all would be possible. However, in taking this action, agents (typically unintentionally) reproduce and transform the resources, mechanisms and structures that they employ and draw upon. These resources, mechanisms and structures become what Bhaskar (1989a, 34–5) refers to as the 'ever present condition . . . and the continually produced outcome of human agency'. Put simply, agents cannot initiate action that might bring about a desired goal without working with resources, mechanisms and structures; and yet in working with them, they are reproduced and transformed. The TMSA therefore presupposes a transformational ontology. What exists does so only in virtue of its continual reproduction and transformation via production.

Note that it is in virtue of the transformative nature of social being that no termination point in the process is ever reached. Whilst what exists is continually reproduced, it is also, typically, transformed in the process so that it is not reproduced exactly.[15]

Let us set out this argument for a transformational understanding of a market-based socio-economy in slightly more concrete terms. We might suggest that for Hayek agents, being equipped with the cognitive apparatus that facilitates rule-following action, in possession of resources in the form of localised knowledge, and motivated by (amongst other things) the desire to increase their chances of becoming wealthy, initiate courses of action and attempt to bring about consequences that are likely to be relatively co-ordinated with the actions and consequences of others. This necessitates drawing upon social rules of conduct. The combination, then, of intended and unintended consequences of the totality of agents' actions brings about a spontaneous order, which is, of course, not part of their original intention. In the absence of formal mechanisms that facilitate the production, communication and storage of knowledge (for example, the trade press), access to a range of knowledge would be severely limited. In the absence of the telecom system, communication would be so cumbersome that no one would know enough to be able to bring about their intended consequences, or even begin to co-ordinate their plans and actions with others. In the absence of social rules of conduct, however, no social action at all would be possible, since agents can only act at all by following rules.

Of significance here is the fact that in taking social action agents (typically unintentionally) reproduce the formal mechanisms, the telecom system and the social rules of conduct that they employ and draw upon. Social structures in the form of rules, and the mechanism of the telecom system, then, are the 'ever present condition . . . and the continually reproduced outcome of human agency'.

This transformational social ontology is presupposed in Hayek's elaboration of the evolution of social systems. He is trying to show that the functioning of a socio-economic order depends upon agents drawing upon a (in some sense correct or adapted) set of pre-existing social structures, which in turn are reproduced and transformed via action. Thus in his 'Notes on the Evolution of Systems of Rules of Conduct' he writes:

> Although the existence and preservation of the order of actions of a group can be accounted for only from the rules of conduct which the individuals obey, these rules . . . have developed because the individuals have been living in groups whose structures have gradually changed . . . Thus for the explanation of the functioning of the socio-economic order at any one time, the rules of individual conduct must be assumed to be given.
>
> (Hayek, 1967a, 72)

> We can judge and modify all our views and beliefs only within a framework of opinions and values which, though they will gradually change, are for us a given result of that evolution.
>
> (Ibid., 75)

Although Hayek generally keeps discussion of rules separate from that of the telecom system, the articulation between them noted in the previous chapter implies that they cannot really be separated. Together they comprise a set of social structures that give rise to the flux of events given in sense experience and become the focus of social scientific inquiry. It is possible to conclude, then, that Hayek adopts a layered ontology and focuses attention on the domain of the deep. He therefore abandons the social ontology that accompanies his earlier philosophical synthesis, and adopts a transformational social ontology.

Switch in the mode of theorising

With this quasi-critical-realist social ontology, an extremely important development in Hayek's thought occurs. The mode of theorising switches from a focus upon the fused domains of the empirical and actual to the domain of the deep. Socio-economic theory ceases to be (solely or even primarily) concerned with the definition of end states, and instead switches to the investigation of the resources, mechanisms and deep structures that make socio-economic activity possible. Put another way, Hayek switches the focus of investigation away from the fused domains of the empirical and actual, and thereby from a preoccupation with events/actions given in sense experience, to the domain of the deep and thereby to a preoccupation with underlying structures. This is due to the recognition that the event/actions given in sense experience that constitute the final outcome are (a) merely the starting point for investigation, (b) governed in part by underlying structures, which are (c) typically out of phase with these underlying structures.

The relation between underlying causal structures and mechanisms, and the events/actions they govern is recognised as non-isomorphic. Similarly, the relation between the events/actions themselves is recognised as non-regular. And yet something does govern these events/actions: whilst not displaying perfect regularity, they are not (typically) a mere chaotic flux. Some form of non-isomorphic relation must exist between the deep structures and the events/actions they govern if the latter are in any way orderly or systematic. Underlying deep structures acting with (material) causal, trans-factual necessity give rise to events/actions, but the nature of this connection cannot be read off from the events/actions themselves. Hence the domain of the deep is where investigation must focus. Metaphorically speaking, the task of science is not to move (horizontally) between actions/events, trying to discover or engineer regular conjunctions, but to move (vertically) from events/actions to the deep structures that govern them.

Hayek's mature quest for an explanation of socio-economic order is no longer the positivist-inspired investigation focusing upon events/actions (as, say, an econometric investigation) or a description of the outcome or consequences of socio-economic activity (as, say, general equilibrium investigation) as is the case with Hayek I. Both of these are examples of economists operating horizontally and with a flat ontology – encouraging the adoption of equilibrium as an organising principle. It even ceases to be the augmented empirical-realist-inspired approach of composing social categories from the conceptions held by agents and obtained by accessing agents' understanding, as is the case with Hayek II. Rather, the task of social science switches to become an inquiry into, and explanation of, the various resources, mechanisms and structures that are drawn upon and produced and thereby make spontaneous order possible. Put another way, the emphasis switches from describing an end state in terms of a set of co-ordinated expectations, plans, actions or consequences (equilibrium) to elaborating upon the conditions for action and thereby upon the transformational processes that are involved in establishing socio-economic order.

With the categories mentioned above all in place it is now both necessary and possible to step beyond this model and illuminate the real processes that this TMSA has grasped at a high level of abstraction. This will demonstrate Hayek's understanding of the actual processes that are involved in establishing spontaneous socio-economic order. His understanding of these processes is illustrated in his elaboration of the operation of the catallaxy.[16]

THE MARKET PROCESS OR CATALLAXY

Hayek uses the term 'catallaxy' because the term 'economy' appears to have been tainted by what he calls constructivist thinking. In 'The Errors of Constructivism', Hayek defines constructivism to be the notion that 'since man has himself created the institutions of society and civilisation, he must also be able to alter them at will' (1970a, 3). Hayek thinks 'an economy' refers to a created institution, a household, firm or a socialist system, any entity in which a given set of means are allocated in accordance with a unitary and consciously formulated plan among competing ends whereby an optimal outcome can be described. The term catallaxy invokes no such ideas of a single order of consciously formulated ends and an optimal end state, but rather a spontaneously emerging phenomenon. Catallaxy, then, is the term used to describe the market order, that is 'the order brought about by the mutual adjustment of many individual economies in the market' (1976, 108–9).

A catallaxy is characterised by a multitude of agents living in what he calls an 'extended order' (1988, 19), with four main or important characteristics. First, whilst the agents in Hayek III's work are isolated, they are not *asocial* but *social* individuals. They are situated within, and depend for their social activities upon, a web of social rules of conduct. Hayek offers a social theory rather than a set of claims about the behaviour of abstract atomised individuals.[17]

Second, as Chapter 5 demonstrated, each agent possesses differing fragments of knowledge. The precise extent of their knowledge is dependent upon the type of knowledge they have, lack or seek. For example, an agent may have fairly extensive knowledge of the immediate environment, be virtually ignorant of the remote environment, and radically ignorant of the future.

Third, agents have expectations, formulate plans, and subsequently initiate courses of action purposefully to pursue their own goals, possibly selfishly, possibly with great altruism; the motive makes no difference. The point is that there is no one mind in control that directs agents to initiate certain actions, or to pursue certain goals, and thereby attempts to make their actions and goals compatible with one another.

At first glance this looks like a recipe for chaos: isolated individuals with small parcels of localised, fragmented and partial knowledge, and on occasion ignorant, pursuing their own (possibly) self-serving goals, with no conscious co-ordinating agency in control.

It is, however, the fourth important characteristic which prevents this slide into chaos and holds the key to establishing socio-economic order, namely social rules of conduct. Since agents are only able to initiate social action by drawing upon social rules (which do not of course determine exactly what they do), their actions are simultaneously individually motivated and socially sanctioned. According to Hayek:

> What reconciles the individuals and knits them into a common and enduring pattern of a society is that . . . they respond in accordance with the same abstract rules . . . What . . . enables . . . men to live and work together in peace is that in the pursuit of their individual ends the particular monetary impulses which impel their efforts . . . are guided and restrained by the same abstract rules. If emotion or impulse tells them what they want, the conventional rules tell them how they will be able and be allowed to achieve it.
>
> (Hayek, 1976, 12)

> A catallaxy is thus the special kind of spontaneous order produced by the market through people acting within the rules of the law of property, tort and contract.
>
> (Hayek, 1982b, 109)

Because of a set of deep underlying structures in the form of social rules of conduct a high degree of compatibility of actions and consequences, where *in*compatibility of actions and consequences and hence chaos initially appears to be the likely outcome, is ensured. Hayek's use of the term catallaxy is extremely illuminating here. The word derives from ancient Greek, and means not only to exchange but, more importantly, 'to change from an enemy into a friend' (Hayek, 1976, 108). The harnessing of a potentially destructive force lies at the heart of Hayek's spontaneous socio-economic order.

To explain how the catallaxy functions to bring about order, Hayek invokes the analogy of a game,[18] the outcome of which will depend upon a mixture of skill and chance. It is rather like a sporting competition in which, although the officials can formulate rules to ensure that no one cheats and that all have an equal chance, there is no way to prevent a lucky winner or an unlucky loser.

The outcome of the game is not seen as in any sense just or fair. In fact these terms are quite meaningless, given the recognition that elements of luck and chance play a part in bringing about this order (Hayek, 1976, 117). Whilst the lure of high returns might bring agents into the market, how is it possible that agents continue to remain in it? For not only may an individual perceive his or her reward as unjust or unfair, but the possibility of making an error of judgement or simple bad luck might be sufficient to force them into severe financial difficulties. The answer lies with two factors. The first relates to the wealth-creating power of the catallaxy. The second relates to the way all agents, by following the market rules of conduct, increase their chance of succeeding in obtaining a greater portion of that increased wealth.

On the first point, the peculiarity of the catallaxy, or so it is claimed, is that it is a wealth-creating, non-zero-sum game, open to any agent who has relevant knowledge to contribute or, one supposes, who knows how to access knowledge. Whilst players enter the game and take action solely to satisfy their own wants, they may also satisfy the wants of others as an unintended consequence. According to Hayek, wealth is created because the game

> supplies to each player information which enables him to provide for needs of which he has no direct knowledge and by the use of means of the existence of which without it he would have no cognizance, thus bringing about the satisfaction of a greater range of needs than would otherwise be possible. Thus in the market, each is made by the visible gain to himself to serve needs which to him are invisible, and in order to avail himself of to him unknown particular circumstances which put

him in the position to satisfy those needs at as small a cost as possible.
(Hayek, 1976, 115)

By increasing the flow of knowledge, every agent is able to increase his or her financial return and simultaneously increase the stream of goods available to society at large. This is supposed to have the benefit of ensuring that costs are minimised since 'no need is served at the cost of withdrawing a greater amount of means from the use of other needs than is necessary to satisfy it' (ibid., 113). The extent of the returns will determine whether individuals' actions are contributing to increased wealth and, if returns turn out to be meagre, they have an incentive to take corrective action. Price signals and profit margins will alert agents to problems, agents then draw upon their stock of rules to decide upon a suitable course of action. The result is that agents do not waste their energy producing or supplying goods and services which are unwanted, or producing those that are wanted by using inefficient techniques. The overall result, Hayek claims, is greater wealth generation than would be the case were this knowledge not free-flowing.

It appears that the particular mode of organisation that increases society's wealth-generating power endures only because agents draw upon its structures and mechanisms in order to increase their own chances of wealth, and in the process produce and transform that mode of organisation.

On the second point, agents remain in the game of catallaxy because the rules that facilitate playing the game are in some sense acceptable. And they are acceptable for two reasons. First, rules are, typically, known tacitly, in the sense that agents know 'how' to follow the rule without necessarily knowing ('that') anything about the function of these rules. In this case agents are not conscious of even playing the game, but they must in some tacit sense be satisfied with the rules, otherwise, I suspect, they would begin to question the structure of society.

Second, the rules are acceptable when, if the game and the rules *are* reflected upon by agents, they perceive that it delivers greater opportunities than would otherwise be the case, i.e. than any other 'game'. The socio-political ideology that implies, for example, that capitalism is the only society compatible with human freedom is accepted even by those that might not do well via that system because they perceive that there is always the opportunity of advancement. Agents accept the rules, Hayek alleges, because they apply equally to all members, giving each one an equal chance of success. The rules, then, are the result of tradition and evolution. They embody the collected wisdom of a historically evolving society. Evolution selects the rules of the game, informing on those aspects of activity that society considers to be asocial.

Moreover, it appears that in an uncertain and continually changing world the only rules that can be followed are abstract or general ones. It is simply inconceivable to suggest that there can be rules so specific as to cover every eventuality. Flexibility is required. Again Hayek appears to be employing a transformational conception, whereby rules are both the condition and outcome of action.

As we noted in Chapter 8, social rules have two important characteristics: they relate not to specific but to general action and are, more often than not, limiting in the sense that they forbid certain classes of action. The rules, then, relate not to what *specific* but to what *general* action an agent may take, and often to what *general* action an agent *may not* take. As Hayek puts it:

> The rules of conduct ... are thus not designed to produce foreseen benefits for particular people, but are multi-purpose instruments developed as adaptations to certain *kinds* of environment because they help to deal with certain *kinds* of situations.
>
> (Hayek, 1976, 4; see also ibid., ch. 7; 1960 ch. 4)

> the rules which guide an individual's action are better seen as determining what he will not do rather than what he will do'.
>
> (Hayek, 1962, 57; see also 1988, 12)

The kind of rules Hayek has in mind are not of a kind that specify that a particular commodity must sell at a particular price, or that a certain distribution of income must be maintained, or that a particular bankruptcy must be avoided, and so on (1976, ch. 10). These are examples of. constructivist, i.e. consciously invented, rules.

The rules he usually has in mind are those discussed at the macro level of analytical abstraction, relating, for example, to private property rights, the discharge of legally binding contracts, or those which inform agents of the channels that may legally be used. Thus, for example, laws making illegal certain forms of 'insider dealing' assist agents to deal with uncertainty since everybody knows what type of communication is not permitted. The rules of conduct within which the catallaxy functions appear, then, as a complex web of rules of the laws of property, tort and contract, not to mention a series of tacit, unwritten rules such as integrity, honesty, keeping promises, and so on

Hayek, then, does tend to emphasise the negativity, i.e. the limiting or constraining nature, of rules, and rules discussed at the macro level of abstraction. However, although Hayek does not specify it in his elaboration of the operation of the catallaxy, agents must also be drawing upon positive, i.e. enabling, rules, and rules discussed at the micro level. Playing the game is a skilled accomplishment, and all agents, especially entrepreneurs have to be able to draw upon the range or hierarchy of rules that are often known only tacitly in order to compete. Recall the discussion in Chapter 8 of Ebling's paper on this matter.

Whilst the complex web of rules acts to decrease uncertainty in general, it will almost inevitably increase uncertainty in particular instances. Rules can only ensure that agents have the potential to interact in a potentially fruitful manner; they cannot guarantee that they will do so. This is particularly so, though at first it appears rather paradoxical, with respect to value or price. By following rules agents are able to utilise the knowledge content of prices or values and thereby decide upon a course of action that at least stands a chance of being compatible with decisions made by others. But the rules do not extend as far as stating what the price should be. According to Hayek, there are no, or ought not to be, rules that are consciously constructed, i.e. that state (in effect) 'commodity *X* must sell at £10'.

> The abstract rule of conduct can (and, in order to secure the formation of a spontaneous order, should) thus protect only the expectations of command over particular physical things and services, and not the expectations concerning their market value.
>
> (Hayek, 1978 124)

> It may at first appear paradoxical that in order to achieve the greatest attainable certainty it should be necessary to leave uncertain so important an object of expectations as the terms at which things can be bought and sold.
>
> (Ibid., 125)

This brings in the telecom system and its signalling function. Prices have a very important temporal aspect, captured in Jevons's phrase 'bygones are forever bygones' (Hayek, 1976, 121). Only current prices are important, since they inform on what action ought to be taken in the present; that is they inform on how much time, effort, resources, and so on it is currently worth putting into a product. Resources already expended cannot be recovered if, over the passage of time, conditions which we thought stable, actually change. In this case, there is a likelihood that the action will lead to disappointed expectations.

Prices, then, will very often be the 'wrong' ones, they will contain the 'wrong' information, they will in orthodox terminology be 'disequilibrium' prices. This does not mean, however, that they are of no use. In fact it is rather odd, given the thoroughly dynamic nature of socio-economic activity and the creativity of human beings, that prices could ever be conceived of as the 'right', i.e. equilibrium, prices. For example, by drawing consciously upon a range of localised knowledge of time and place, as well as a range of tacitly known social rules of conduct which enable him or her to 'go on', an entrepreneur may form an expectation that a piece of machinery will produce commodities of a certain quality, and that expectation may be explicitly underwritten by a legal contract between him and the supplier and implicitly underwritten by rules of honesty, promise-keeping, and so on. Both of these rule types will allow the entrepreneur to reduce uncertainty with regard to the eventual commodity and the actions of the supplier. Such rules, then, severely limit the scope for disappointed expectations of this type.

By contrast, however, the entrepreneur may also have an expectation that the final commodities will sell at a certain price, yet there is not, cannot be, and ought not to be a rule to ensure that his pricing expectation is not disappointed. As Ebling noted, entrepreneurs have to decide to act based upon a stock of ideal typifications. At any particular moment in time, particular entrepreneurs will constantly be formulating expectations that will be disappointed, although the overall result will be one where most entrepreneurs, most of the time, will formulate expectations that turn out to be correct.

The outcome is that, whilst following general rules, agents will have to proceed by trial and error, and this must inevitably involve a constant stream of disappointed expectations for a number of them. Only via the existence of specific uncertainty can general uncertainty be minimised. As Hayek puts it: 'The best we can attain . . . is not certainty but the elimination of avoidable uncertainty' (1976, 125).

The continual process of trial and error, disappointed expectations and the communication of failure to others triggers a process of adaptation as agents strive to correct them. Wrong expectations on the part of the individual entrepreneur, for example by acting on poor or wrong information, reading the market wrongly, making a wrong decision, or simply being unlucky, might mean that the commodity price obtained in the market is not what was expected. This will necessarily affect the firm's returns. Market-determined rewards then, are:

> incentives which as a rule guide people to success, but will produce a viable order only because they often disappoint the expectations they have caused when relevant circumstances have unexpectedly changed. It is one of the chief tasks of competition to show which plans are false.
>
> (Hayek, 1976, 117)

But, once certain plans or expectations are shown to be false, the consequences are perceived by other agents who might attempt to avoid acting on the same false expectations. As Lachmann says: 'Nobody can profitably [or, one might add, unprofitably] exploit his knowledge without conveying hints to others' (1976, 59).

As the title of one of Hayek's essays, 'Competition as a Discovery Process' (1968a), indicates, in a changing world price signals indicate not only what circumstances to exploit, but also which ones to avoid. Thus, not only price signals, but also bankruptcy and/or loss-making are as much part of the discovery process as high profits and act to inform agents of what courses of action to avoid.

That some agents will be severely harmed by this process is an unfortunate side-effect which cannot be prevented since intervention allegedly impedes the discovery, communication and storage of knowledge, and thereby impedes the wealth-creating process and harms the chances of all:

> What is required if the separate actions of individuals are to result in an overall order is that . . . in those respects in which the success of the action of the individuals depends on some matching action by others, there will be at least a good chance that this correspondence will occur. But all that rules can achieve in this respect is to make it easier for people to come together and to form that match: abstract rules cannot actually secure that this will always happen.
>
> (Hayek, 1973, 99)

> In a spontaneous order, undeserved disappointments cannot be avoided . . . It is only because countless others constantly submit to disappointments of their reasonable expectations that every one has as high an income as he has.
>
> (Hayek, 1982a, 128)

The possibility of overall spontaneous order therefore can only arise because there is continual disorder; at every point in time, some agents are inevitably in a situation of disorder in the form of having disappointed expectations.

In summary, then, Hayek appears to be arguing that agents enter the game of catallaxy with resources in the form of knowledge, for the purposes of improving their own interests. They play by drawing upon deep structures and mechanisms in the form of a hierarchy of cognitive rules, social rules and the telecom system that facilitate the discovery, communication and storage of knowledge. This ensemble of structures and mechanisms facilitates the discovery, communication and storage of the requisite knowledge to ensure that something approaching co-ordinated activity occurs. In the process of using sources, engaging mechanisms, and drawing upon structures, the socio-economy is reproduced and transformed.

The principle of order at work here appears to be the principle of reproduction and transformation of the ensemble of social structures which constitute both the conditions and outcome of market-based action. Hayek, it appears, explains order by explaining how the conditions for orderly activity endure through reproduction and transformation via production.

However, because the ability of the mechanisms and structures that facilitate the discovery, communication and storage of knowledge are far from 'perfect', co-ordination is far from perfect, efficient, optimal or some such. Activity in the market place proceeds by trial and error and therefore via the necessity of continual disappointment, generating a spontaneous socio-economic order which, whilst impossible to describe as an equilibrium or perfect co-ordination of plans, actions or consequences, is far from mere chaos.

CONCLUSION

By 1960 Hayek has abandoned his earlier subjective idealism and adopted a layered and transformative ontology, and thereby a range of categories appertaining to knowledge, ignorance and social rules of conduct. This new ontology also allows for the possibility of refocusing socio-economic inquiry away from the fused domains of the empirical and actual, and towards the domain of the deep. This encourages a shift in the mode of theorising. Socio-economic theory ceases to be concerned with the generation of constant conjunctions of events, i.e. Humean law, the deduction of consequences from axioms buttressed by assumptions, and the definition of end states via equilibria. Instead, socio-economic theory becomes an inquiry into, and explanation of, the conditions that make co-ordinated socio-economic activity possible. Hayek's theory of socio-economic order focuses upon the various resources, mechanisms and structures that are drawn upon, reproduced and transformed by agents in their attempt to co-ordinate their plans, actions and consequences.

Hayek, it appears, adopts what one might call a *transformational conception of spontaneous socio-economic order.* The conditions for socio-economic order, namely: resources in the form of knowledge; mechanisms such as the telecom system that facilitate the discovery, communication and storage of this knowledge; and structures in the form of social rules of conduct, are the ever-present condition, and the continually reproduced and transformed outcome of, market-based socio-economic action. His elaboration of the market process or catallaxy is the substantive manifestation of this transformative social ontology.

NOTES

1 INTRODUCTION

1 See Kay and Mott (1982) on feudal society; Spengler (1948) and Clark (1989) on the origin of a quest for order throughout history.

2 See especially Rubin (1990).

3 Arrow and Hahn (1971) write the following of Smith's invisible hand: 'The notion that a social system moved by independent actions in pursuit of different values is consistent with a final coherent state of balance . . . is surely one of the most important intellectual contributions that economic thought has made to the general understanding of social processes.' See also Hahn (1982), illuminatingly entitled 'Reflections on the Invisible Hand'.

4 Before claiming this novelty, a note of caution is necessary since Bosanquet has already coined the (very close) phrase, namely the 'three main phases' in Hayek's work. Bosanquet understands Hayek's thought as a 'development of consistent perceptions on a number of issues starting from a few central propositions about knowledge and behaviour. There would seem to be three main phases' (1983, 28).The first 'subjectivist' phase (1936–53) focuses upon knowledge, particularly its partial and subjective nature, psychology, the confusion arising out of the failure to differentiate clearly between the natural social sciences, collectivist planning, and the negative role of intellectuals. It also sees Hayek formulating his views on social science. The second phase (1960 to the early 1970s) focuses upon political philosophy and the law. The key theme here is freedom or liberty and how this is best preserved: by the state or by the submission to undesigned rules, conventions and traditions. The third phase appears to be marked by the volumes of *Law, Legislation and Liberty*, 1973–9 and focuses upon spontaneous order, catallaxy, social rules of conduct, the evolution defence of individualism, the negative impact on democracy, constitutional form and the dangers of inflation. Bosanquet locates the underlying shift as one from the 'minor key' of psychology to law.

Whilst Bosanquet's periodisation is quite different to the one presented in this study, I feel it is unsatisfactory. However, a detailed critique would rapidly become tangential to my concerns. Bosanquet touches on so many aspects of Hayek's work which span over fifty years in one short chapter that addressing them all would require a more substantial paper. I opt therefore to pick out a few points to indicate the main areas of disagreement. Hayek never ceases to work on psychology. He continued working in this area beyond the first phase, publishing on it in 1962, 1968, 1978 (ch. 19) and 1982a. Moreover, these contributions must not be seen as outside his social economic, political and legal work, but rather as underpinning all this by grounding human behaviour in the mind's capacity to internalise a variety of abstract rules, particularly social rules of conduct – which form the basis of Hayek III's work. Hayek's subjectivism is not grounded in his work on psychology but in his philosophy. Hayek's subjectivism does not disappear with his psychology, but changes its form: a *verstehen* approach supplants a subjective idealist one sometime in the 1960s. Although I agree that Hayek displayed a subjectivist phase, the reasons I offer are different, and I see this phase extending beyond 1953. Bosanquet never mentions philosophy, which is a serious omission not only because Hayek himself considers it extensively, but also because the failure to locate Hayek's shifts in substantive theory to underlying philosophical shifts leads to a rather superficial approach to periodising Hayek's work on the basis of listing his stated preoccupations.

Hayek's explicit argument against scientism continued in his 1955, 1961 and 1975 papers. It is also implicit every time he attacks the use of statistics in planning and it is continually mentioned as 'constructivist rationalism' in 1988. Whilst Hayek certainly did formulate 'views' on 'social science' in the first phase, the idea that these constitute 'the Hayekian views' is incorrect. There is no one 'Hayekian' view of social science; this changes considerably from the extreme subjectivism of the scientism essay to the quasi-transcendental realism of his post-1960 work.

Bosanquet's suggested second phase corresponds roughly to my Hayek III, although his preoccupation is primarily with matters of political science. However, without understanding the theory underlying the substantive work on political science, the latter remains superficially understood. Moreover, in relation to theory, the themes of knowledge and ignorance are of crucial importance, since without them one cannot grasp the *raison d'être* for social rules of conduct as devices for allegedly securing liberty: rules are the means for communicating relevant knowledge when it is possessed and for coping with ignorance when it is not. The reason for Bosanquet's (virtual) omission of the themes of knowledge and ignorance is that he appears to draw his ideas primarily from *The Constitution of Liberty*, and not from other papers written in the 1960s which are not concerned primarily with political philosophy, but with psychology, rules, evolution and order (for example, Hayek, 1964a). In trying to go straight for political matters, Bosanquet jumps over the theoretical foundations that allow these matters to be grasped in their fulness.

Bosanquet's suggested third phase is problematic partly because his previous two phases are problematic. So, for example, aspects of Hayek's subjectivism (whilst no longer of the radical kind) are still evident in the late 1970s. There are also factually incorrect claims such as that notions of taxis, cosmos, nomos and catallaxy first appear in Hayek's work in the 1970s, when they actually appear in 1967 (see Hayek, 1978, ch. 6). Whilst it is not entirely clear what is meant by the comment that Hayek's 'defence of an individualist approach' is developed 'much more strongly' (ibid., 36), I shall in any case argue that in his later work, Hayek abandons his earlier methodological individualist position. Bosanquet's claim that the third phase sees law raised to prominence above psychology is plausible, provided one recognises that psychology still plays an important theoretical underlabouring task, grounding the social rules upon which legal rules are based. Bosanquet sees psychology as a 'detour' taken in the first phase as an attempt to establish subjectivism, then abandoned. Psychology allows Hayek to develop a notion of human behaviour as rule-following and therefore as procedurally rational rather than instrumentally rational.

Whilst Bosanquet focuses upon *Law, Legislation and Liberty* as the backbone of the third phase, much of what he discusses is already contained in *The Constitution of Liberty* and various papers of the 1960s such as 1967d. The third phase might be better conceived of as a change in emphasis rather than a break with past themes, since many of the themes Bosanquet identifies as located in phases two and three are still present.

I believe the Hayek II/III periodisation is more powerful, first because it focuses upon key aspects rather than attempting to include every aspect that Hayek mentions. Second, it pursues these key aspects in more depth, ultimately grounding Hayek's substantive work in his philosophical position. It is not merely a question of my asking different questions, but of engaging a method that can establish more than superficial shifts in emphasis. I shall give one example. Whilst Bosanquet's claim that the 'thesis', by which he means the basic explanation of the socio-economic mechanisms of a market order, 'remains unchanged' (ibid., 28) is not exactly incorrect since Hayek always emphasises the efficacy of the telecom system, there is far more to it than this. After 1960 Hayek is able to show how the telecom system articulates with the network of social rules of conduct to give a far more sophisticated understanding of the operation of the catallaxy. And the development of social rules of conduct is only possible once Hayek III abandoned his previous philosophic position and adopted something that I style a quasi-transcendental realist philosophy.

5 For a defence of this sweeping statement and a critical realist critique of (i) econometrics, see Lawson (1989a and b, 1995); and (ii) of formalism in general, see Sayer (1991, chs 4 and 6).

6 For an elaboration of Hayek's positivism, see Lawson (1994c, 1995a).

7 'I myself originally approached my subject [i.e. social science] thoroughly imbued with the belief in the universal validity of the methods of the natural sciences. Not only was my first technical training largely scientific in the narrow sense of the word but also what little training I had in philosophy or method was entirely in the school of Ernst Mach and later of the logical positivists' (Hayek, 1942b, 57–8). In 1964, Hayek describes himself in the pre-1936 period as a 'very pure and narrow economic theorist' dealing with 'technical economics' (1964a, 91).

8 The link between positivism (i.e. empirical realist ontology) and the use of equilibrium will be discussed in Chapter 10.

2 PHILOSOPHY

1 Since metaphysics includes far more topics than will be discussed in this book, after elaborating its meaning and significance I shall not use the term, opting to retain the more general term 'philosophy'.

2 According to Bhaskar: 'in the absence of the concept of an ontological realism, the implicit realism generated implies that whatever is experienced in sense experience is an event and whatever constant conjunctions are experienced are causal laws' (1978, 42).

3 In fact Kant, rejecting what he calls 'material idealism', contrasts his own position to the 'dogmatic idealism of Berkeley' and the 'problematic idealism of Descartes' (Beck, 1988, 122). Thus Kant, unlike the solipsist, has no problem in accepting the existence of an external world: he only doubts our ability to know it. I note this to highlight the fact that there are numerous versions of idealism, so that later, when I claim that Hayek is a subjective idealist, it will not implicitly be presumed that this refers to Berkeleyan idealism or even solipsism. To repeat the point for emphasis, *subjective idealism does not imply the denial of the external world.*

4 Throughout this book, unless otherwise stated, the term 'epistemology' will refer to the derivation of knowledge, that is how knowledge can be derived, when the object of that knowledge remains unknowable, a Kantian preoccupation. This is

distinct from the neo-Kantian preoccupations of either (a) what is to count as knowledge (Vienna Circle); or (b) the reliability to claims of knowledge (confirmation and falsification). See Hamlyn, 1987, 21–3; Parsons, 1990, 296–9; and Stern, 1990, ch. 1, for elaboration of the Kantian version of epistemology; and Caldwell, 1991, chs 2 and 3, for neo-Kantian versions.

5 I shall return to this later in the chapter, but wish to emphasise the importance of understanding what is meant by subject idealism and the claim that the subject structures the object. If this is not understood, the description of Hayek II as a subjective idealist is apt to be misinterpreted.

6 Smith and Nyiri (1990, 271) agree.

7 Note that these terms and categories are not always Hayek's own. In fact many of them appear to be unknown to him. They are necessary, however, in discussion of the requisite philosophical issues.

8 Social entities such as rules are in fact known to agents in a rather special way, requiring an understanding of the difference between knowing 'how' and knowing 'that'. This cannot, however, be developed until Chapter 7.

3 THE PHILOSOPHY UNDERLYING HAYEK II's SOCIO-ECONOMIC THEORY

1 I strongly suggest that if the reader is unsure of what is meant either by the term artifact, or by the claim that subjective idealism involves the subject structuring the object, the section entitled 'Clarification of categories and terminology' in Chapter 2 is re-read.

2 See also Hayek (1942b), especially section 2.

3 It can actually be interpreted in three ways, if the possibility is included that there is nothing wrong with Hayek's argument, that is, he opts to remove the external domain from the interest field of the social scientist, but could replace this domain if we wished. I shall attempt to show indirectly, however, that this interpretation cannot be sustained.

4 Marx, for example uses the notion of commodity fetishism to ascertain why and how certain phenomena actually appear to agents in an inverted form. Their misconception becomes a subject for inquiry. Commodity fetishism forms a central part of Marx's *economics*; it is not an esoteric, sociological side-issue.

5 Mark Peacock (1993) uses the policeman as an example of Hayek's transcendental realism in that the latter appears to display a relational conception of social structure. I think Peacock overlooks the fact that what Hayek refers to as 'structures' turn out to be merely conceptions held by agents. Thus, whilst Hayek II holds a relational conception, it is a relation between ideas. It is based, therefore, upon extremely subjective social theory, subjective-idealist ontology, and therefore cannot be cited as an example of transcendental realism.

6 Note that this is claiming far more than the obviously true point that the mind is involved in cognition.

7 See Lawson (1994c) for similar comments on this matter.

8 Whilst it would be useful for purposes of exposition to elaborate upon Hayek's cognitive psychology at this point, it would break the flow of the thesis, since it is dealt with in depth in Chapter 8.

9 Herrman-Pillath (1992) even goes so far as to suggest that the relations between neurons or linkages are weeded out by natural selection to become 'the conceptual equivalent of the re-interpretation of Kantian a priori categories . . . Referring to Hayek, (1952, 71), Agonito suggests that: 'What we have here is an open-ended set of Kant's categories, neurologically specified (Agonito 1975, 165). After a brief

discussion of Hayek (1952), Gray (1984, 7) writes of 'Hayek's Kantianism, so prominent in his theory of knowledge'. According to Kukhatas (1989, 5): 'Hayek's thought is Kantian in its denial of our capacity to know things as they are or the world as it is. It is in this denial that we can know things as they are, and his insistence that the order we find in our experiences, including even our sensory experiences, is the product of the creative activity of our minds rather than a reality given to us by the world that Hayek's Kantianism consists. It follows from this sceptical Kantian standpoint that the task of philosophy cannot be that of uncovering the necessary character of things.'

4 THE METHODOLOGY UNDERLYING HAYEK II's SOCIO-ECONOMIC THEORY

1 I shall not be concerned here with the traditional debates on Hayek's methodology that focused upon Hayek as a praxeologist (Barry, 1979; Hutchison, 1981; Gray, 1985; Caldwell, 1984, 1988; Pheby, 1988); Hayek as a Popperian and/or falsificationist (Hutchison, 1981; Gray, 1985; Barry, 1979, 1981); Hayek as a hypothetical deductivist (Nishiyama, 1979). Neither shall I comment upon more recent claims such as: Hayek as Aristotelian (Smith, 1986b; Smith and Nyiri, 1990); Hayek as Anti-Constructivist (Paque, 1990).

2 See 'Clarification of categories' in Chapter 2 for a definition.

3 Kuninski uses Hayek's notion of the similarity of the structure of minds (noted in the previous chapter) to show two things. First, he shows that Hayek's 'early writings' (1942 to 1952) display what he refers to as 'Cartesian verstehen'. The Cartesian element lies in the 'false conception [that] the direct knowledge of our mental events (and minds) which are then projected or read into other people's minds under the assumptions of their similarity' (1992, 353). Second, he shows that Hayek undergoes a 'hermeneutical shift' (ibid.) to adopt a hermeneutic version of *verstehen* whereby the 'understanding of other people's actions is based . . . upon our perception of a rule governing that action' (ibid., 358). Whilst Kuninski does not explore the possibility of hermeneutic foundationalism, the fact that he perceives a shift away from a notion of Cartesian dualism strengthens my claim that Hayek II adopts a subjective idealist epistemology. As Hamlyn (1987, 17) puts it:

> what is fundamentally wrong is . . . the thought introduced by Descartes that we have direct access only to ideas or mental representations. Since these do not constitute a reality of public and physical objects, they can be thought of as a realm of appearances only. Idealism stems from this with the additional thought that, since we do not have access to anything beyond ideas, the only reality which we have any justification in assuming is those ideas . . . [I]dealism is the only rational position for one who embraces the distinction between appearance and reality on the Cartesian basis.

4 See Hayek's discussion of the theory of rent (1942a, 282–3).

5 See Nishiyama (1964, 113–18).

6 It will be noted (in passing) in the next chapter that Hayek does discuss what he refers to as explanation in his 1941 book (ch. 2). However, here he appears (arguably incorrectly) to equate explanation to some form of deduction via causal sequences. He suggests that if events turn out differently from what the entrepreneur expected, provided we know the direction of the difference, we can deduce the entrepreneurs' action (1941, 23).

7 The section entitled 'Hayek's philosophical position in natural sciences' in Chapter 3 also argues that Hayek accepts a Humean conception of law.

8 In the ensuing exposition, I shall break the Hayek II/III periodisation and draw upon a paper from 1961. This is not actually an abrogation of my thesis on Hayek II and III, primarily because the point I wish to make turns on Hayek II adopting (a version) of Humean law which he does not abandon even after 1960.

9 Pareto arguably captures the dominant ideas when he writes: 'Human actions present certain uniformities, and it is only thanks to this property that they can be studied scientifically. These uniformities have another name; one calls them laws' (1966, 15).

10 Since my task is primarily to ascertain Hayek's approach to the matter, I shall not offer an elaboration of this controversial area which has traditionally touched upon the following defining characteristics of methodological individualism: the recognition that only individual agents but not wholes have (a) existence, and (b) purpose; the irrelevance of social structures; the usefulness of psychology in investigating economic behaviour; individual and purposive action as the causal steam driving the socio-economic engine; and that wholes are reducible to parts. See Hodgson (1988, ch. 3); see also Nozick (1977).

11 See Chapter 3, the sub-section entitled 'How science establishes the possibility of knowing the object', where I discussed incorrigibility with respect to natural science and re-classification.

12 Recall Chapter 2, the section entitled 'Empirical realism'.

5 THE IMPLICATION OF HAYEK II's PHILOSOPHY AND METHOD FOR HIS SOCIO-ECONOMIC THEORY

1 Note the tension here between objective and subjective facts. In 1936, Hayek claims both that knowledge is about objective existents and also about what agents merely 'believe to exist'. By 1942 this tension is overcome by Hayek's removal of objective, mind-independent phenomena from the interest field of the economist. This indicates that Hayek's shift towards subjective idealism occurs after 1936 and before 1942. Certainly the 1942a paper is far more subjectivist than the 1936 paper.

2 Whilst Hayek does not explicitly mention this in 1936, it is implied since he does think agents come to see the objective world in similar terms. Whilst he does not attempt to explain this until 1942, and again in 1952, we must note that the latter work was drafted in the 1920s. The implication is that Hayek was aware of the 'similarity of minds' argument even in 1936.

3 O'Driscoll and Rizzo (1985) also recognise the heterogeneity of knowledge, noting five characteristic features which (with the exception of their characteristic of surprise) are subsumed under my five agent–knowledge headings.

4 So adequate that Desai has recently remarked that the 'problem of knowledge is a non-problem . . . Hayek discovered by 1945 that the problem was solved by the price system' (1994, 49). Arguably Desai's acceptance of Hayek II's exaggerated claims for the telecom system, and his neglect of Hayek III's more sociological work leads him to close the argument before it has really begun. It is one of the tasks of this thesis to show that Hayek gradually becomes aware that the telecom system cannot single handedly solve the 'knowledge problem', hence the need for social structures in the form of social rules of conduct.

5 This matter will be returned to in more depth in Chapter 10.

6 A recent paper by Desai (1994) entitled 'Equilibrium, Expectations and Knowledge' looks closely at Hayek's notion of equilibrium in the period from the late 1920s to 1945. Desai illustrates some of the conceptual difficulties Hayek wrestles with.

7 It has little to say about the agent–knowledge relations discussed in the preceding section.
8 The term 'reality' is used here in a common-sense way, and carries none of the philosophical connotations discussed in earlier chapters.
9 Littlechild (1982) would profoundly disagree with the argument put forward here. He claims that in his 1936 paper Hayek sketches out two alternative research programmes: the first entails an elaboration of the market process and the conditions for convergence to equilibrium; the second focuses upon the existence and efficacy of equilibrium. He then goes on to claim that Hayek opts for the second research programme. Now this is indeed a remarkable and incorrect claim – as this book will show. It is possible, however, that the source of Littlechild's error lies in his failure to spot any development in Hayek's work. Thus, all his references (with one exception) are to Hayek II's work, where as noted above, due to ambivalence, Hayek could be construed as retaining some notion of equilibrium. This simply cannot be sustained if Hayek post-1960 is considered. This is a good example of the necessity to periodise Hayek's work. The 'one exception' is taken from Hayek's 1970 paper, where he claims that mathematical techniques have been useful. Whilst this cannot be elaborated upon here, Littlechild merely appears to be trading upon the odd comments made by Hayek that suggest a neoclassical bent.
10 Desai (1994, 48) might have a point in his observation that after posing a number of serious questions on knowledge and the tendency towards equilibrium, 'in the end Hayek's commitment to the price system overrides his analytical doubts'.
11 See also Hayek (1945, 525, 527; 1946, 100; 1968a, 185; 1976, 116; 1978, 302; 1988, 76, 95–9).
12 On p. 72 I cited one example from 1945. The following example is drawn from the post-1960 period simply because it is the clearest one available. It does not affect the periodisation adopted here because Hayek retained the often-exaggerated and ambiguous claims for the role and efficacy of the telecom system throughout his career.
13 I have edited this comment slightly to make the point more succinct – since it spans two pages.
14 This argument was suggested by Bruce Caldwell, commenting on an earlier draft.
15 Nowhere does Hayek advance a thoroughly subjectivist theory of value along the lines of Menger, Thirlby or, more recently, Buchanan, as Streissler (1994) and Vaughan (1980) suggest. In fact, Buchanan (1969a) criticises Hayek for not being sufficiently subjective in his treatment of value and cost.

6 HAYEK III's QUASI-TRANSCENDENTAL REALIST PHILOSOPHY

1 Whilst I wish to claim that Hayek approaches transcendental realism, I do not wish to overstate the case. There are certain quite crucial aspects of transcendental and critical realism that Hayek cannot embrace. If we were to give the major obstacle to Hayek's embracing transcendental realism in full, it would have to be that he does not abandon the use of Humean law. As was illustrated in Chapter 4, he does not abandon this notion of law, he simply allows it to operate within loose tolerances. Transcendental realism's assault on all aspects of empiricism begins with the rejection of Humean law, replacing it with a notion of law (social or natural) as the existence of a power or disposition to act, or (in more essentialist–realist terms) as the manifestation of an entity's essence. Hayek simply cannot get

anywhere near this type of conception, and so cannot fully embrace what one might call the 'heart' of transcendental realism.

2 There have been attempts made recently to locate (at least parts of the work of) a number of economists who, typically, do not fall into the category of 'mainstream' under the rubric of critical realism. For example: N. Kaldor (Lawson, 1989b), Marx (Pratten, 1993) A. Marshall (Pratten 1994), J. Commons (C. Lawson 1994), post-Keynesians in general (Lawson, 1994b), Hayek (Peacock, 1993).

3 Ontological matters were the preoccupation of Aristotelian-inspired philosophy, which went out of fashion after Spinoza, Marx and Engels.

4 Bhaskar (1978, chs 1, 2 and postscript); Collier (1994, ch. 2) and Lawson (1994a).

5 Note that *empirical* realism implicitly recognises the domains of the empirical and the actual, although it fuses them so that what is given in sense experience is what is.

6 Recall (Chapter 2) that Hayek's notion of 'complex phenomenon' leads to his rejection of the notion of constant conjunctions of events – although his rejection, grounded as it is in epistemology, not ontology, is not the same as the rejection formulated by transcendental realism.

7 If this is unclear, refer to the section entitled 'Clarification of categories and terminology', in Chapter 2.

8 He also shifts his attention away from individuals to the overall social order of actions. This is perhaps best illustrated by his emphasis upon group as opposed to individual selection in evolutionary theory – although I shall not deal with this topic.

9 Reification refers to the notion that society exists independently of human action. Put bluntly, agents' actions are merely the result of their being buffeted by social structures. Schematically: structures →(create)→ agents actions.

10 'Voluntarist' here refers to the notion that agents merely produce society in their actions. Not only are constraints on action taken seriously, structures that enable action are also ignored. Schematically: agents' actions →(create)→ structures.

11 'Dialectical' here refers to the notion of reciprocal causality where agents' action causes structure, which then causes agents action and so on. Schematically: agents' actions →(create)→ structures →(create)→ agents' actions →, and so on. On this, see Bhaskar (1989a, 27–44).

12 This is, actually, to claim that the mode of inference switches from deduction to *retroduction*. For a comparison of deduction and retroduction, see Lawson (1994), and for an elaboration of retroduction, see Collier (1994, 160–7).

13 This will be elaborated in Chapter 10.

7 KNOWLEDGE, IGNORANCE AND SOCIAL RULES OF CONDUCT

1 What this 'special sense' entails will be developed later in the chapter.

2 The term 'relative spatio-temporal co-ordination' is used here to signify that any co-ordination that does occur within the socio-economic system is not perfect, optimal or total, but only approximate. For brevity, however, I shall simply use the term 'co-ordination' to mean its relative form unless otherwise stated.

3 Knowledge and ignorance are, of course, always about something: agents cannot possess knowledge or be ignorant *per se*. To claim that agents possess knowledge is to claim that they possess knowledge of some thing, event or state of affairs and thereby to claim by implication that they are ignorant of other things . . . (and so on). To claim that an agent possesses knowledge invites me to state (a) exactly this knowledge consists of, and (b) exactly what the agent is ignorant of. In the

context of an investigation into Hayek's notion of socio-economic order and thereby co-ordination of plans, we are concerned with the quality and quantity of knowledge of things (and so on) produced, acquired and communicated by and between agents for the purpose of formulating plans that co-ordinate with the plans of others. I shall refer to the quality and quantity of knowledge necessary for this purpose as *requisite* knowledge. This avoids the necessity of continually specifying (a) and (b) above; an impossible task anyway, because they are different in each context. Similarly, the term ignorance does not imply that agents are totally ignorant of all things, merely that they do not possess the *requisite* knowledge. That is, agents are not in possession of the quality and quantity of knowledge of things (and so on) necessary for the purpose of formulating a plan that co-ordinates with the plans of others. I deliberately avoid Hayek's term 'relatively ignorant' (in the epigraph), since this implies that agents have partial knowledge of the thing (and so on) in question, when in fact I shall want to deny that they possess any requisite knowledge of the thing (and so on) in question. Once this is understood, phraseology such as 'agents possess requisite knowledge' or 'agents are ignorant' can be used without continually specifying what it is that they possess or are ignorant of.

4 Hayek (1988, 139) notes the linguistic difficulties surrounding the term knowledge.

5 Boehm (1989, 211); Hodgson (1989, 6–7, 108–9); Lachman (1988, ch. 3) and Ioannides (1992, 36–7) have all noted that knowledge and information are not quite the same thing, although only Lachman has attempted an elaboration. Whilst Lachman's comments are interesting, his ultra-subjectivist approach differs from Hayek's, making his elaboration problematic in assisting an interpretation of Hayek. Hayek's rare comments on the matter do not really clarify matters either. For example, he writes:

> When we spoke of the transmission and communication of knowledge, we meant to refer to the two aspects of the process of civilisation . . . [namely] the transmission in time of our accumulated stock of knowledge and the communication among contemporaries of information on which to base their action.
>
> (Hayek, 1960, 27)

Does Hayek really mean to imply that the distinction between knowledge and information is that knowledge is communicated across time, whereas information is communicated between agents? I doubt that this distinction is what he wants to maintain. His concern here is really with issues of tradition, not with concerns of distinguishing knowledge from information, and it is therefore misleading to infer things about the latter from this sort of comment.

It is, however, probably more in keeping with common usage of the terms to use knowledge to refer to a relation between a human agent and an object, event or state of affairs such that the agent uses the faculty of understanding and prior knowledge to transform some sense data into knowledge. At this point the agent may be said to possess knowledge. Information, on this common understanding, is used to refer to the form in which the sense data is transmitted or communicated. But even this is not so clear-cut. The information, the sense data, is itself knowledge in the process of being communicated. If, for example, the Meteorological Office knows that it will rain tomorrow and they issue a weather bulletin, then lay agents come to know that it will rain tomorrow. The weather bulletin contains, and can thereby communicate, knowledge. Does it enhance our understanding to claim that the weather bulletin contains and communicates information? Irrespective, then, of the merits of this argument, and countless others like it, it is quite obvious that we get rather quickly into a complex debate about these categories. Moreover, this is not a debate that adds significantly to the arguments presented in this book. Rather than go off on a possibly fruitless tangent, I shall follow Boehm (1989, 211), who does not see the distinction as very important, and use the term knowledge to include information. This might in any case be close to Hayek's understanding, since for most of the time he uses the terms virtually interchangeably. For example in his 1945 paper, 'The Use of Knowledge in Society', he writes in one place of 'communicating all this knowledge', followed a couple of sentences later by 'communicating to him such further information' (Hayek, 1945, 524–5).

6 Whilst recognising that local non-tacit knowledge is an important (and under-researched) source of knowledge for social action, no more will be said about it. Tacit knowledge will be the focus of attention instead.

7 There are similarities here between Hayek's notion of the knowledge of circumstances and Alfred Marshall's notion of the 'atmosphere' of 'industrial districts' (1923, 284–5; see also 1947, ch. 10). These categories refer to the spatial organisation of knowledge within which each firm operates. Referring explicitly to Marshallian competition as a 'Hayekian discovery process', Loasby (1989, 55) succinctly sums up the importance of the spatial organisation of knowledge that characterises Marshallian competition:

> The second factor [that facilitates a more intimate connection between producing units] is the concentration, not just of single industries, but often of clusters of industries in particular localities . . . Each locality develops a 'special industrial atmosphere' in which the inhabitants unconsciously absorb the aptitudes which its industries require. Moreover, within an industrial district, it is easier for each firm to create the network of personal contacts which will give it the confidence to integrate its activities with others – relying perhaps as much on moral sentiments as financial incentives. As Richardson was to remind us, personal contact is especially important when goods and services are not standardized. This network also forms an invisible college, which fosters the development, appraisal, and application of new ideas.
>
> (Ibid., 59)

Note, however, that Marshall explored neither the social structures in the form of rules of conduct that facilitate the discovery, acquisition and communication of knowledge, or tacit knowledge. And it is these two notions that take Hayek's understanding of knowledge beyond that of Marshall. For a discussion of the possibility of Marshall as a critical realist, see Pratten, (1994).

8 This is a contentious area, although one that I shall not discuss in this book. Cf. Herrman-Pillath (1992); Hodgson (1991), Vanberg (1986).

9 I think what is most difficult to accept in the claim that rules embody knowledge is the fact that knowledge is of, or about, some thing or object, it is not itself a thing or object. In this case, then, knowledge cannot be embodied in a rule because this makes knowledge a thing or object. By claiming to have knowledge of a rule, we end up claiming to have knowledge of knowledge and this sounds absurd. If, however, we use the distinction between knowledge and information, then claim that rules contain information, it does not sound absurd to claim that we have knowledge of information. Whilst this does admittedly sound better, it is not easy to say why it is better, since the distinction between knowledge and information is not a clear-cut one. Ignoring the distinction, then, consider the following example. If a friend possesses knowledge that commodity *X* is available at a lower

price in Liverpool than in Cambridge and communicates this knowledge to me by writing a letter, can it not be said that the letter contains knowledge? And if so, then upon my reading the letter, I have knowledge of knowledge. The peculiarity of all this lies in the fact that in this case, and in this case only, the object of knowledge (rule) is itself tied up with knowledge (it embodies it). One therefore has knowledge of an object, and this object is itself a container of knowledge. This does not occur with other objects of knowledge. For example, one can have knowledge that grass is green, and since green grass is not tied up with knowledge there is no problem. I submit that the difficulties here are semantic, having more to do with the peculiarity of the case in point and perhaps the lack of a clear-cut distinction between knowledge and information than with the underlying argument.

10 This is well known in labour process theory. Cf. Kusterner (1978) and the collection of essays in Wood (1989), especially the one by Jones.

8 RULES AND THE COGNITIVE PSYCHOLOGY UNDERPINNING RULE-FOLLOWING

1 For a detailed summary of Hayek's cognitive psychology, see Hayek in Weimer and Palermo (1982, ch. 12); Weimer (ibid., ch. 13); Agonito (1975); and for an extremely erudite and concise summary, see Runde in Earl (1985, 119–20). The latest contribution is Vries (1994).

2 See Chapter 4 'The goal of social science, 2: explanation' and Hayek's curious attachment to the Humean notion of scientific law.

3 See Hodgson (1988, 110) on the mind as a multi-layered hierarchy.

4 Smith (1995) has noted the similarity between Hayek's (and Hebb's) pioneering work in cognitive psychology and developments in connectionism which appear to underpin recent developments in neural network modelling.

5 All social rules of conduct, as well as the meta-conscious rules of the mind, are of course abstract and general – this is what distinguishes rules from commands. Any variation is in terms of the degree of abstractness or generality.

6 Note that the terms micro and macro do not involve any aggregation, as is perhaps the norm in economics. Usage is more in keeping with sociology, where the differentiation is between small- and large-scale social interaction.

7 Recall the comments quoted in Chapter 1 where Hayek is laying out his multidisciplinary credentials.

8 In a paper entitled 'Tacit Knowledge in Managerial Success', Wagner and Sternberg (1987) develop a model of managerial tacit knowledge that is in part what I have been driving at with Ebling's ideal types. They appear to be getting down to the semi-conscious processes that managers are continually drawing upon in order to initiate any kind of managerial action. To give one example: 'Tacit knowledge with a *pragmatic* orientation . . . is knowing when you should politely decline an invitation to do something that you have no time to do'.

9 THE ARTICULATION BETWEEN SOCIAL RULES OF CONDUCT AND THE TELECOMMUNICATIONS SYSTEM

1 O'Driscoll and Rizzo do not, however, build upon their recognition of the necessity of rules as Hayek does. In a paper entitled 'Subjectivism, Uncertainty and Rules', rules are dealt with in half a page. Even in their book they are more

concerned to extol the virtues of rule-following over continuously maximising choice at the margin (1985, 119–22).

2 A similar argument could, I think, be formulated by considering the work of other Austrians, for example, Garrison (1982, esp. 133); High (1986, esp. 117); Littlechild (1982). See also Kirzner (1982b). What all these commentators lack is anything like Hayek's notion of social rules of conduct. They are then forced into overplaying or exaggerating the efficacy of whatever mechanisms they suggest are responsible for order. Vaughan, in places, gets closest to Hayek but even she cannot quite see the efficacy of social rules (Vaughan, 1982, esp. 23).

3 One of the best examples of overplaying the hand is given by O'Driscoll, who, in a book entitled *Economics as a Coordination Problem* (1977), writes: 'The missing link . . . is the mechanism that tends to bring decisions into closer correspondence: the price system. Hayek, in a classic metaphor, suggested that "we look at the price system . . . as a mechanism for communicating information if we want to understand its real function". The price system is the mechanism to be focused on in a study of the co-ordination problem.' Note that the quote from Hayek is from his 1945 paper; the mature Hayek has moved way beyond this narrow economic purview, as the next chapter will demonstrate.

10 HAYEK III's TRANSFORMATIONAL CONCEPTION OF SPONTANEOUS SOCIO-ECONOMIC ORDER

1 I introduced this with the TMSA in Chapter 6, but will elaborate upon it more fully in the course of this chapter.

2 Let me deal with a possible critical response to this *modus operandi*. One could object that if Hayek does not advance such a claim, then I have no right to advance one for him. I reject this on two counts. First, advancing such a claim is quite legitimate if it improves our understanding of how socio-economic order occurs. Since this book is not an exercise in the history of economic thought, I have no hesitation in going beyond Hayek's rhetoric if need be. Second, however, there does appear to be enough ideas implicit in Hayek's work to suggest that he is presupposing something similar to a transformational conception. Even if, then, I am going beyond Hayek, I am doing so on the basis of some very strong clues left by him.

3 Oliver is a philosopher cited by Hayek (1964b).

4 There are, of course, many diverse notions of equilibrium (and its close relative disequilibrium) within mainstream economics. Weintraub (1986) usefully discusses: Walrasian equilibrium and disequilibrium; Edgworthian equilibrium and disequilibrium; the macroeconomic equilibrium of the Z–D and IS/LM models, and the more general notion of General Systems Theory. The notion of equilibrium is also used in Sraffian-influenced Marxian economics.

5 I shall not elaborate upon the *spontaneous* nature of the socio-economic order or the comments on Taxis and Cosmos (Hayek, 1973, ch. 2), because the point Hayek is making is moot. The argument that the Great Society is the result of human design (at least in terms of nineteenth- and twentieth-century thought) is an argument without an opponent. As Kukhatas puts it: 'There can surely be no doubt the Hegel and Marx did not think of society as the product of conscious design' (1989, 208; see also ch. 6.2). See also Diamond (1980) for a discussion of Hayek's ambiguous notion of constructivism.

6 Recall the discussions of empirical realism in Chapter 2, and the transcendental realist notion of a structured ontology in Chapter 6.

7 Note that the move into statistical theory does not overcome the problem that

event regularities cannot be discovered outside the (theoretically) closed system. The 'Whenever event *X* then event *Y*' format is essentially the same as the 'Whenever event *X* then event *Y* on average' format. Stochastic closure is still closure. On closure, see Lawson 1989a.

8 According to Dow, GE theory 'abstracts from intractable aspects of reality to provide a watertight rigorous framework for analysis of those aspects which are tractable. . . . [It] is not clear how one translates a statement expressed in terms of a GE model into a statement about a world which it does not describe. The precision refers to the model, not the economic events which reflect theoretically intractable elements' (1985, 123).

9 Coordination might relate to a partial equilibrium context, or more importantly for the purposes of this book, i.e. investigating the notion of socio-economic order, to a general equilibrium context. Recall the initial discussion of equilibrium in Chapter 5, where I refer to Hahn's suggestion that GE theory is really a theory of order.

10 This generic equilibrium state could be rephrased in terms of agents' plans rather than actions, might or might not involve a set of market-clearing prices; or be extended to a situation where the action of one actually does frustrate the outcome of the other but for some reason neither has a tendency to change their expectations or actions.

11 Whilst it is true that notions of *process* can be used without adopting critical realism, many such uses are, upon closer scrutiny, quite vacuous. Fisher, for example, claims the following equation 'characterises the *process* known as tatonnement' (1989, 20–3):

$$P_i = F^i\,[Z_i(P)]$$

P_i is the price of the *i*th commodity, Z_i is the total excess demand, and $F^i(.)$ is a continuous sign preserving function (*sic*). He explains this as follows: '[T]he price of the *i*th commodity adjusts in the same direction as the excess demand for that commodity, the exact adjustment being a continuous function of the excess demand (and therefore price).' Whilst the notion (or metaphor) of tatonnement is no doubt intended to refer to the market processes involved in the formation of socio-economic order, the reduction of these multidimensional processes to (a) a relation between price and quantity, and (b) the one dimension of an equation is banal – although absolutely necessary if the positivist economist is to *close the system*. We only have to compare this notion of process against the quasi-critical realist notion of market process elaborated by Hayek to understand that describing the former as a process is misleading and vacuous.

12 Note the similarity here between positivist economics and positivist natural science. Recall Chapter 3, where Hayek II treats 'atomic structures' and 'magnetic fields' as merely conceptual constructs, aids to theorising.

13 Drawing no more than the logic of a recognition of the truly dynamic nature of the economy, Kregel writes: 'If individuals generate information through their actions rather than just acquiring it, there is no reason for expectations to converge' (1986, 163). In a similar vein, Vaughan criticises Kirzner's vision of co-ordinating entrepreneur action: 'The problem with this argument, however, is that it fails to supply arguments about why entrepreneurs in an uncertain world should on balance be correct enough to drive the system towards equilibrium. If the data are constantly changing, what does equilibrium mean anyway?' (1992, 259).

14 Paque, who understands that Hayek is concerned with processes, cannot break free of the mind set of equilibrium. He writes: 'Austrian economics focuses on the *process* of moving towards a dynamic equilibrium in the Hayekian sense.' He then adds: 'A system of interdependent markets is regarded as a social institution

that generates new information and thus allows market participants to gradually improve their knowledge and correct prior errors . . . [This] has been a recurrent theme in Hayek's writings' (Paque, 1985, 421). Arguably, this kind of misunderstanding of Hayek's rejection of equilibrium is encouraged by an historic treatment of Hayek's work that allows a thinker like Paque to take bits and pieces from Hayek's work irrespective of the time of writing and assemble them in a way that appears coherent. What Hayek wrote on equilibrium in the 1940s, however, is simply not applicable to his work of the 1960s and beyond.

15 This is sufficient to violate a key requirement of mathematics, namely that the variable under consideration does not change in the act of computation – algebraic or empirical. In critical-realist language we could say that the variable is intrinsically closed, i.e. its internal state is completely defined and unchanging in the course of computation. As Sayer, drawing upon Georgescu-Roegen, observes:

> Only if the objects are qualitatively invariant is the order in which we measure or change them irrelevant. The transformation of coal into ashes or the socialization of a child are irreversible processes involving qualitative change . . . [If] the objects referred to by the variables of an equation interact in a way which produces qualitative change (for example, through a learning process), the variables will not be able to make stable reference.
>
> (Sayer, 1992, 177)

The transformational nature of social being, of course, means that a mathematical treatment of Hayek's notion of spontaneous socio-economic order is quite impossible.

16 In a paper illuminatingly entitled 'Cognition, Competition and Catallaxy', Streit (1993) presents an argument that in many ways resembles that put forward in this book – although there are also many differences. Streit's main point is that Hayek's epistemology and cognitive psychology provide the foundations upon which his analysis of the socio-economic phenomena are based. Issues of knowledge (particularly its limitations) and rule-following behaviour, then, are seen as inextricably linked to the operation of the catallaxy.

17 Note that Hayek does not discuss anything like Bhaskar's notion of positioned practices, a feature that is necessary to complete the understanding of the TMSA by establishing a relational conception of sociology. Bhaskar defines the positioned-practices notion as

> a system of mediating concepts . . . designating the 'slots', as it were, in the social structure into which active subjects slip in order to reproduce it; that is, a system of concepts designating the 'point of contact' between human agency and social structure. Such a point . . . must both endure and be immediately occupied by individuals. It is clear that the mediating system we need is that of positions (places, functions, rules, tasks, duties, rights, and so on) occupied . . . by individuals, and of the practices (activities, and so on) in which in virtue of their occupancy of these positions . . . they engage . . . [R]elations . . . hold between the positioned-practices, not between the individuals who occupy them.
>
> (Bhaskar, 1989a, 40–1)

This is one example of Hayek's inability to embrace the TMSA fully, thereby demonstrating the correctness of the ascription 'quasi- TMSA'.

18 Hayek (1976, ch. 10; and 1968a). See also O'Driscoll and Rizzo (1985, 95).

BIBLIOGRAPHY

Note: To allow the historical development of Hayek's thought to be readily seen, dates of his work refer to either the date of its conference presentation or of publication, whichever is the earlier.

Addleston, M. (1986) 'Radical Subjectivism and Austrian Economics', in Kirzner.

Agonito, Y. (1975) 'Hayek Re-visited: Mind as a Process of Classification', *Behaviourism* 3(2).

Arrow, K. and Hahn, F. (1971) *General Competitive Analysis*, New York: Holden-Day.

Bacharach, M. (1989) 'The Role of Verstehen in Economic Theory', *Ricerche Economiche*, 42, 1–2.

Bakhurst, R. (1991) *Consciousness and Revolution in Soviet Philosophy: From the Bolsheviks to Evad Ilyenkov*, Cambridge: Cambridge University Press.

Barry, N. (1979) *Hayek's Social and Economic Philosophy*, London: Macmillan.

—— (1984) *Hayek's Serfdom Re-visited: Essays by Economists, Philosophers and Political Scientists*, London: Institute of Economic Affairs.

Beck, L. (1988) *Kant: Selections*, London: Macmillan.

Bhaskar, R. (1978) *A Realist Theory of Science*, Brighton, Sussex: Harvester Wheatsheaf.

—— (1989a) *The Possibility of Naturalism*, Brighton, Sussex: Harvester Wheatsheaf.

—— (1989b) *Reclaiming Reality: A Critical Introduction to Contemporary Philosophy*, London: Verso.

Birner, J. and Van Zijp, R. (1994) *Hayek, Co-ordination and Evolution*, London: Routledge.

—— (1994) 'Hayek and Knowledge: Some Question Marks'.

Boehm, S. (1989) 'Hayek on Knowledge, Equilibrium and Prices: Context and Impact', *Wirtschafts Politische Blatter*, 2.

—— (1994) 'Hayek and Knowledge', in Colona and Hageman (eds) (1994).

Boetke, P., Horowitz, S. and Prychitko, D. (1986) 'Beyond Equilibrium Analysis: Reflections on the Uniqueness of the Austrian Tradition', *Market Process* 4 (fall).

Bosanquet, N. (1983) *After the New Right*, London: Heinemann.

Buchanan, J. (1969a) *Cost and Choice*, Markham Publishing.

—— (1969b) 'Is Economics the Science of Choice?', in Streissler (1969).

Butler, E. (1983) *Hayek: His Contribution to the Political and Economic Thought of Our Time*, London: Temple Smith.

Butos, W. (1985) 'Hayek and General Equilibrium Analysis', *Southern Economic Journal* 52 (October).

Caldwell, B.(1984) 'Praxeology and its Critics: an Appraisal', *History of Political Economy* 16(3).

—— (1988) 'Hayek's Transformation', *History of Political Economy* 20(4).
—— (1990) *Carl Menger and his Legacy in Economics*, Durham, N.C.: Duke University Press.
—— (1991) *Beyond Positivism: Economic Methodology in the Twentieth Century*, London: Unwin Hyman.
Clark, C. (1987–8) 'Equilibrium, Market Process and Historical Time', *Journal of Post Keynesian Economics* 10(2).
—— (1989) 'Equilibrium for What? Reflections on Social Order in Economics', *Journal of Economic Issues*, 23.
Collier, A. (1994) *Critical Realism: An Introduction to Roy Bhaskar's Philosophy*, London: Verso.
Colona, M. and Hageman, H. (1994) *The Economics of Hayek*, vol. 1: *Money and Business Cycles*, Aldershot, Hants.: Edward Elgar.
Desai, M. (1994) 'Equilibrium, Expectations and Knowledge', in Birner and Van Zijp (1994).
Diamond, A. (1980), 'F. A. Hayek on Constructivism and Ethics', *Journal of Libertarian Studies* 4.
Dictionary of Philosophy, (1983) London: Pan Books.
Dow, S. (1985) *Macroeconomic Thought: A Methodological Approach*, Oxford: Basil Blackwell.
Dreyfus, H. and Dreyfus, L. (1987) *Mind Over Machine: The Power of Human Intuition and Expertise in the Era of the Computer*, Oxford: Basil Blackwell.
Earl, P. (1985) *Psychological Economics: Developments, Tensions, Prospects*, Amsterdam: Kluwer.
Eatwell, J. and Milgate, M. (1994) 'Competition', Prices and Market Order', in Colona and Hageman (eds) (1994).
Ebling, R. (1986) 'Towards a Hermeneutical Understanding of Economics', in Kirzner (1986).
Eriksson, R. (1993) 'Hayek, Realism and Idealism', Abo Akademi University, Finland, unpublished manuscript.
Fisher, F. (1989) *Disequilibrium Foundations of Equilibrium Economics*, Cambridge: Cambridge Univerisity Press.
Foreman, F. (1989), *The Metaphysics of Liberty*, Amsterdam: Kluwer.
Frowen, S. (1995) *Hayek the Economist and Social Philosopher: A Critical Retrospect*, London: Macmillan.
Galeotti, A. (1987) 'Individualism, Social Rules, Tradition: The Case of F. Hayek', *Political Theory* 15.
Garrison, R. (1982) 'Austrian Economics as the Middle Ground', in Kirzner (1982a).
Gray, J. (1984) *Hayek on Liberty*, Oxford: Basil Blackwell.
Hahn, F. (1973) *On the Notion of Equilibrium in Economics*, Cambridge: Cambridge University Press.
—— (1982) 'Reflections on the Invisible Hand', *Lloyds Bank Review*, April.
Hamlyn, D. (1987) *Metaphysics*, Cambridge: Cambridge University Press.
Hargreaves-Heap, S. (1989) *Rationality*, Cambridge: Cambridge University Press.
Harré, R. (1988) *The Philosophies of Science*, London: Oxford University Press.
Hayek, F. (1931) *Prices and Production*, London: Routledge.
—— (1936) 'Economics and Knowledge', *Economica*, February.
—— (1941) *The Pure Theory of Capital*, London: Routledge and Kegan Paul.
—— (1942a) 'Scientism and the Study of Society', *Economica*.
—— (1942b) 'The Facts of the Social Sciences', in Hayek (1949).
—— (1943) 'Scientism and the Study of Society, Part II', *Economica*, February.
—— (1944) 'Scientism and the Study of Society, Part III', *Economica* February.
—— (1945) 'The Use of Knowledge in Society', *American Economic Review*, 35(4).

—— (1946) 'The Meaning of Competition', in Hayek (1949).
—— (1947) 'Free Enterprise and Competitive Order', in Hayek (1949).
—— (1949) *Individualism and the Economic Order*, London: Routledge and Kegan Paul.
—— (1952) *The Sensory Order*, London: Routledge and Kegan Paul.
—— (1955) 'Degrees of Explanation', in Hayek (1967a).
—— (1960) *The Constitution of Liberty*, London: Routledge & Kegan Paul.
—— (1961) 'The Theory of Complex Phenomena', in Hayek (1967a).
—— (1962) 'Rules, Perception and Intelligibility', in Hayek (1967a).
—— (1964a) 'Kinds of Rationalism', in Hayek (1967a).
—— (1964b) 'Kinds of Order in Society', *New Individualist Review*, 1(3).
—— (1967a) *Studies in Philosophy, Politics and Economics*, London: Routledge and Kegan Paul.
—— (1967b) 'Notes on the Evolution of Systems of Rules of Conduct', in Hayek (1967a).
—— (1967c) 'The Economy, Science and Politics', in Hayek (1967a).
—— (1967d) 'The Confusion of Language in Political Thought', in Hayek (1967a).
—— (1968a) 'Competition as a Discovery Process', in Hayek (1978).
—— (1968b) 'The Primacy of the Abstract', in Hayek (1978).
—— (1970a) 'The Errors of Constructivism', in Hayek (1978).
—— (1970b) 'The Pretence of Knowledge', in Hayek (1978).
—— (1973) 'Rules and Order', in Hayek (1982b).
—— (1976) 'The Mirage of Social Justice', in Hayek (1982b).
—— (1978) *New Studies in Philosophy, Politics and Economics*, London: Routledge and Kegan Paul.
—— (1979) 'The Political Order of Free People', in Hayek (1982b).
—— (1982a) 'The Sensory Order after 25 Years', in Weimer and Palermo (1982).
—— (1982b) *Law Legislation and Liberty*, London: Routledge and Kegan Paul.
—— (1983) *Knowledge, Evolution and Society*, London: Adam Smith Institute.
—— (1988) *The Fatal Conceit*, London: Routledge.
Heath, E. (1992) 'Rules, Function, and the Invisible Hand: an Interpretation of Hayek's Social Theory', *Philosophy of the Social Sciences*, 22(1).
Heilbronner, R. (1986) *The Essential Adam Smith*, London: Oxford University Press.
Herrman-Pillath, K. (1992) 'The Brain, its Sensory Order and the Evolutionary Concept of the Mind: On Hayek's Contribution to Evolutionary Epistemology', *Journal of Social and Biological Structures* 15(2).
—— (1993) 'Evolutionary Rationality, economic Man and the Foundations of Social Order', paper presented at the F.A. Hayek Memorial Symposium, Bleiburg, Germany, June.
High, J. (1986) 'Equilibration and Disequilibration in the Market Process', in Kirzner (1986).
Hodgson, G. (1988) *Economics and Institutions*, Oxford: Polity Press.
—— (1989) *Economics and Institutions*, Cambridge: Polity Press.
—— (1991) 'Hayek's Theory of Cultural Evolution: an Evaluation in the Light of Vanberg's Critique', *Economics and Philosophy* 7.
—— (1993) 'The Economics of Institutions', *European Association for Evolutionary Political Economy, Newsletter* July.
Hollis, M. (1987) *The Cunning of Reason*, Cambridge: Cambridge University Press.
Hutchison, T. (1981) *The Politics and Philosophy of Economics*, Oxford: Basil Blackwell.
Ioannides, S. (1992) *The Market, Competition and Democracy*, Aldershot, Hants.: Edward Elgar.
Kay, G. and Mott, J. (1982) *Political Order and the Law of Labour*, London: Macmillan.

Kirzner, I. (1982a) *Method Process and Austrian Economics*, New York: Lexington Books.
—— (1982b) 'Uncertainty, Discovery, and Human Action', in Kirzner (1982a).
—— (1986) *Subjectivism, Intelligibility and Economic Understanding*, New York: New York University Press.
—— (1992) *The Meaning of Market Process: Essays in the Development of Modern Austrian Economics*, London: Routledge.
Koestler, A. and Smithies, A. (1969) *Beyond Reductionism: New Perspectives in the Life Sciences*, London: Hutchinson.
Kregel, J. (1986) 'Conceptions of Equilibrium: the Logic of Choice and the Logic of Production', in Kirzner (1986).
Kukhatas, C. (1989) *Hayek and Modern Liberalism*, Oxford: Clarendon Press.
Kuninski, M. (1992) 'F. A. Hayek's Theory of Spontaneous Order: Between 'Verstehen' and 'Invisible Hand Explanation', in J. Lee Auspitz *et al.*, *Praxiologies and the Philosophy of Economics: The International Annual of Practical Philosophy and Methodology*, vol. 1, London: Transaction Publishers.
Kusterner, K. (1978) *The Important Working Knowledge of 'Unskilled' Workers*, Boulder, Col.: Westview Press.
Lachman, L. (1969) 'Methodological Individualism and the Market Economy', in Streissler (1969).
—— (1976) 'From Mises to Shackle: an Essay on Austrian Economics', *Journal of Economic Literature* 54(14).
—— (1986) *The Market as an Economic Process*, Oxford: Basil Blackwell.
Lavoie, D. (1986) 'The Market as a Procedure for Discovery and Conveyance of Inarticulate Knowledge', *Comparative Economic Studies* 28(1).
Lawson, C. (1994) 'The Transformational Model of Social Activity and Economic Analysis: A Reinterpretation of the Work of J.R. Commons', *Review of Political Economy*, 6 (2).
Lawson, C., Peacock, M. and Pratten, S. (1995) 'Realism, Underlabouring and Institutions', *Cambridge Journal of Economics* forthcoming.
Lawson, T. (1988) 'Probability and Uncertainty in Economic Analysis', *Journal of Post Keynesian Economics*, 11(1).
—— (1989a) 'Abstraction, Tendencies and Stylised Facts: a Realist Approach to Economic Analysis', *Cambridge Journal of Economics* 13 (1).
—— (1989b) 'Realism and Instrumentalism in the Development of Econometrics', *Oxford Economic Papers* 41(1).
—— (1994a) 'A Realist Theory for Economics', in R. Backhouse, *New Directions in Economic Methodology*, London: Routledge.
—— (1994b) The Nature of Post-Keynesianism and its Links to Other Traditions: a Realist Perspective', *Journal of Post Keynesian Economics* August.
—— (1994c) 'Realism and Hayek: a Case of Continuous Transformation', in Colona and Hageman (eds) (1994).
—— (1995a) 'Developments in Hayek's Social Theorising', in Frowen (ed.) (1995).
—— (1995b) 'The Lucas Critique: a Generalisation', *Cambridge Journal of Economics*.
Littlechild, S. (1982) 'Equilibrium and Market Process', in Kirzner (1982a).
Loasby, B. (1989) *The Mind Method of the Economist*, Aldershot, Hants.: Edward Elgar.
—— (1991) *Equilibrium and Evolution*, Manchester: Manchester University Press.
Maki, U. (1990a) 'Scientific Realism and Austrian Explanation', *Review of Political Economy* 2(3).
—— (1990b) 'Mengerian Economics in Realist Perspective', in Caldwell (1990).
Marshall, A. (1923) *Industry and Trade*, London: Macmillan.

—— (1947) *Principles of Economics*, 8th edn, London: Macmillan.
Meikle, S. (1985) *Essentialism in the Thought of Karl Marx*, London: Duckworth.
Nishiyama, S. (1964) 'Hayek's Theory of Sensory Order and the Methodology of the Social Sciences', *Journal of Applied Sociology* 7.
—— (1979) 'Anti-Rationalism or Critical Rationalism', in F. Mayer *et al.* (eds), *Verfassung der Freiheit: Festgabe für F. Hayek zur Vollendung seines achtzigsten Lebensjahres*, Stuttgart: Fischer.
Nozick, R. (1977) 'On Austrian Methodology', *Synthese* 36.
Nyiri, J. (1988) 'Tradition and Practical Knowledge', in Smith and Nyiri (1988).
O'Driscoll, G. (1977) *Economics as a Coordination Problem*, Kansas City: Sheed Andrews and McMeel.
O'Driscoll, G. and Rizzo, M. (1985) *The Economics of Time and Ignorance*, Oxford: Basil Blackwell.
—— (1986) 'Subjectivism, Uncertainty and Rules', in Kirzner (1986).
Oliver, W. (1951) *Theory of Order*, Yellow Springs, Ohio: Antioch Press.
K.-H. Paque (1985) 'How Far is Vienna from Chicago? An Essay on the Methodology of Two Schools of Dogmatic Liberalism', *Kyklos* 38.
—— (1990) 'Pattern Predictions in Economics: Hayek's methodology of the Social Sciences Revisited', History of Political Economy 22(2).
Pareto, V. (1971) *Manual of Political Economy*, New York: Augustus M. Kelley.
Parsons, S. (1990) 'The Philosophical Roots of Modern Austrian Economics: Past Problems and Future Prospects', *History of Political Economy* 22(2).
—— (1994) 'Hayek and the Limitations of Knowledge: Philosophical Aspects', (forthcoming) 'Developments in Hayek's Social Theorising', in S. Frowen (ed.) *Hayek the Economist and Social Philosopher: A Critical Retrospect*, London: Macmillan.
Peacock, M. (1993 forthcoming) 'Hayek, Realism and Spontaneous Order', *Journal for the Theory of Social Behaviour* 23.
Peters, R. (1958) *The Concept of Motivation*, London.
Pheby, J. (1988) *Methodology and Economics: A Critical Introduction*, London: Macmillan.
Polanyi, M. (1958) *Personal Knowledge*, London: Routledge and Kegan Paul.
—— (1966) *The Tacit Dimension*, Anchor Books.
Popper, K. (1972) *Conjectures and Refutations*, London: Routledge and Kegan Paul.
Pratten, S. (1993) 'Structure, Agency and Marx's Analysis of the Labour Process', *Review of Political Economy*, 5(4).
—— (1994) 'Marshall on Tendencies, Equilibrium and the Statistical Method', unpublished paper, Cambridge University.
Prisching, M. (1989) 'Evolution and Design of Social Institutions in Austrian Theory. Austrian Economics: Roots and Ramifications Reconsidered, Part 2', *Journal of Economic Studies* 16(2).
Rizzo, M (1990) 'Hayek's Four Tendencies Towards Equilibrium', *Cultural Dynamics* 3 (1).
Rubin, I. (1990) *Essays on Marx's Labour Theory of Value*, Detroit, Mich.: Black Rose Books.
Rubinstein, D. (1981) *Marx and Wittgenstein: Social Praxis and Social Explanation*, London: Routledge and Kegan Paul.
Runde, J. (1985) 'Subjectivism, Psychology and the Modern Austrians', in P. Earl (ed.), *Psychological Economics*, Amsterdam: Kluwer.
Ryle, G. (1945) 'Knowing How and Knowing That', *Proceedings of the Aristotelian Society* 46.
—— (1949) *The Concept of Mind*, London: Hutchinson.

Sayer, A. (1992) *Method in Social Science*, London: Routledge.
Sayers, S. (1985) *Reality and Reason*, Oxford: Basil Blackwell.
Smith, B. (1986) 'Austrian Economics and Austrian Philosophy', in Smith and Grassl, (1986).
—— (1990a) 'Aristotle, Menger, Mises: an Essay in the Metaphysics of Economics', in Caldwell (1990).
—— (1990b) 'On the Austrianness of Austrian Economics', *Critical Review* 4.
—— (1995) 'The Intellectual Order: a Study of Hayekian Psychology', in Frowen (ed.) (1995).
—— and Grassl, W. (1986) *Austrian Economics: A Historical Background*, London: Croom Helm.
—— and Nyiri, J. (1988) *Practical Knowledge: Outlines of a Theory of Traditions and Skills*, London: Croom Helm.
—— (1990) 'Aristotle, Menger, Mises: an Essay in the Metaphysics of Economics', in Caldwell (1990).
Spengler, J. (1948) 'The Problem of Order in Economic Affairs', *Southern Economic Journal* 15.
Stern, R. (1990) *Hegel, Kant and the Structure of the Object*, London: Routledge.
Streissler, E. (1969) *Roads to Freedom: Essays in Honour of F. von Hayek*, London: Routledge and Kegan Paul.
—— (1994) 'Hayek on Information and Socialism', in Colona and Hageman (1994).
Streit, M. (1993) 'Cognition, Competition and Catallaxy', *Journal of Constitutional Political Economy* 4.
Thompson, J. (1989) 'The Theory of Structuration', in J. Thompson and D. Held, *Social Theory and Modern Societies: A. Giddens and his Critics*, Cambridge: Cambridge University Press.
Thomsen, E. (1992) *Prices and Knowledge: A Market Process*, London: Routledge.
Tomlinson, J. (1990) *Hayek and the Market*, London: Pluto Press.
Ullman-Marglit, U. (1978) 'Invisible Hand Explanations', *Synthese* 39.
Vanberg, V. (1986) 'Spontaneous Market Order and Social Rules: a Critical Examination of F.A. Hayek's Theory of Cultural Evolution', *Economics and Philosophy*, 2.
Vaughan, K. (1980) 'Economic Calculation under Socialism', *Economic Enquiry* 18.
—— (1982) 'Subjectivism, Predictability, and Creativity: Comment on Buchanan', in Kirzner (1982a).
—— (1984) 'The Constitution of Liberty from an Evolutionary Perspective', in Barry 1984.
—— (1992) 'The Problems of Order in Austrian Economics: Kirzner vs. Lachmann', *Review of Political Economy* 4(3).
Vries, R. de (1994) 'The Place of Hayek's Theory of Mind and Perception in the History of Philosophy and Psychology', in Birner and van Zijp (1994).
Wagner, R. and Sternberg, R. (1987) 'Tacit Knowledge in Managerial Success', *Journal of Business and Psychology* 1(4).
Weimer, W. and Palermo, D. (1982) *Cognition and the Symbolic Process*, London: Lawrence Erlbaum.
Weintraub, E. (1986) *Microfoundations*, Cambridge: Cambridge University Press.
Wood, S. (1989) *The Transformation of Work*, London: Unwin Hyman.
Woolfson, C. (1982) *The Labour Theory of Culture*, London: Routledge and Kegan Paul.

INDEX